AF701186

Hunger *in a* Global Economy

HUNGER 1998

Eighth Annual Report
on the State of World Hunger

Bread for the World
INSTITUTE
1100 Wayne Avenue, Suite 1000
Silver Spring, Maryland 20910
USA

Printed on recyled paper.

Bread for the World Institute

President
David Beckmann

President Emeritus
Arthur Simon

Director
Richard A. Hoehn

Editor
Marc J. Cohen

Co-Editor
Don Reeves

Design
Marcos I. Ballestero

© 1997 by Bread for the World Institute
1100 Wayne Avenue, Suite 1000
Silver Spring, MD 20910, USA
Telephone: (301) 608-2400 Fax: (301) 608-2401
E-mail: institute@bread.org
WWW: http://www.bread.org
All rights reserved. No part of this book may be reproduced in any form without permission from the publisher except for brief passages quoted in a review.

Printer: HBP, Hagerstown, MD

Photos: Cover: Food and Agriculture Organization of the United Nations (FAO); Page 54: The World Bank; Page 68: WFP; Page 80: The World Bank; Page 88: Rick Reinhard

Manufactured in the United States of America
First edition published October 1997
ISBN 1-884361-06-4

Table of Contents

Acknowledgments

We are deeply grateful for the valuable insights provided by sponsors, cosponsors and colleagues at three consultations related to this report and in response to earlier drafts. Those who provided comments include:

Mark Anderson, American Federation of Labor and Congress of Industrial Organizations; Professor George Ayittey, The American University; Manfred Bardeleben, Friedrich Ebert Foundation; Karen Bloomquist, John Halvorson and John Stumme, Evangelical Lutheran Church in America; Robert Brauning, International Monetary Fund; Professor Carolyn Campbell, Cornell University; Carol Capps, Church World Service/Lutheran World Relief; John Cavanagh, Institute for Policy Studies; Vern Conaway, Catholic Relief Services; Mike Degan and Perry Lester, Agricultural Cooperative Development International/Volunteers in Overseas Cooperative Assistance; Jennifer Dec, Save the Children Federation/U.S.; Christopher Dunford, Freedom from Hunger; Robert Fisher; Timothy Frankenberger, CARE; Anthony Freeman and Sandra Polaski, International Labor Organization; Jean Hirshart; Keir Jorgensen, UNITE; Julie Kimbrough, International Fund for Agricultural Development; Louis Knowles, Ecumenical Development Cooperative Society; Barbara Kohnan, U.S. Catholic Conference; William Levine, Abt Associates; Peter Mann, World Hunger Year; Martin McLaughlin, Center of Concern; Lynn McMullen, RESULTS; Joseph Mettimano, U.S. Committee for UNICEF; Aziz Ali Mohammed, Group of 24; Paul Montacute, Baptist World Alliance; Walter Owensby, Presbyterian Church (U.S.A.); Shubh Kumar Range and Isabell Grunberg, United Nations Development Programme; Howard Rosen, Competitiveness Policy Council; Robin Shell, Food for the Hungry International; Lisa Smith, U.S. Agency for International Development; Professor Luther Tweeten, Ohio State University; Flavio Luiz Shiek Valente, Association for Projects to Combat Hunger (AGORA, Brazil); Susan Weaver Van Lopik, Christian Reformed World Relief Committee; Lori Wallach, Public Citizen; Rob Weissman, *Multinational Monitor*.

We appreciate assistance from the following people in obtaining data: Ezzedine Boutrief, F.L. Zegarra and Rick Sutton, Food and Agriculture Organization of the United Nations; Masataka Fujita, United Nations Conference on Trade and Development; Sakiko Fukuda-Parr and Gül Tanghe-Gülluova, United Nations Development Programme; Saba Beyene, Office of the United Nations High Commissioner for Refugees; Shaohua Chen, David Cieslikowski, Kris Martin, Sulekha Patel and Martin Ravallion, The World Bank; Suki McClatchey, Mercedes de Onis, Monika Blössner and Yun Ling, World Health Organization; Jean Tash, U.S. Bureau of the Census; Howard Hayghe, U.S. Department of Labor; Penny Fowler, Catholic Institute for International Relations; Jeff Whisenant, Lutheran World Relief; John Cook, Center on Hunger, Poverty and Nutrition Policy, Tufts University; Susan Davis and Lee Murphy, Gallaudet University; Michael Lipsey and Randall Fotiu, Michigan State University; Faith Lai, University of Idaho; Katherine Ross, Syracuse University; Koen Vleminckx, Stephan Wagner and Carolyn Tombeur, Luxembourg Income Study; Peter Saama, University of California at Los Angeles; Steven Hansch, Refugee Policy Group; Sandra Sellers, Software Publishers Association; and Lucilla Li Tan.

ESRI generously donated the ARCVIEW geographic information system software used to generate the maps.

Dennis and Sackett Designs assisted in producing figures and tables.

The following Bread for the World members and Bread for the World/Bread for the World Institute board members and staff provided comments and assistance: Ron Cunningham, Sam Folin, Kay Furlani, Paul Gloeckner, Janet Green, Frances Johnson, Steve Miller, David Miner, Maria Otero, Jim Shields, Arthur Simon, Donna Wenstrup, Ray Almeida, Mark Barwick, Mai Bull, Margaret Cohen, Sarah DeBolt, Lynette Engelhardt, Larry Goodwin, Donna Hodge, Larry Hollar, Barbara Howell, Ellen Jennings, Bhavna Patel, Mimmy Polan, Susan Kay Park, Shohreh Kermani Peterson, Dorothy Pilkington, Sam Rao, Michael Rubinstein, Niloufer De Silva, Katherine Simmons, Carole Southam, David Suley, Michele Tapp, Donald Williams, Lynora Williams, Mizanekristos Yohannes and Dolly Youssef.

BREAD FOR THE WORLD INSTITUTE

Hunger *in a* GLOBAL ECONOMY

Give priority to the needs of hungry and poor people when making economic decisions.

Introduction

By Richard A. Hoehn

The global economy is not just a political slogan or an advertiser's dream. This amazing new reality is here, there, almost everywhere, to the tune of $24 trillion a year. A trillion has 12 zeroes – $24,000,000,000,000 or $24,000 billion.

The scale and momentum are stunning. Foreign direct investment more than tripled from the mid-1980s to the mid-1990s. General Motors' annual sales are higher than the total value of goods and services of Norway. "Of the world's hundred largest economies, 51 are now economies internal to corporations. A mere 200 corporations, linked together by strategic alliances and interlocking boards, account for 29 percent of world economic activity."[1]

Consider: If trade were evenly spread around the land surface of the world, the inhabitants of each square mile, including Antarctic penguins and Saharan camels, would have more than $62,000 in products to trade each year. But it is not. The thousands of women who sew sneakers in Indonesia together make less than Michael Jordan gets for endorsing them.

This is certain. The global marketplace has replaced the Cold War as the structure dominating international behavior. Global communications and the global economy are manufacturing the largest social change since the industrial revolution and the rise of the modern state.

Love it or hate it, we can't leave or ignore it. We're all caught up in it one way or another – clothes, cars and cat food. Tourists use ATM cards as readily in Bangkok as in Berlin.

And, television affects how people perceive each other all over the globe.

So, how many cheers for the global economy? Three? Two? Or, the sound of one hand clapping? Reactions are mixed.

Market advocates cite new and better paying jobs in shoe factories in Indonesia. Critics point to difficult working conditions there and a loss of jobs in the United States. Proponents of freer trade and investment applaud wealth generation that contributes to longer lives, less illness, decent homes, healthy kids staying longer in schools and worldwide reductions in poverty. Skeptics speak of pirate economics and the global casino in which rich people get richer and more powerful, some people on the margins are shoved into the abyss and nature conducts a trial to see whether humans are a sustainable project on this earth.

Bread for the World Institute is committed to examine and share information that helps people shape a global economy that serves human hopes and dreams.

10 Ways to Make the World Economy Work Better for Hungry People

1. Give priority to the needs of hungry and poor people when making economic decisions.
2. Complement markets with government and civic action to ensure secure livelihoods for all.
3. Include hungry and poor people in decisions that affect their lives.
4. Coordinate policies among nations to foster full employment and other social goals.
5. Promote international trade – with safeguards for labor rights, the environment and food security.
6. Foster food security through more liberal agricultural trade coupled with sound agricultural policies and safety nets.
7. Encourage responsible investing through policies that are good for businesses, workers and consumers.
8. Focus the World Bank and other international financial institutions on reducing poverty, and make them accountable to the low-income communities they affect.
9. Relieve the debts of poor-country governments committed to reducing poverty, and expand foreign aid programs that help hungry and poor people.
10. Exercise our influence as responsible citizens, consumers, employers, workers and investors to make the world economy work for everyone.

Concerned about the welfare of all people, our special mission begins with the world's most vulnerable people.

Nearly a quarter of humanity – 1.3 billion people – live in absolute poverty with incomes of less than a dollar a day. About one in seven – 841 million people – are chronically undernourished. We strive to view policies, systems and solutions through their eyes; and to suggest ways in which individuals and groups can act to meet their needs.

"Poverty means that God forgives our thefts." Tony, homeless "street kid," age 10, Angola[2]

Hunger in a Global Economy views the global economy much like a pharmacist looks at a powerful drug. It can work a miracle of healing, but wrongly used can kill.

The market-oriented global economy creates great wealth for a few, provides benefits and reduces hunger for many, while increasing hunger, misery and insecurity for many others. Since this economy is likely to prevail for the near future, *Hunger 1998* focuses on feasible reforms to make the world economy work better for hungry people.

Chapter 1 surveys the global economy and the persistence of widespread hunger. It describes key actors in the global economy and argues that markets should be balanced by government and civil society.

The second chapter examines how the triumph of the global economy has upset what balance had been achieved within nations. Governments need to coordinate their policies to foster full employment and other social goals.

Chapter 3 shows that international trade contributes to economic growth and that growth can contribute to the reduction of poverty. But trade and growth may not help poor people unless governments and trade agreements assure that they do. The chapter outlines key policies governments can adopt to channel the benefits of trade toward secure livelihoods for all. It analyzes child labor, GATT, the World Trade Organization, NAFTA and the arms trade.

A Catholic **Framework** for Economic Life

1. The economy exists for the person, not the person for the economy.
2. All economic life should be shaped by moral principles. Economic choices and institutions must be judged by how they protect or undermine the life and dignity of the human person, support the family and serve the common good.
3. A fundamental moral measure of any economy is how the poor and vulnerable are faring.
4. All people have a right to life and to secure the basic necessities of life (e.g., food, clothing, shelter, education, health care, safe environment, economic security).
5. All people have the right to economic initiative, to productive work, to just wages and benefits, to decent working conditions as well as to organize and join unions or other associations.
6. All people, to the extent they are able, have a corresponding duty to work, a responsibility to provide for the needs of their families and an obligation to contribute to the broader society.
7. In economic life, free markets have both clear advantages and limits; government has essential responsibilities and limitations; voluntary groups have irreplaceable roles, but cannot substitute for the proper working of the market and the just policies of the state.
8. Society has a moral obligation, including governmental action where necessary, to assure opportunity, meet basic human needs and pursue justice in economic life.
9. Workers, owners, managers, stockholders and consumers are moral agents in economic life. By our choices, initiative, creativity and investment, we enhance or diminish economic opportunity, community life and social justice.
10. The global economy has moral dimensions and human consequences. Decisions on investment, trade, aid and development should protect human life and promote human rights, especially for those most in need wherever they might live on this globe.

A Catholic Framework for Economic Life Copyright©1996 United States Catholic Conference, Washington, DC 20017. Reprinted with permission. All rights reserved. No part of this work may be reproduced or transmitted in any form without permission in writing from the copyright owner. The framework is available in English and Spanish as a poster and a palm card. All may be ordered by calling 800-235-8722 and asking for the following publication numbers: English poster (5-137), Spanish poster (5-138), English card (5-139), Spanish card (5-140).

Trade in agriculture is being liberalized more than ever before. Chapter 4 says that agricultural trade can contribute to food security. Developing-country governments need to adopt policies focused on food security. In addition, the industrial countries should make good on their promises of aid to Low-Income Food Deficit Countries.

Chapter 5 describes the current growth of international investment. It outlines what governments have to do if they want to attract investment. It argues that governments can opt for a mix of policies that will attract foreign investment and, at the same time, improve livelihoods for their people.

Chapter 6 describes the World Bank and the International Monetary Fund, and argues that these institutions should focus on reducing poverty and promoting democratic participation. It includes a call for relief of the impossible debt burdens of some of the poorest developing countries.

Chapter 7 provides up-to-date information on the extent of hunger in different parts of the world.

Finally, Chapter 8 shows how individuals can help make the world economy work better for hungry people.

Economic systems are rooted in beliefs and values: wealth and growth should come first; or not. The needs of vulnerable people should come first; or not. You get what you deserve in life; or not. Safety nets are worth what they cost; or not. We should let the private sector develop without interference; or not.

Religious people hold a full spectrum of beliefs about the pluses and minuses of the global economy.

And yet, most of the religious and ethical traditions of the world would affirm certain core values – "the priority of God's reign over both individual decisions and institutional forms; the love of neighbor and its implications in a preferential option for the poor; a commitment to environmental sustainability; a concern for both fellow citizens and foreigners."[3] The National Conference of Catholic Bishops in the United States has articulated 10 principles on economic life that can guide religious and secular people alike (see "A Catholic Framework...," p. 4).

Regional, national and international organizations have gone on record to assert the priority of the needs of hungry and poor people in political and economic policy decisions. In 1976, Bread for the World initiated a Right to Food Resolution in the U.S. Congress. Congress declared:

> It is the sense of Congress that:
>
> - the United States reaffirms the right of every person in this country and throughout the world to food and a nutritionally adequate diet; and
> - the need to combat hunger shall be a fundamental point of reference in the formulation and implementation of United States policy in all areas which bear on hunger including international trade, monetary arrangements, and foreign assistance.[4]

Statements from Christian, Jewish, Muslim, Buddhist or secular sources all affirm the fundamental responsibility of human beings toward one another and nature; and, in particular, toward people in need.

Responsibility is a core value behind all these specific guidelines. Spouses should be responsible to one another and their children. People have a responsibility to carry their own weight in society. But consumers and corporations, citizens and governments also have responsibilities to society. Responsible citizens, businesses and governments will give priority to the needs of hungry and poor people when making economic decisions.

Responsibility is about "respecting and enhancing the integrity of life."[5] Every time we act to affirm the well being of another person – when we hug our child, when we share our resources, when we work for justice – we affirm the meaningfulness of the other peoples' existence; and ours. We bring life where otherwise death might prevail. Such acts are an expression of, and feed, our deep wellsprings of meaning.

Ruth Fowler

"Poverty ... means powerlessness and low status. It means a culture of silence. It means bearing children on the street. It means the lack of privacy, dignity and any kind of security."

Mahila Milan, an association of homeless women in Bombay, India[6]

People of faith experience such acts as spiritual moments because they respond to the bountiful blessing of creation and unite us with the whole human community.

This book is not just about a global economy, but the search for a responsible global economy, responsible trade practices, responsible investment policies, responsible corporations; responsibility toward hungry and poor people; responsibility toward generations to come; and, finally, our responsibility to act.

The bountiful earth, human ingenuity and now global communications have enhanced our ability to respond. The global economy is spectacularly rich. The task in front of us is to assure access to its wonderful gifts by the whole human family and protect the earth that sustains us. Native American author Vine Deloria says: "The future of [humans] lies in waiting for those who will come to understand their lives and take up their responsibilities to all living things."[7]

Dr. Richard A. Hoehn is director of Bread for the World Institute.

World Hunger in a Global Economy

By Marc J. Cohen

Complement markets with government and civic action to ensure secure livelihoods for all.

Include hungry and poor people in decisions that affect their lives.

This chapter outlines the extent of hunger in the $24 trillion world economy. Who are the key players? How can we make use of markets to promote efficiency and growth, but also assure equity?

Growing Globalization

The global economy is a coin with contrasting sides. One is bright and shiny: explosive expansion of trade and investment, integrated financial markets in which phenomenal sums change hands daily, instant communications, new breakthroughs in science and technology. But the flip side is tarnished and corroded: 1.3 billion people (nearly a quarter of humanity) living in absolute poverty, with incomes of less than a dollar a day; 841 million people chronically undernourished; rising inequality within and between nations. On one side, the Internet offers exciting possibilities for breaking down distinctions based on class, race, gender, age, ability/disability and culture. On the other side, over 90 percent of the people on earth do not have telephones.

Economic globalization is the integration of world markets for goods, services and money. It broadens and deepens links across national borders, and powerfully affects hunger, for good and ill.

The double edges of globalization are evident in the United States: on one side, $60 billion in foreign direct investment (FDI, i.e., investment from abroad in productive activities, as opposed to stocks and bonds) poured in during 1995, or nearly as much as flowed to the entire developing world (excluding China).[1] Such ventures as the Toyota plant in Georgetown, Kentucky, have created jobs and stimulated economic activity.

But imports of manufactured goods from lower-wage countries and the shift of production facilities to those countries have contributed to declining real wages and economic insecurity for low-skilled U.S. workers (see Chapters 2 and 3).

Newcastle in Northern England – famous for the expression, "It's foolish to carry coals to Newcastle" – offers more evidence of globalization's ambiguities. The coal deposits are exhausted, and Asian competition has bankrupted the shipyards. But the available work force has attracted East Asian firms seeking European bases. For Ken Chapman, assembly work in the Korean-owned Lucky Goldstar microwave oven plant pays less than his old job in the coal pits, but is preferable to unemployment. For Mandy Little, a school dropout, full-time work for Lucky Goldstar and a part-time barmaid job offer a higher standard of living than work in a British-owned garment factory.[2]

Globalization has had mixed effects in developing countries as well. In the Cavite Export Processing Zone near Manila Bay in the Philippines, workers who make blue jeans for sale in U.S. department stores can earn $480 monthly in wages and piece-rate bonuses. That's four times what the bay's struggling fisherfolk could expect even in good times. But pollution from the zone and overfishing drive boats ever farther from shore for a meager catch. Arnulfo Plocios, a fisherman in the town of Rosario, can only feed his family one meal a day of rice and dried fish.[3]

Over the past decade, the volume and growth rate of cross-border flows of goods, services and capital have increased dramatically. According to the World Bank:

> Between 1985 and 1994, the ratio of world trade to GDP [gross domestic product, i.e., total production] rose three times faster than during the previous decade. During the same 10-year period foreign direct investment (FDI) doubled as a share of global GDP. Developing countries have participated extensively in the acceleration of global integration. Over the past decade their ratio of trade to GDP has increased, and their share of global FDI has risen to more than one-third.[4]

A closer look, however, reveals sharp differences among countries. Although the developing world as a whole kept pace with the growth of world trade, the poorest countries have seen trade decline as a proportion of their economies, and have not received much foreign investment. The ratio of trade to GDP fell in 44 of 93

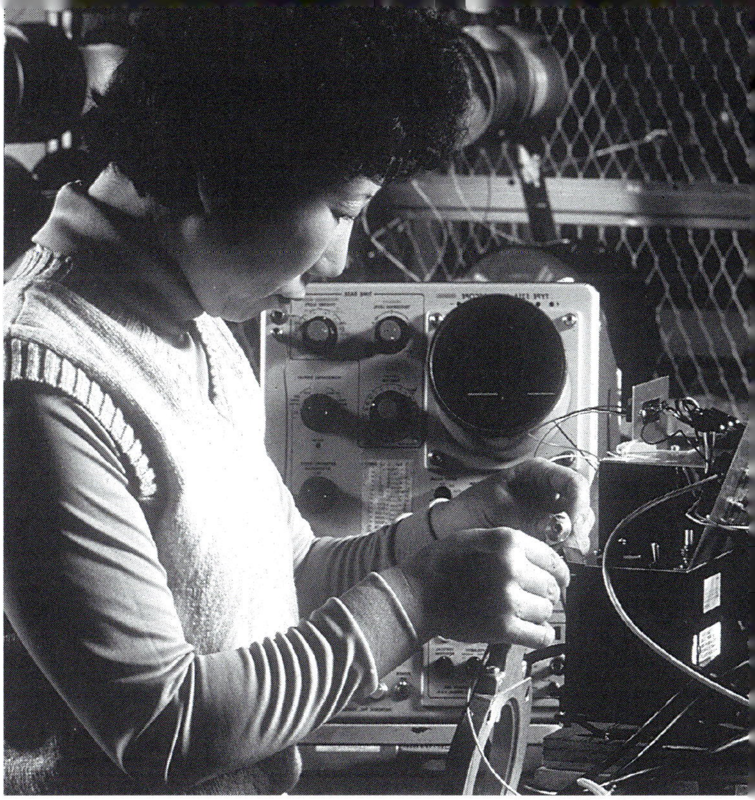

John Zoiner/Pictor Uniphoto

The work of young women, such as this Thai electronics worker, has been essential to East Asia's "miracle."

developing countries over the past 10 years. Similar disparities exist in private investment flows: two-thirds of FDI in the developing world went to just eight countries; half the countries received little or none. Globalization has by-passed much of sub-Saharan Africa.

Some developing countries that have enthusiastically joined the global economy – notably those in East and Southeast Asia – have experienced rapid economic growth. China has enjoyed double-digit economic growth in the 1990s, compared to average annual global economic growth of under 2.5 percent. Increasingly, Asian countries are exporting higher technology manufactured goods, which are more insulated from business cycles than the raw agricultural product and mineral exports upon which Africa depends. Prices for many of Africa's commodities have experienced long-term decline or stagnation.

Global Hunger: Scope & Trends[5]

In the period from roughly 1970 to 1992, the number of people in the developing world afflicted by hunger (see "Hunger: Key Concepts, p. 8 for

HUNGER: **Key Concepts**

Hunger is a condition in which people do not get enough food to provide the nutrients (carbohydrate, fat, protein, vitamins, minerals and water) they need for fully productive, active and healthy lives. *Malnutrition*, which can impair physical and mental health, results from inadequate consumption (*undernutrition*) or excessive consumption of one or more nutrients. Infectious diseases are both a cause and an effect of malnutrition. Thus, clean water, safe sanitation and access to health care are essential to good nutrition.[1]

Food security means assured access for every person, primarily by production or purchase, to enough safe, nutritious and culturally acceptable food to sustain an active and healthy life with dignity. It includes food *availability*, food *access* and appropriate *food utilization*.

Human existence depends upon food. But food is not the only necessity of life. *Livelihood security* refers to adequate and sustainable access to income and other resources to enable households to meet *all* of their basic needs, including housing, health care, access to clean water and safe sanitation, community participation, education and training, adequate time for proper child care and knowledge of good dietary practices (see figure below).[2] And, as the Nobel Prize-winning South African novelist, Nadine Gordimer, has written, the arts, the world of ideas and spirituality are also essential to "truly human fullness of existence."[3]

Livelihood Security

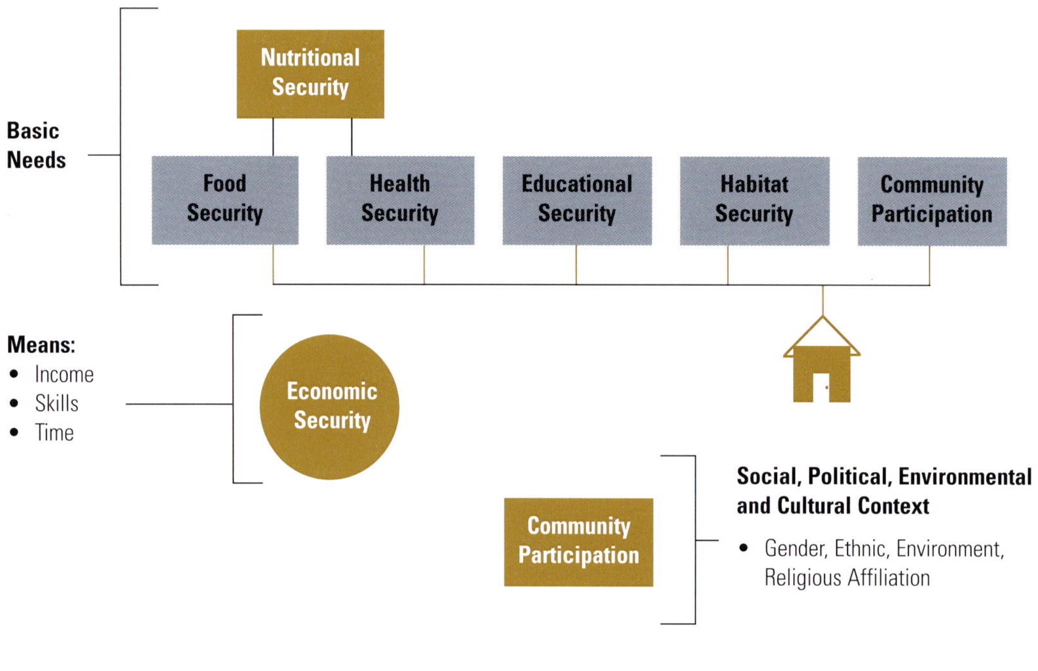

Source: CARE-USA

Notes: 1) See also Eleanor Noss Whitney, Eva May Nunnelley Hamilton and Sharon Rady Rolfes, *Understanding Nutrition, Fifth Edition* (St. Paul, MN: West Publishing, 1990). 2) CARE-USA Household Livelihood Security Working Group, "Household Livelihood Security: A Unifying Conceptual Framework for CARE Programming," mimeo, September 20, 1995. We are also grateful to Timothy R. Frankenberger, CARE's senior food security advisor, for many hours of conversation and explication of the concept of livelihood security over the past three years.
3) Nadine Gordimer, "The Sum of All Our Hungers," *Choices*, October 1996, 11.

definitions) fell from 918 million to 841 million, while the proportion dropped from 35 percent to 20 percent. But, one in every five people in developing countries (one in seven worldwide) remains undernourished. The 1996 World Food Summit, organized by the Food and Agriculture Organization of United Nations (FAO), declared, "This situation is unacceptable," and pledged concerted international action to reduce the number of hungry people by half by no later than the year 2015 (see "The World Food Summit," pp. 16-17).

Figure 1.1 indicates the proportion of national populations suffering from chronic undernutrition in 98 developing countries in 1990-1992, along with anecdotal information about some industrial and transition countries. Figure 1.2 shows the proportion of undernourished children under age 5 in 82 developing countries; Table 1.1 gives regional figures.

For many countries, undernutrition rates for children are considerably higher than those for the population as a whole. For example, in India, 21 percent of the overall population was chronically undernourished in 1990-1992, but 53 percent of the preschool children were underweight in 1996. Undernutrition often adversely affects children's physical and mental development, undermining their future as productive and creative members of their communities and nations.

The aggregate figures – a mixture of modest progress toward food security and stubborn persistence of hunger – tell only part of the story. There are substantial regional differences, as summarized in Figure 1.3 and detailed in Chapter 7. Hunger has increased in many countries since 1970, especially in Africa. Figure 1.4 shows that the "center of gravity" of hunger (i.e., where the majority of hungry people live) has shifted from East and Southeast Asia, where export-led growth helped many people out of hunger, to South Asia and sub-Saharan Africa. The proportion of the population that is hungry declined in South Asia, but jumped 13 percent in Africa over the past quarter century. The absolute number of hungry Africans more than doubled. FAO predicts that if current trends persist, 265 million Africans will suffer hunger in the year 2010.

The Low-Income Food Deficit Countries

Of particular concern is the group of nations known as the "Low-Income Food Deficit Countries" (LIFDCs). FAO defines these countries as nations that have been net importers of food over a three-year period and whose net income per person is below the eligibility threshold ($1,395 in 1996) to receive assistance from the World Bank's "soft loan window," the International Development Association (see Chapter 6, pp. 70-71).

In 1996, 82 countries fit this description, half of them in Africa (see Table 1.2). These LIFDCs are home to the vast majority of the world's chronically undernourished people. Many lack foreign exchange for commercial food imports.

Globalization's Impact on Hunger

People in East and Southeast Asia have shared widely in the fruits of export-led growth. Since China embarked on its "open door" economic policy in 1978, its poverty rate has fallen 60 percent, freeing 170 million people from poverty. The infant mortality rate fell 25 percent.[6]

China has attracted more foreign investment in recent years than any other country except the United States. Yue Yuen, a Taiwanese company, employs 40,000 workers in Southern China to make athletic shoes for Nike, Reebok and Adidas. The company has arrangements with local governments to provide junior high school graduates to staff its lines, thus providing

Table 1.1 **Estimated Percentage and Number of Underweight Children Under 5 in Developing Country Regions, 1990**

Region	Percent Underweight	Number Underweight (millions)	Total Number of Children Under 5
Sub-Saharan Africa	30	26	88
Middle East	25	12	49
South Asia	58	91	156
E. & S.E. Asia	24	42	180
Latin America & Caribbean	12	6	55
Economic Group:			
Low Income	38	148	388
Middle to High Income	22	31	140
Total	34	179	528

Source: World Health Organization.

employment opportunities. Wages are about average, but benefits, including medical care, are equal in value to cash compensation. The company also provides opportunities for advancement, sending the best and brightest workers to Beijing's Foreign Language Institute. Because China has a huge market and relatively low costs for educated workers, it has the leverage to obtain foreign investment on favorable terms.[7]

The proportion of hungry people in China fell from 45 percent in 1969-1971 to 16 percent in 1990-1992. Despite this remarkable progress, 189 million Chinese remain chronically undernourished.

Other Asian countries have similarly channeled export-fueled growth into reduced poverty and hunger, while maintaining relatively modest levels of income inequality. But, as in China, not everyone has benefitted equally.

In Thailand, economic expansion and public policies aimed at improving health and nutrition have helped reduce the absolute poverty rate to less than 1 percent. But in March 1997, over 10,000 impoverished farmers and landless laborers demonstrated at the prime minister's office in an effort to obtain land titles and financial compensation for those displaced by dam, forestry and industrial projects. "Only the rich, who already own a lot of land and have the money to bribe officials to register it, have proper land titles," said a protest organizer. Average incomes in the poverty-stricken northeast are just 10 percent of those in the capital city, Bangkok. The city's high levels of pollution threaten public health. And the share of national income of the poorest 20 percent has declined by almost half over the last 20 years to 3.4 percent. In 1990-1992, about a quarter of the population (over 14 million people) were chronically undernourished.[8]

Table 1.2 **Low-Income Food Deficit Countries**

Sub-Saharan Africa		**Eastern Europe/NIS**
Angola	Senegal	Armenia
Benin	Sierra Leone	Albania
Burkina Faso	Somalia	Azerbaijan
Burundi	Swaziland	Georgia
Cameroon	Tanzania	Kyrgyz Republic
Cape Verde	Togo	Former Yugoslav
Central African	Zaire(Congo-Kinshasa)	Republic of
Republic	Zambia	Macedonia
Chad	Zimbabwe	Tajikistan
Comoros		Turkmenistan
Congo (Brazzaville)	**Asia-Pacific**	Uzbekistan
Côte d'Ivoire	Afghanistan	
Djibouti	Bangladesh	**Latin America-**
Equatorial Guinea	Cambodia	**Caribbean**
Eritrea	China	Bolivia
Ethiopia	India	Dominican
Gambia	Indonesia	Republic
Ghana	Laos	Ecuador
Guinea	Maldives	Guatemala
Guinea-Bissau	Mongolia	Haiti
Kenya	Nepal	Honduras
Lesotho	Pakistan	
Liberia	Philippines	**Middle East &**
Madagascar	Sri Lanka	**North Africa**
Malawi	Kiribati	Egypt
Mali	Papua New Guinea	Jordan
Mauritania	Samoa	Morocco
Mozambique	Solomon Islands	Syria
Niger	Tuvalu	Yemen
Nigeria	Vanuatu	
Rwanda	Bhutan	
Sao Tome and		
Principe		

Source: FAO.

A recent U.N. report notes that "economic growth ... remains the main channel through which the standard of living is raised and the benefits of a larger volume and wider variety of goods and services are made available to all segments of the population."[9] Negative economic growth has devastating consequences for poor people: increased infant mortality rates, lowered life expectancy and decreased school enrollment.

Yet growth can have adverse side effects. The East Asian countries have raised living standards, but they have generally neglected environmental protection until quite recently. Authoritarian government contributed to this; popular participation in policy making might have led to earlier attention to environmental issues.

As affluence has increased in East and Southeast Asia, many people have adopted Western-style diets high in animal fat and refined carbohydrates. Seung Kyung Lee, a manager in a department store in Seoul, South Korea, grew up on a rice farm 60 miles from the city. Her family ate lots of rice and vegetables. They only ate meat on special occasions. Today, she serves her family meat from the supermarket almost every day, along with wheat bread. Her son, 13-year-old Chul Soo, loves Western-style fast food and is overweight.[10]

And, while economic growth is necessary to reduce hunger and poverty, it is not sufficient. Brazil experienced overall economic growth of around 3 percent annually in both the 1980s and 1990s. Exports grew much more quickly, 5 percent in the 1980s and

Figure 1.1

Global Hunger, 1997

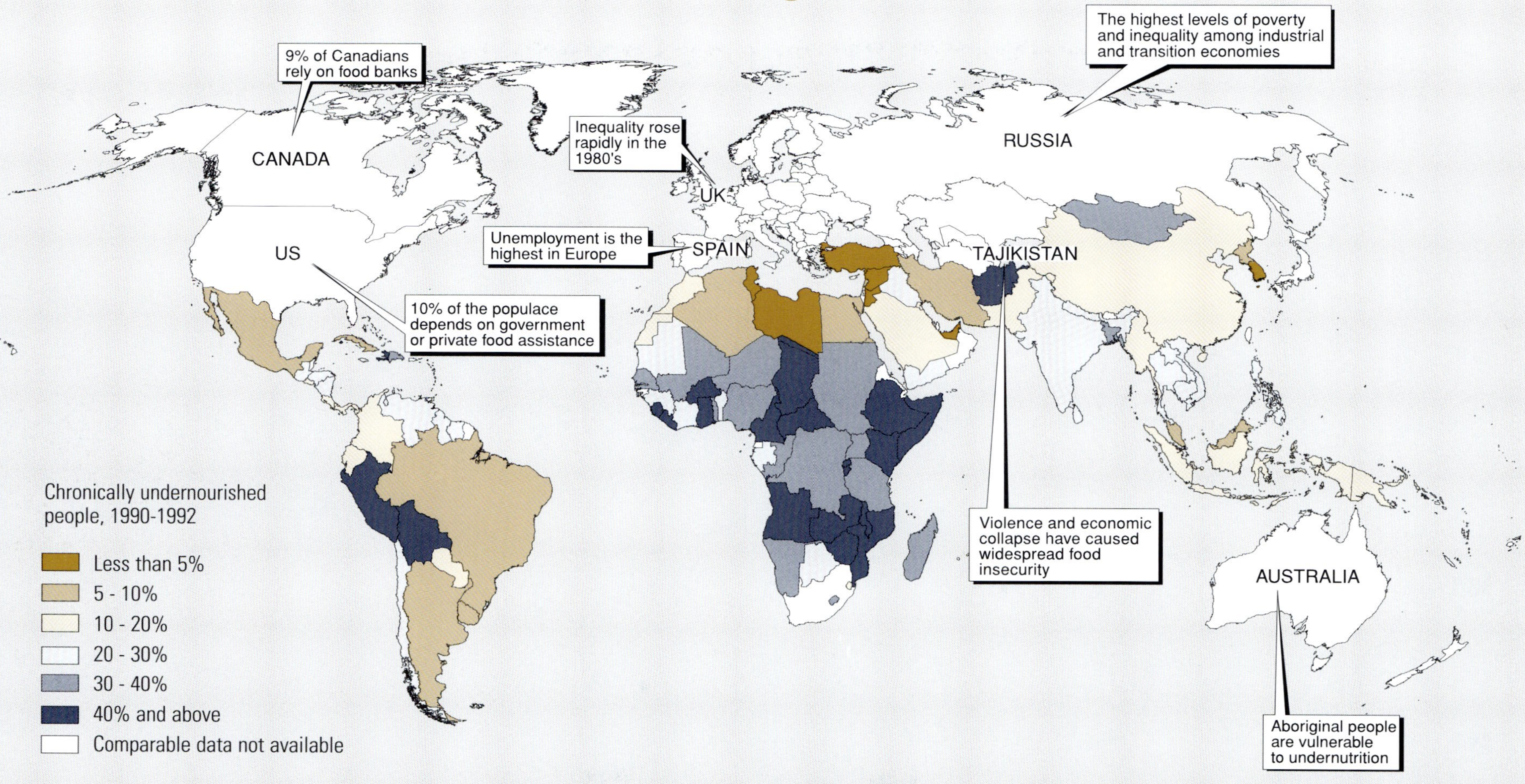

Sources: FAO; Luxembourg Income Study; *First World Hunger*, USDA; Second Harvest.

Figure 1.2

Hungry Children in Developing and Transition Countries, 1997

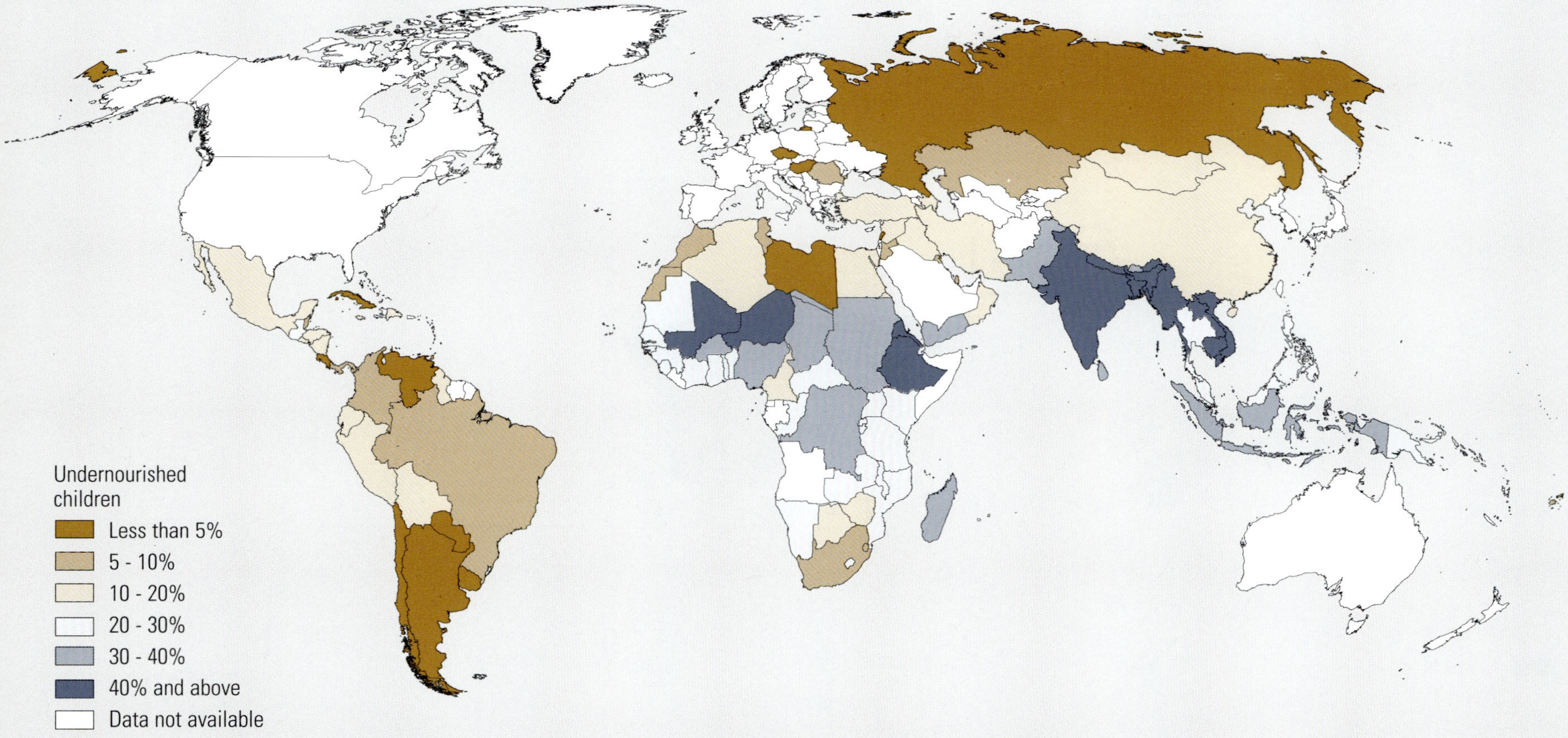

Sources: WHO Global Database on Child Growth and Malnutrition, 1997; UNICEF. Notes: "Undernourished" indicated by low weight for age. Estimated from surveys conducted in 1981-1996.

Figure 1.3 **Trends in Number and Proportion Undernourished People by Developing Region**

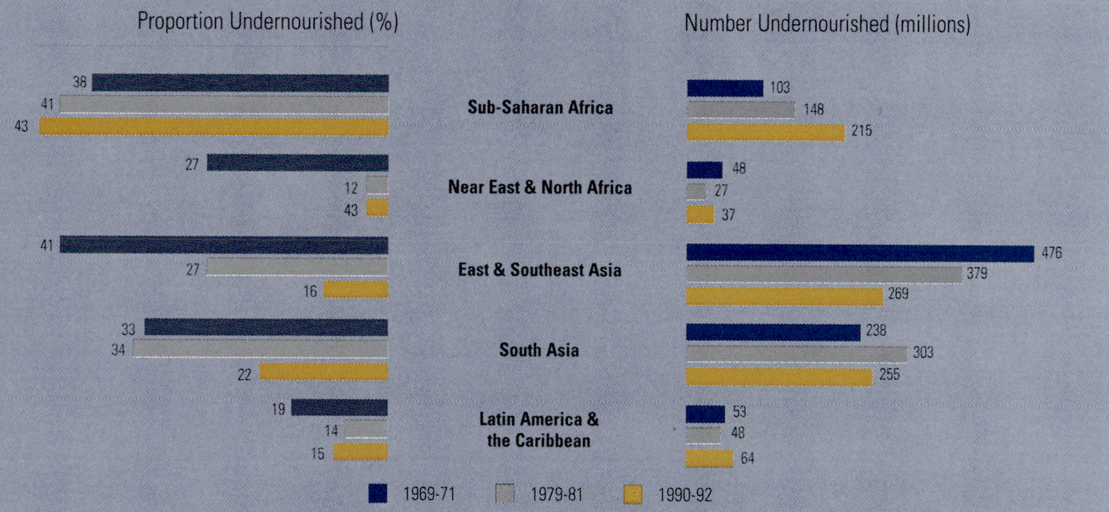

Source: Food and Agriculture Organization of the United Nations, *The Sixth World Food Survey* (Rome: FAO, 1996), 46. Reprinted with permission.

9 percent in the 1990s. The country is one of the major foreign investment targets within the developing world. Yet 32 million Brazilians (20 percent) are poor, 25 million to 26 million face hunger. The gap between rich and poor is the highest in the world, with the top 20 percent earning 32 times the income of the poorest 20 percent.[11] Hence, development economists increasingly stress the importance of *broad-based* growth for food security.[12]

Globalization is not the only, or primary, source of economic growth. In China, reduced poverty and hunger stem as well from domestic economic policies, notably the move away from collective agriculture to family farming after 1978. Yet the global economy can contribute to growth that, if properly channelled, will indeed reduce hunger.

Hunger: Causes & Solutions

The causes of hunger often include: lack of economic opportunity; political disempowerment; income inequality; inadequate public social spending; discrimination based on race, ethnicity, gender and age; violence; and environmental degradation. The solutions often include: sustainable development, including expanded income-earning opportunities for poor people; democratic participation and community empowerment; government programs to assure that everyone meets their basic needs; environmental protection; demilitarization; and policies that promote gender equality, cultural pluralism and social inclusion.

This report argues that international trade and investment can help expand income-earning opportunities for hungry and poor people, but that in order to overcome hunger, governments and civil society need to work actively on other strategies too. Political empowerment of poor people is especially important.

The Players

This section discusses some key players in the global economy – from massive transnational corporations, to national governments, to struggling low-income community organizations.

Transnational Corporations

The world's 40,000 transnational corporations (TNCs) are the main actors moving goods, services and funds across borders. The combined sales of the 200 largest companies account for 29 percent of global economic activity. One-third of world trade consists of transactions among various units of single corporations.[13] Most TNCs are headquartered in the industrial world, although developing-country TNCs are gaining significance.

TNCs offer efficiencies in matching supply and demand; moving goods and services over long distances on a timely basis (including emergency food aid); assuring improvements in product quality, as well as production of appropriate quantities; transferring capital, knowledge and technology; and research and development.

At the same time, trade in most products is dominated by five or fewer companies. The top five firms account for 30 percent to 60 percent of global sales in automobiles, electronics, airplanes, aerospace, steel, oil, personal computers, chemicals and the media. Sixty percent to 90 percent of global grain trade is controlled by six firms. Cargill alone supplies over 60 percent of the world cereal market, and its coffee revenues exceed the GDP of each of the African countries from which it buys coffee beans.[14]

Figure 1.4 **Distribution of Undernourished People by Developing Region, 1969-71 and 1990-92**

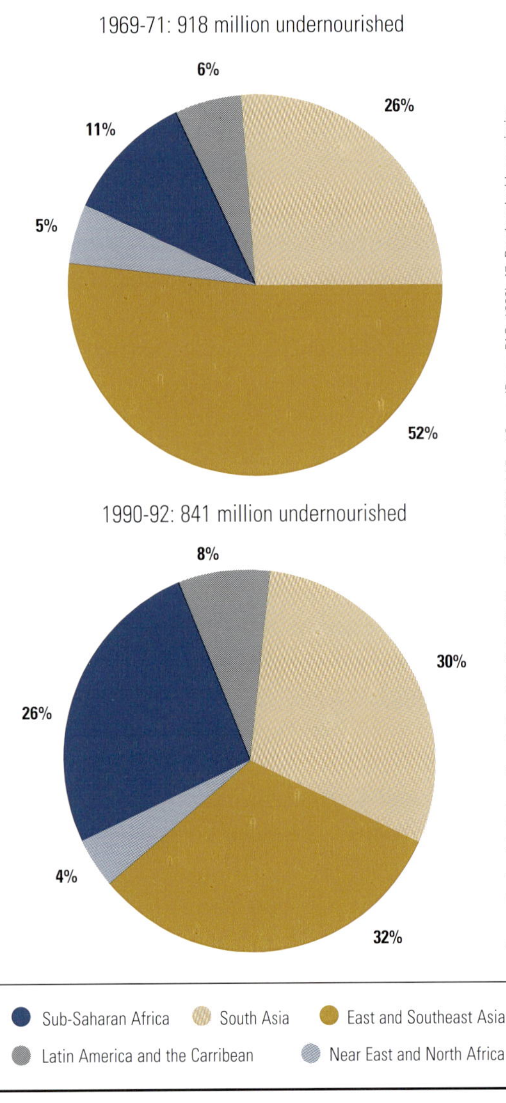

Source: Food and Agriculture Organization of the United Nations, *The Sixth World Food Survey* (Rome: FAO, 1996), 47. Reprinted with permission.

TNCs' market power gives them increasing political leverage. Their ability to shape national and international policies related to their interests was seen clearly in negotiations leading up to the 1994 global trade agreement. Industrial country corporations successfully pressed their home governments to assure strengthened intellectual property rights protection (see Chapter 4, pp. 50-51).

This political power has serious implications for popular participation in development and democratic decision making. The ability of national governments to impose social and environmental restrictions on transnationals' activities is limited in the absence of global standards and cooperation. Companies can always threaten to move in search of lax regulations.

In the United States in recent years, anti-hunger advocates have sought alliances with corporate leaders on such issues as full funding of domestic nutrition programs, adequate funding of foreign assistance (especially aid to agricultural and rural development) and education. While some executives support such policies on the grounds of humanitarianism or social responsibility, others consider such policies to be useful to their public image or in their own "bottom line interest" in having healthy consumers and skilled workers available at home and abroad. Considerable room also is available for anti-hunger advocates to press for responsible corporate policies through consumer and investor action (see Chapter 3, p. 45; Chapter 5, pp. 65-66).

Smaller Businesses

Mid-sized, small and micro-enterprises and "informal" economic activity account for a disproportionate share of global employment. Despite their vast economic weight, the top 200 TNCs employ only 18.8 million workers, or 0.8 percent of the global work force.

Small enterprises employ over 40 percent of the new entrants into the work force over the past 10 years in Botswana, Kenya, Malawi, Swaziland and Zimbabwe. In China, self-employment and enterprises with eight or fewer workers put 29 million people to work in 1993. That same year, small enterprises accounted for 22 percent of non-agricultural employment in Latin America. Small private businesses and the informal sector likewise are the main source of new jobs in the former communist countries, and small businesses are the main creators of employment opportunities in the United States. By enhancing the well-being of poor households, creating jobs and allowing for human capital formation, these enterprises contribute to their nations' ability to encounter globalization in ways that are positive for poor and hungry people (see Chapter 5, pp. 62-65).[15]

Government

Governments establish the framework within which national economies develop. It is up to governments to establish a stable political, legal and monetary context. Governments shape private sector development through regulations, taxes and subsidies. They provide physical infrastructure such as roads. Governments play a major role in education, health and social welfare.

Governments also affect the level of national engagement in globalization. They influence the competitiveness of exports and the relative cost of imports by setting exchange rates. Governments decide how much to protect domestic industries from import competition. A government's fiscal and monetary policies and the provision of physical infrastructure can help attract foreign investment.

Beginning in the early 1960s, the South Korean government promoted export-oriented industrialization and directly encouraged the growth of giant trading companies (*chaebol*) such as Samsung and Hyundai. The government promoted these companies' investment in labor-intensive activities to assure job creation. Policies stressed education and training and public works employment for workers who lost their jobs. This contributed to effective participation in the global economy. It brought growth and the rapid reduction of hunger and absolute poverty. Korea had also undertaken land reform, and the government invested in agriculture and rural development. Just 1 percent of South Koreans are chronically undernourished, whereas at the end of the Korean War, 44 years ago, most were poor peasants.[16]

Still, globalization puts new pressures on the economic and social policies of national governments. The Korean government recently responded to growing competition from other developing countries by trying to modify longstanding rules guaranteeing job security – a policy that provoked widespread protests.

Inter-governmental policy coordination and standard setting are needed to maximize what globalization can contribute to secure livelihoods (see Chapter 2). One promising blueprint for policy coordination is the 20:20 initiative, endorsed at the World Summit for Social Development and Fourth World Conference on Women in 1995. It encourages developing countries to spend 20 percent of government budgets and donors to allocate 20 percent of their aid to basic education, primary health care, nutrition, low-cost water supply, sanitation and reproductive health. This could mobilize $30 billion to $40 billion a year. Though substantial, this is just 25 percent of what developing countries now spend on debt service and military activities.

Globalization also means that domestic policy decisions can have major international implications and vice versa. The U.S. government's decision to end the Farmer Owned Reserve – a farm program aimed at stabilizing domestic grain supply and prices – has exacerbated global food price volatility. Liberalized agricultural trade under the North American Free Trade Agreement has undermined livelihood security for both small grain farmers in Mexico and tomato growers in Florida who face competition from cheap imports.

International Organizations

The World Bank and International Monetary Fund influence the economic policies of developing countries, and their "seal of approval" influences private capital flows (see Chapter 6, pp.73-74).

The World Trade Organization is a powerful new intergovernmental agency that sets trade rules and settles disputes (see Chapter 3, pp. 43-44; Chapter 4, pp. 49-50).

U.N. agencies play significant roles: the International Labor Organization promotes minimum international labor standards; the U.N. Conference on Trade and Development provides valuable information and fora for discussing how to make global economic activity equitable among nations and people. The U.N. Children's Fund works on all areas of children's well-being, including child labor. The U.N. Development Programme is a major funder of sustainable development. Its *Human Development Report* and Development Studies units conduct influential research on the impact of globalization on human well-being.

FAO seeks "to alleviate poverty and hunger by promoting agricultural development, improved nutrition and the pursuit of food security."[17] It serves as a forum on international efforts to reduce hunger. Its staff collects and disseminates information on agricultural production, agricultural trade, food consumption, world nutritional status and food emergencies. FAO also sets global food safety and quality standards, and provides technical assistance to agricultural and rural development and agrarian reform in developing countries.

The World Food Summit

The November 1996 World Food Summit set a concrete goal and timetable for reducing hunger. But it pledged no financial or organizational resources.

In contrast to the 1974 World Food Conference, also held in Rome, the 1996 gathering recognized that hunger seldom results from food shortages. Nearly always it grows out of poverty, inequality, violence, discrimination and environmental despoliation. The 1996 Declaration and Plan of Action commit national governments to work toward "food for all." The documents stress equitable access to resources, gender equality, sustainable development and the active engagement of poor and hungry people themselves in combatting hunger. The United States government worked to strengthen language in these last three areas.

Governments should assure hungry and poor people access to resources such as land, water and credit, and promote racial and gender equality.

The Summit Plan of Action commits the world's governments, in collaboration with all actors of civil society, to: establish an enabling environment for development; reduce poverty and facilitate access to food; adopt sustainable and participatory development practices; ensure trade policies conducive to food security; improve forecasting and respond to food emergencies; and encourage investment. To carry out the plan, governments agreed to draw up national strategies and programs and improve international cooperation.

The summit did not make much of an ethical case against hunger. Its documents display little passion, let alone moral outrage, that hunger exists in a multi-trillion dollar global economy and even in the world's wealthiest countries (city authorities had rousted homeless Romans from the summit site before the meeting). This was another contrast with the 1974 Conference, which featured ardent rhetoric and promises of both increased *– continued next page*

Farmers & Rural Workers

Despite rapid urbanization, agricultural activities still employ 60 percent of the work force in the developing world. Continued investment in agriculture is essential, not only to assure adequate food production for a growing population, but to provide adequate incomes for the majority of the populace.

Globalization and commercialization have had mixed results for farmers and farm workers, as for others (see Chapter 4, pp. 46-47). The United States is the world's leading grain exporter, with family-run farms accounting for most of the crops. But family farmers increasingly produce on contract to large agribusiness companies, with the crop, seed variety and input package specified in advance.[18]

In developing countries, women account for much of domestic food production – 80 percent in Africa. But development efforts too often focus on male-controlled export crops.

In Bolivia, Lutheran World Relief is working with the Bolivian Integral Development Foundation to make organic agriculture a source of sustainable livelihoods for mostly indigenous highland people. Since the 1960s, falling global tin prices have devastated highland communities that looked to the mines for jobs. The highlands cannot support extensive agriculture as an alternative. The government has encouraged migration to the lowlands, but slash and burn agriculture there has led to deforestation and depleted soils. The organic agriculture project helps 540 poor farm families in the lowland Department of Santa Cruz produce tropical fruits for export to Europe and other Latin American countries. Organic produce is also popular locally, assuring financial viability.[19]

Many poor farmers are independent and scattered, and so they do not have cohesive organizations. The largest global farmers' organization is the International Federation of Agricultural Producers (IFAP). It stresses the importance of family farms to "the social tissue of resources and new institutions to achieve the ambitious goal of ending hunger altogether in a decade.

In 1996, governments sought a blueprint for food security on the cheap. At the insistence of the U.S. government, the documents portray trade liberalization, free markets and private investment as key pieces in the food security puzzle. They call for agricultural development in the developing countries but do not analyze potential tradeoffs between strengthening local agriculture and liberalization.

In contrast, the Nongovernmental Organization (NGO) Forum, which paralleled the summit, put small farmers at the center of food security and stressed sustainable and participatory development.

Most prominent heads of state and government from both North and South declined to attend. President Bill Clinton chose to go instead to the Asia Pacific Economic Cooperation Forum to negotiate greater access to Asian markets for U.S. electronics firms.

In 1974, members of Congress played a prominent role on the U.S. delegation. This time, only Representative Tony Hall, a leading anti-hunger advocate, showed up. He provided a more nuanced view of trade liberalization than the official U.S. delegation, and spoke out on the right to food.

On the last day of the summit, the U.S. delegation filed an "interpretative statement." This says that the United States does not regard language in the documents about the right to food as creating enforceable international obligations. In addition, the United States rejected the need for stronger international legal mechanisms to advance this right. U.S. officials feared litigation by food insecure people in the United States and demands for more foreign aid.

The NGO forum had placed considerable emphasis on food as a human right. Bread for the World President David Beckmann and leaders of 30 other U.S. NGOs sent a letter to Secretary of Agriculture Dan Glickman, the head of the U.S. delegation, expressing "surprise and disappointment" at the U.S. statement. The groups called it "inconsistent with longstanding U.S. policy" of unqualified support for the right to food.

Ending hunger, at home and abroad, will require money, political will and appropriate institutions. It is heartening that the Clinton administration appears serious about using follow-up to the Summit to help address problems created by the welfare reform law of 1996. But mending the national social safety net will not be cheap or easy. Nor will creating a global economy that assures everyone secure livelihoods.

The author, **Marc J. Cohen**, represented Bread for the World at the World Food Summit, the NGO Forum, and at preparatory meetings in Canada, the United States and Italy.

rural communities" and as an equitable engine of growth for national economies. Established in 1946, IFAP includes 82 organizations in 58 countries (28 in the developing world) and hundreds of millions of farm families. These range from small, subsistence-oriented operators to huge commercial ranchers.

Cooperatives offer small producers and consumers alike a measure of countervailing market power vis-à-vis TNCs in both the developing and industrial world. In 1994, farmer cooperatives were responsible for $452 billion in global production. The International Cooperative Alliance brings together 220 member organizations from 90 countries representing 760 million members.[20]

Workers

Free-moving capital, which roams the globe in search of new profit opportunities, may be the piston that drives the global economy, but the 2.7 billion member global labor force provides the steam. In the developing world, the overwhelming majority of the workers in garment, footwear and electronics assembly are women between the ages of 16 and 25.

Export zones are common in developing countries, and offer a mixed blessing. The jobs almost always represent gains for workers' households, and the factories can stimulate additional economic activity in such areas as supplies, services and marketing. But the zones encroach on land that could support more traditional sources of livelihood such as fishing and farming. They may force older manufacturing enterprises out of business, although they sometimes provide new business for local enterprises. The zones frequently harm the surrounding environment. Workers in export zones typically work long hours for modest pay under poor or even dangerous conditions. Governments often declare these zones off-limits to labor unions in order to attract investors.

Daniel Cima/IAF

A cooperative farmer in Costa Rica displays organically grown blueberries.

Workers in the industrial world face serious challenges to their livelihood security as well, at least partly due to global competition (see Chapter 2, pp. 25-29). In the United States and United Kingdom, real wages for low-skilled workers have declined, while most other industrial countries face chronic unemployment. Meanwhile, governments have cut back on safety net spending.[21]

Hundreds of millions of children are part of the global work force, some of them as young as 5 or 6. Many work in the informal sector, in domestic service, at home, in the fields. Poverty is a key factor driving children into employment. Many child workers have unemployed or underemployed parents. They often do not have the chance to go to school (see Chapter 3, pp. 38-39).

Worldwide, unions make a positive difference for workers, not only through collective bargaining for better wages, hours and working conditions, but also by affecting broader social policy. In the United States, the labor movement was instrumental in gaining passage of Social Security and civil rights legislation.

In India, the Self-Employed Women's Association (SEWA) is a trade union with 150,000 members. It is affiliated with the International Union of Food, Agricultural, Hotel, Restaurant, Catering, Tobacco and Allied Workers' Associations (IUF), an International Secretariat joining 322 unions with 2.6 million members in 107 countries. SEWA has always stressed the food security of its members and their families. Members engage in artisanal activities, salt farming, water management, nursery plantation and dairy cooperative activities. SEWA also provides microloans, and members pool their incomes so they can purchase food during droughts.

IUF's rules commit it to seeking worker and consumer participation in policy making at all levels related to the production, processing and distribution of food. The Secretariat is associated with the International Confederation of Free Trade Unions, a worldwide alliance of 194 union bodies in 136 countries with 124 million members.[22]

Consumers

Consumer organizations help assure fair prices, safe products, healthy food and socially responsible corporate behavior (see Chapter 3, p. 45). In the United States, Consumers Union, the Consumer Federation of America and Public Citizen have helped pass consumer protection legislation and continue to foster consumer awareness. In the developing world, Malaysia has long had a strong consumer movement.

Consumers International (formerly the International Organization of Consumers Unions) issued a seven-point manifesto of consumer rights in conjunction with the World Food Summit. It stressed the right to adequate food, food safety, information, fair settlement of consumer claims related to food, education on food issues, a healthy environment and participation in decision making.

Civil Society

"Civil society" consists of voluntary popular organizations and associations through which individuals work together to pursue interests, values and ideas for the common good. It includes community, farmer, labor and consumer organizations, as well as religious, humanitarian, business, professional and public-interest groups.

The active engagement of civil society organizations at all levels – local, national, regional, international – is essential to democratic decision-making and patterns of economic globalization that foster well-being for everyone. Ordinary people have considerable ability to influence the course of the global economy, despite power imbalances, especially as they work through organizations of civil society.

As Carnegie Endowment President Jessica Mathews has pointed out, nongovernmental organizations (NGOs) have in recent years had increasing influence on international negotiations and organizations. They are "bringing new priorities, demands for procedures that give a voice to groups outside government and new standards of accountability." The 1992 Earth Summit was a watershed, with civil society organizations playing a strong role in setting the global sustainable development agenda.[23]

During preparations for the World Food Summit in 1996, NGOs influenced many provisions in the Plan of Action, including those relating to food emergencies, breastfeeding and sustainable agriculture. Some 1,300 NGOs from all regions joined together in November to issue a declaration, "Profit for Few or Food for All?," which was read to the summit on its last day. When violence exploded in Zaire during the course of the summit, African NGOs in Rome issued a powerful call for a demilitarized, African-led response.

Via Campesina, formed in 1993, is a movement of peasants, small and medium-sized farmers (including many women farmers), agricultural workers and indigenous communities, seeking equality and social justice in economic relationships, sustainable agriculture and self-reliance in food production. During the World Food Summit, Via Campesina challenged governments and NGOs alike to support agrarian reform and "food sovereignty," the right "of each nation to maintain and develop its own capacity to produce its basic foods respecting cultural and productive diversity."[24]

In the Asia-Pacific region, the Asian NGO Coalition for Agrarian Reform and Rural Development has brought together organizations from around the region to promote food security, self-reliance and the rights of small farmers and rural poor people. It has also stressed gender equality and sustainability.

In Brazil, Citizens' Action, the national anti-hunger movement, has engaged people from all walks of life and all social backgrounds in the struggle against that country's pervasive hunger. Since 1993, the movement has established 5,000 local committees around the country with over 3 million members. An estimated 30 percent of all Brazilians have participated in some aspect of the campaign, which includes direct services, efforts to create economic opportunities for poor people and advocacy aimed at convincing the government to make food security a priority. Citizens' Action successfully pressed the government of Brazil to establish a Food Security Council, which includes civil society representatives, and a national community food security program.[25]

In the United States, national, state and local anti-hunger organizations have collaborated closely since 1996 in the Hunger Has a Cure Campaign. It seeks to reverse cutbacks in federal food programs, strengthen state-level anti-hunger advocacy, encourage private charitable responses to hunger and seek policies to improve job prospects for low-income people. Bread for the World, the largest national grassroots anti-hunger organization, made Hunger Has a Cure its major 1997 campaign.

Markets Aren't Magic

The market-oriented global economy is likely to prevail for the foreseeable future. So while some social critics articulate alternative visions for the future (see "Alternative Visions," p. 20), this report focuses on feasible reforms to make the world economy more supportive of secure livelihoods for everybody.

Markets mobilize businesses to meet consumer demand. So markets are powerful instruments for human betterment. Businesses turn ideas into opportunities, organize people into jobs and meet their customers' shifting interests. Market competition typically compels businesses to operate efficiently and try to improve productivity.

Active engagement of civil society is essential to end hunger.

Alternative Visions

Current proposals for drastic alternatives to the global market economy often focus on strengthening local communities and addressing environmental concerns. David Korten, of the People-Centered Development Forum, has called for a development strategy based on "self-reliance and needs," including:

> restructuring our economic institutions to create the kinds of market economies that are efficient, democratic and accountable. These are likely to be local economies in which the ownership of productive assets resides with local people whose well-being depends on the health and vitality of their community and ecosystem.[1]

Korten calls upon people in industrial countries to end their overconsumption, which drives extraction of resources and cheap labor from developing countries.

In a similar vein, ecofeminist Vandana Shiva, of Third World Network, urges people to "think globally, eat locally." She contrasts what she calls the "outmoded values of the capitalist patriarchy propelling globalization" with "emerging values of ecological feminism for food security" (see "Old and New Food Systems").

Former World Bank economist Herman Daly argues that economic growth is still needed in the developing world. But he calls for "steady state" national economies in the industrial world, in which growth becomes qualitative rather than quantitative.[2]

Futurist Hazel Henderson stresses the need to base global economic activity not on unfettered markets, but an ethical and cooperative framework, taking the full social and environmental costs into account. This will foster a sense of legitimacy for the global economy among people around the world and thus make the system more long-lasting. Voluntary codes of conduct, agreed upon rules, and public-private-civil society partnerships will allow much more room for socially innovative entrepreneurship to promote human well-being.[3]

Notes: 1) David Korten, "Global Growth at Too High a Cost," *Choices*, January 1997, 7; see also 4-6, 8, and David Korten, *When Corporations Rule the World* (West Hartford, CT: Kumarian Press, 1995). 2) Herman Daly, *Beyond Growth: The Economics of Sustainable Development* (Boston: Beacon Press, 1996). 3) Hazel Henderson, *Building a Win-Win World: Life Beyond Global Economic Warfare* (San Francisco: Berrett-Koehler Publishers, 1996).

Old and New Food Systems

OLD	NEW
Maximization of long-distance trade with erosion of democratic control and increase of greenhouse gases and climate destabilization	Maximization of short-distance trade to nuclear democratic control and reduced environmental impact
Intensification of external chemical inputs	Intensification of internal biological inputs
Monocultures	Biodiversity
Monopolies on knowledge	Sharing of knowledge
Industrial production	Ecological production
Global control	Local control
Dependency	Self-reliance
Dispensability of small farmers	Protection of small farmers
People only as consumers	People as producers, consumers and free citizens
Supermarket democracy	Ecological democracy

Source: Dr. Vandana Shiva, "Caliber of Destruction: Globalization, Food Security and Women's Livelihoods," *No Short-Cut to Food Security Monograph* No. 3 (Manila: Isis International-Manila, 1996), p. 27. Reprinted with permission of the publisher.

But it is necessary to complement markets with government and civic action to ensure secure livelihoods for all.

Last year's report in this series, *What Governments Can Do: Hunger 1997*, argued against the currently widespread cynicism about governments. It stressed two roles of governments.

First, governments can help provide a framework to assure that markets provide opportunities for everyone. Macroeconomic policies can encourage full employment. Only public policies can assure universal access to basic education and primary health care, which is critical to productivity and well-being. Measures such as an increased minimum wage and an expanded Earned Income Tax Credit can make sure that workers in the United States receive a living wage.

A second key role of government is to maintain a social safety net to provide a secure livelihood to those people who cannot otherwise support themselves.

Public policies make all the difference about whether economic growth contributes to food security, as in East and Southeast Asia, or takes the form of "unaimed opulence," as in Brazil.[26] The appropriate public policies are more important than growth alone; many countries with only modest growth rates (Sri Lanka, the Indian state of Kerala) have reduced hunger substantially because of public investment in human well-being.

Poor countries can often afford to put resources into public health services and basic education because these labor-intensive activities are relatively cheap in a low-wage country. These areas are also ideal targets for development assistance from wealthy governments and international organizations. The evidence is overwhelming that improving health and education among poor people, with a particular emphasis on gender equality and improved female literacy, contributes enormously to economic growth and poverty reduction.

Many of sub-Saharan Africa's social indicators improved during the 1960-1990 period, despite economic decline, based in large part on "indigenous capacities to organize and innovate." This holds out hope for future progress in the region.[27]

Civil society has a vital role, too. Religious groups and other social organizations care for people. They provide substantial and personalized help for people in need. They also influence what government does (see Figure 1.5).

Even under authoritarian regimes, an active civil society can assure that government makes hunger reduction a policy priority. In Chile, the military dictatorship of Augusto Pinochet (1973-1989) drastically reduced the role of the state in the economy and reduced spending on health, housing and education. But the government expanded child health and nutrition programs and provided public works employment for jobless workers. These policies resulted from strong pressure from labor unions and other popular organizations, and contributed to improved well-being and reduced hunger.[28]

So it is imperative to include hungry and poor people in decisions that affect their lives.

In general, people go hungry because they are poor and powerless. To achieve food security, they need both income and power. In the United States, poor people have suffered disproportionate losses in recent debates over the federal budget. Low-income people tend not to vote, and the organizations that represent them are much weaker than many other interests. As elsewhere, politicians have cut funding from anti-poverty programs at little political cost.

Poor people acquire some power if they can earn money or build assets. They acquire power in governmental structures through voting and building representative associations – farm or labor organizations, community organizations or religious groups.

In both the developing and industrial countries, globalization often causes market forces to overwhelm government and civil society, with negative hunger consequences. The next chapter discusses the need to restore balance among these major sectors of society in order to eradicate hunger.

Figure 1.5 **Governments, Markets & Civil Society**

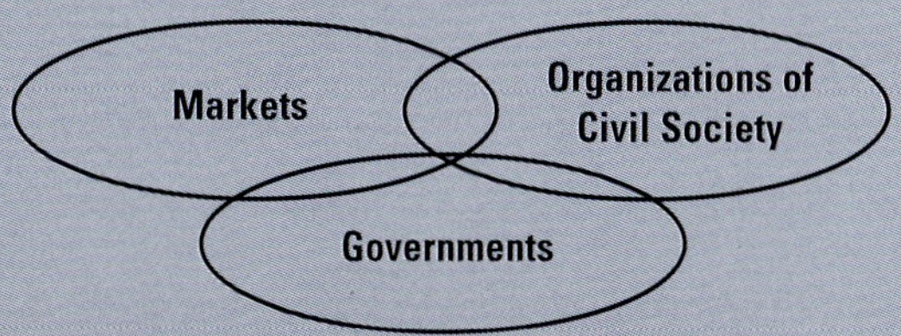

The realms of market, government and civil society are enmeshed with one another. People may be active in all three realms. For instance, a business person may advise and vote for a government while affiliating with organizations of civil society, such as religious, professional, women's groups or a trade union.

Source: Institute for Development Research.

Dr. Marc J. Cohen, senior research associate at Bread for the World Institute, is editor of *Hunger in a Global Economy.* **Dr. Lily Philipose**, BFW Institute intern, and **Jashinta D'Costa**, consultant, assisted in research and writing for this chapter.

CHAPTER 2

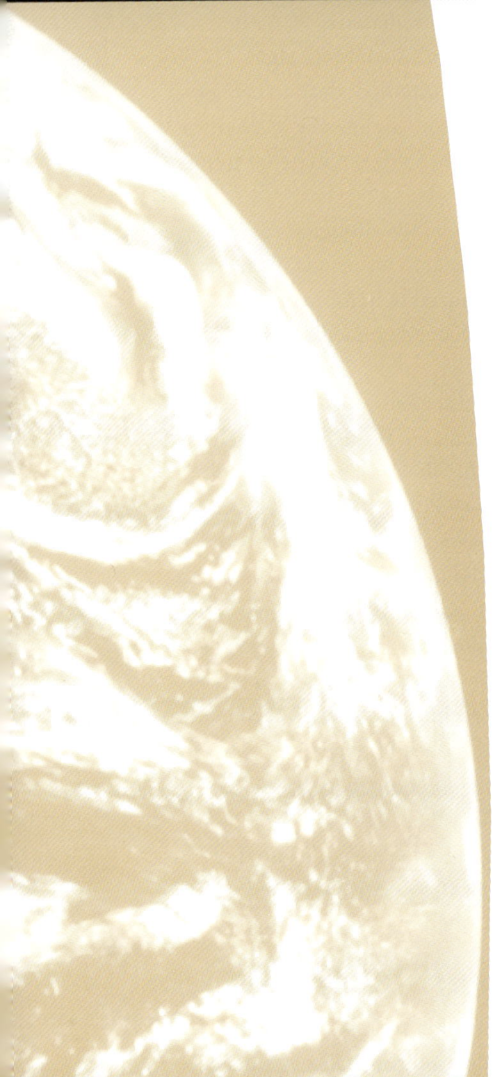

Globalization, Governments & Politics

By Marc J. Cohen & Don Reeves

Coordinate policies among nations to foster full employment and other social goals.

The global economy has replaced the Cold War as the dominant international structure. "Competitiveness" has replaced "national security" as the prevailing principle for fashioning public policies (see "From National Security to Competitiveness," pp. 24-25).

In 1992, Francis Fukuyama reviewed the generally strong performance of market economies since World War II and their positive contribution to human well-being. He contrasted the dramatic changes in China in the early 1980s with the collapse of the Soviet economy in the late 1980s and noted the generally dismal performance of nearly every other centrally planned economy. He declared "democratic capitalism" the wave of the future, on which all nations are surfing.[1]

Much evidence supports this view. From World War II into the 1970s, the industrial nations of the North experienced growth and prosperity undreamed of in human history. Living standards increased for all who had work, and most did. Safety net programs helped those who, for whatever reason, did not. Poverty rates dropped. Income disparity between rich and poor narrowed. Meanwhile, each of the developing nations where poverty has dropped the fastest over the past 35 years, primarily in East and Southeast Asia, have instituted some version of a market economy.

In 1997, William Greider offered a more pessimistic view. He likened the global economy to a giant, wondrously productive, essentially out-of-control machine, leaving great destruction in its wake and quite possibly headed toward its own destruction.[2]

Again, plenty of evidence exists. A bewildering array of goods and services is available, at ever decreasing real prices. But even in the bastions of capitalism, poverty and unemployment are increasing. Real wages for the majority of U.S. workers declined steadily from 1973 to 1994. Unemployment has soared in

Europe. Income gaps are widening within and across national boundaries. Hundreds of millions of hungry people in Africa, Latin America and Asia meanwhile survive in shadow economies. They are barely connected to the dominant global economy, and certainly see none of its presumed benefits (see "The Informal Sector," pp. 64-65).

Both visions contain truth. Zealous market advocates claim too much; critics often miss the dynamism and potential in well-functioning markets.

From the end of World War II through the 1960s, national governments had considerable ability to assure equity and opportunity within their borders. Through such policy mandates as minimum wages, safe working conditions and antitrust laws, they could harness the productivity of markets for most of their citizens. They tried to maintain full employment and provide a social safety net. But the globalization of the economy and the ideological triumph of market economies have made it more difficult for national governments to maintain such policies.

The triumphant and pervasive market economy is also straining civil society. Massive advertising urges all of us to satisfy our individual desires. Community traditions and institutions are under assault.

This chapter looks first at the daunting challenge of providing employment for a growing global labor force. Globalization makes it difficult for any national government, acting on its own, to pursue full employment and other social goals.

The chapter concludes with a discussion of the pressure economic interests bring to bear on politics and civil society. This pressure makes it very difficult to win political approval for even modest steps to reduce hunger.

Globalization & Constraints on National Economic Policies[3]

Historical Perspective

Before World War I, trade and international investments flowed as freely as today. Following that war, financial and monetary problems caused by debts and punitive war reparations, coupled with a retreat into trade protectionism, made it difficult for governments to restore openness. In the absence of a mechanism for coping with worldwide economic crises, the 1929 U.S. stock market crash degenerated into a global depression.[4] Economic hardship contributed to growing political extremism, nationalism and, eventually, another global war.

National Archives

The collapse of the global economy in the 1930s left millions of people hungry.

The rise and fall of this earlier version of the global economy should be a warning that international cooperation and responsiveness to hardship are necessary complements to freewheeling markets.

World economic growth since 1945 has had widespread benefits. Between 1960 and 1991, the proportion of hungry people in developing countries dropped by nearly half. Enrollment in primary school rose to 77 percent of eligible students, while average life expectancy increased by more than a third.[5]

But the development of the global economy has been turbulent and often painful. The international debt crisis in 1982 led to a decade of economic stagnation or decline for most African and Latin American economies. More than 100 countries, with populations totaling 1.5 billion people, experienced zero or negative per capita income growth between 1980 and 1995.[6]

Only a few developing economies, notably in East and Southeast Asia, maintained the pace of widespread gains against hunger and poverty through the 1970s and 1980s. These countries incrementally adopted market-oriented economic policies. Their governments also made crucial decisions, whether or not those decisions matched signals from the global marketplace, to nurture

From **National Security** to **Competitiveness** | *By Marc J. Cohen*

The global economy increasingly shapes political discourse. During the Cold War, advancing "national security" was the litmus test of any U.S. policy. Today, the question is how policy contributes to "competitiveness."

For example, during the 1970s, I financed my post-graduate education through the U.S. government's "National Defense Education Act." My grant required me to learn Indonesian; the government had decided that it was "critical" to national security for people in the United States to gain fluency in certain developing country languages.

My Ph.D. research focused on how national security concerns shaped U.S. food aid to developing countries. I found that the Carter administration wanted to end U.S. food aid to Indonesia because it mainly served as a subsidy for otherwise uncompetitive U.S. rice sales, and did not have an impact on development. The administration kept shipping food aid, nevertheless, because Indonesia wanted the cheap rice. After the Soviet invasion of Afghanistan in 1979, maintaining good relations with a large, strategically located Muslim country became an important U.S. foreign policy priority.

Today, President Clinton says the United States should expand access to education because it boosts productivity and global competitiveness. True, but education *also* enriches human communities in many non-economic ways through the arts, sciences and humanities. Engineers who appreciate poetry and English majors with technological skills are more likely to contribute to the overall quality of life. An educated populace is likely to be more tolerant.

Similarly, in early 1997, J. Brian Atwood, administrator of the U.S. Agency for International Development, recognized the need to couch arguments in global economic terms. He called vigorously for an expanded foreign aid budget not on the grounds of morality or solidarity with the struggle for sustainable development, but because aid helps build U.S. export markets abroad and most of the aid budget gets spent at home. In the past, Cold War considerations shaped foreign aid policy and funding. Since 1990, industrial-country governments have cut back on bilateral aid programs and contributions to multilateral aid agencies. Now that national security is no longer a very convincing rationale, *– continued next page*

industrial development, become more competitive globally and maintain strong emphasis on universal education (see Chapter 5, pp. 58-59).[7]

Transitions to economic openness are nearly always painful. In their shift from planned to market economies, Poland, the Czech Republic and the Baltic states each experienced three or four years of sharply declining incomes. The process is taking longer in Russia and the other former Soviet republics. Most sub-Saharan African nations began with less human resource development and infrastructure. A few of these countries finally appear to be on a growth path after up to a decade of "adjustment." Mexico's attempt at liberalization, complicated by mismanagement, if not actual malfeasance, has contributed to soaring wealth for a few families, but increasing poverty for up to 40 million of its people.[8]

How can the world reap benefits from the current cycle of economic globalization and ensure that these benefits extend to everyone – particularly hungry and poor people?

Employment is Key

The route out of poverty and hunger for most people is through new economic opportunities – jobs or self-employment. Employment provides income to meet basic needs; it also provides social cohesion. When opportunity is lacking, social instability threatens. Family and community bonds fray. The risk of crime increases.

Employment is also key to thriving national economies and general well-being. People with decent jobs buy from each other. Their incomes are a major source of saving for public and private enterprises. Wage-based taxes are a principal source of revenue for public goods such as universal education and health care, good roads and parks. The U.S. War on Poverty advocates for aid put more emphasis on competitiveness and the commercial payoff.

Even anti-hunger advocates have been forced to shift to the language of competitiveness. The persistence of hunger in a world of plenty is one of the most critical moral challenges facing the human community on the brink of the 21st century. But moral arguments alone seldom win the day in policy debates. In the 1980s, anti-hunger groups stressed the national security aspect of hunger – as both a cause and an effect of social tension and violence that can lead to war and refugee flows. Today, the argument has shifted to global economic terms: Dr. J. Larry Brown, director of the Center on Hunger, Poverty and Nutrition Policy at Tufts University, stresses that children in the United States who suffer from mild undernutrition in the first years of life will not achieve full cognitive development, and will be less able to compete personally or contribute to the country's competitive edge. At the same time, care for children creates a moral edge.[1]

Dr. Marc J. Cohen, senior research associate at BFW Institute, is editor of *Hunger in a Global Economy.*

Note: 1) Dr. J. Larry Brown, "The Disease America's Never Cured," *Bread, the Bread for the World Newsletter*, June/July 1997, 5.

and even stronger social compacts throughout western Europe were both financially and politically feasible in the high employment era of the 1960s and early 1970s, when they reached their zenith.

Rising Unemployment and Falling Wages

The global economy is booming in 1997, and sustained growth has finally tightened the job market in the U.S., even for low-income workers. But this good news comes against a backdrop of decades of slack demand for labor in the industrial countries.

In contrast with the prosperity of 1960-1973, unemployment nearly doubled during 1988-1994 in Canada. It did double in Italy and Japan, quadrupled in the United Kingdom, grew fivefold in France and increased by 850 percent in Germany.[9] In the United States, median wages, adjusted for inflation, fell steadily from 1973 through 1995, most sharply for lower-paid workers.[10] (see "Employment Problems in Industrial Countries," pp. 26-27).

High unemployment and underemployment have persisted in the developing countries as well. In sub-Saharan Africa, paid employment in manufacturing declined 0.5 percent per year during the 1980s. Urban unemployment now ranges between 15 percent and 20 percent, compared to around 10 percent in the mid-1970s. In Latin America, paid employment fell at a rate of about 0.5 percent annually during the 1980s.[11]

Only in East and Southeast Asia were there countries that witnessed a consistent improvement in employment, workers' wages, and capacity to maintain or improve social services.

Needed: 2 Billion Jobs

The world's population will grow a third – from 5.9 billion to 8 billion – by the year 2025. The global labor force will grow even faster, from 2.7 billion to more than 4 billion workers. If part of the billion-plus workers presently unemployed or underemployed are added, more than 2 billion new economic opportunities are needed over the next 30 years.

Half these new workers have already been born. There are few new frontiers to settle, and technology is making farming less labor-intensive. So virtually all the added jobs will need to be non-farm. Some of the non-farm opportunities can be in rural areas.

Most of the new jobs will be needed in developing countries, where more than 90 percent of the increase in population and work force is taking place. Improvements in education, health care and public infrastructure may provide some public service jobs. But most new income-earning opportunities, if they come to pass, will be in the private or informal sectors of these economies.

Because of economic globalization, labor surpluses in the developing countries may tend to drive the wages of low-skill workers down further in the industrial countries, as well.

Policy Setting under Global Competition

In this context of need for more and better employment opportunities, we look at some of the policies usually prescribed as necessary in a world of intense

Employment Problems in Industrial Countries

In a globally competitive environment, low- and mid-skilled workers in the industrial countries have taken some losses. Some of their jobs have been exported; some have been eliminated by technology. Other workers face competition from immigrants willing to work for less. Their unions, which helped them capture a full share of productivity gains through the 1960s, have declined in numbers and strength. Wages for many of the remaining jobs in these areas have declined sharply, in real terms, as have wages for new jobs requiring equivalent skills in service industries. The majority of people who have lost manufacturing jobs receive lower pay in their new jobs.

At the same time, increasing trade and technology have generated additional jobs, including some very good ones that require high technical or management skills.

These factors have contributed to rising inequality throughout most of the industrial world, particularly the United States, the other English-speaking countries and Italy.

Trade is one of a number of causes of this growing inequality. Analysts differ widely, but the accompanying table (see Table 2.1) is somewhere near the median among a wide range of assessments of the balance among causes of diverging wages.

In the United States, between 1979 and 1993, real wages for the bottom 10th of male U.S. workers fell 16 percent, while only those for the top 5 percent rose at all, spectacularly for those at the very top. Wages for women workers similarly diverged. Wages for women in the bottom 10 percent fell as sharply as for men, while increasing steeply for a few at the very top. In between, women fared better than men, with real wages dropping for the bottom one-third, while rising modestly for most of the rest (see Figure 2.1). The male-female gap closed significantly, although far from completely, over the period for all except the bottom workers, but largely at the expense of lower wages for men.[1]

In the United States, between 1979 and 1993, real wages for the bottom tenth of male U.S. workers fell 16 percent, while only those for the top 5 percent rose at all, spectacularly for those at the very top.

Household incomes have diverged in the same pattern as wages: down 11 percent for the poorest one-fifth of U.S. households, and up 24 percent for the top one-fifth between 1979 and 1994 (see Figure 2.2). The meteoric rise in income for top households is based on at least three contributing factors: the divergence in wages; an increasing proportion of two-earner families in this group (likely both with high incomes); and much lower taxes on high incomes.

While the U.S. economy has yielded growing inequality, it has also generated several positive outcomes. Overall, the economy has grown steadily, without high inflation, particularly since the middle 1980s. It has created 30 million jobs since 1980. Increases in productivity (output per worker) resumed during the 1990s, after being relatively flat since about 1970. The mid-1990s have enjoyed sustained economic growth with low inflation. Unemployment in spring 1997 reached a 24-year low.

Computer and business graduates in 1997 are overwhelmed with generous offers. But high school dropouts still get *– continued next page*

Table 2.1 **Accounting for the Rise in U.S. Wage Inequality**

Cause	**Estimated Contribution to Rise in Inequality (percent)**
Trade and Immigration	15-20
Lack of investment in education	25
Decline in unionization	20
Decline in minimum wage	5-10
Technological change	25

Source: *When Earnings Diverge.*

Figure 2.1 **Change in Real Hourly Earnings**
United States, 1979-1993, by deciles

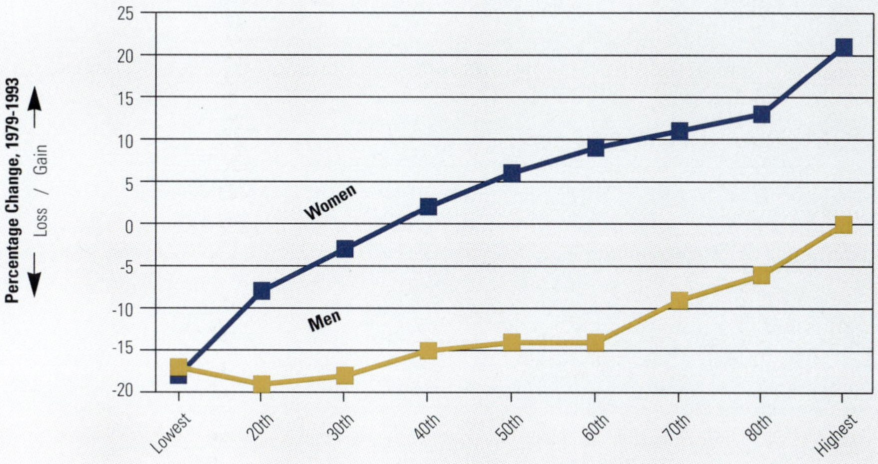

Source: *When Earnings Diverge.*

minimum wages, without benefits, often only for temporary or part-time work.

Policy choices have contributed to a quite different pattern in most of Europe, compared to the United States and, to a lesser degree, Canada and the United Kingdom. The United States has let the minimum wage fall behind inflation and whittled away at safety net and unemployment programs.

In contrast, Europeans more nearly maintained their already stronger unemployment and social safety net programs, and continued full-cost-of-living wage raises throughout the eighties and early 1990s. The bottom 10th of workers in Germany now have twice the income of their U.S. counterparts. Overall, the bottom one-third of workers in Europe and Japan have more purchasing power than the same group in the United States, even though the average of all U.S. citizens is pushed higher by much higher incomes at the top.[2]

But Europe is being pressed to make sharp adjustments. Since employers have to pay relatively high costs to hire someone, no net new jobs have been created for decades. Unemployment has reached record levels. As European governments cope with serious budget constraints, they are curtailing social spending. Currently, they spend 2 percent of gross domestic product (GDP) supporting jobless workers – nearly $150 billion per year.

Figure 2.2 **Changes in U.S. Family Income, 1979-1994**
by income groups

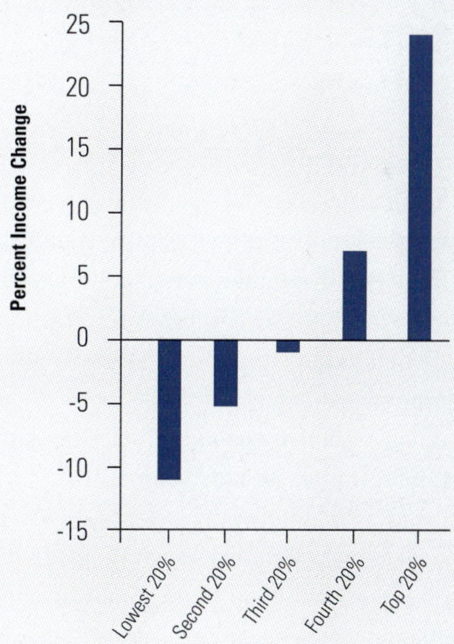

Source: *When Earnings Diverge.*

Both experiences – declining incomes for most U.S. workers and high unemployment in Europe – are rooted in declining demand for labor.

Notes: 1) Richard B. Freeman, *When Earnings Diverge: Causes, Consequences and Cures for the New Inequality in the U.S.* (Washington: National Policy Association, 1997), 26. 2) Ibid., 13-21.

Maria Luiza M. Carvalho/IAF

International cooperation can help assure basic labor rights for these Brazilian factory workers and others worldwide.

global competition. What lessons emerge from contrasting the present global competition with the experiences of the industrial nations from World War II through the early 1970s and of the East Asian countries over the past two decades?

Sound Macroeconomic Policies

The investments necessary for economic growth, productivity gains and job opportunities require a stable economic environment. If inflation is rampant, domestic savings will not be locally invested, nor will foreign capital be attracted. Maintaining a sound currency implies, in turn, that governments balance their budgets, or nearly so; that currency exchange rates find their "market" level; and that interest rates be kept competitive.

But global competition led many governments to put more emphasis on keeping inflation down (to make their national exports competitive) and interest rates up (to attract foreign lending, especially purchase of the government's own bonds). As a result, many governments are putting less emphasis on growth and employment in their macroeconomic management than they did when national economies were more self-contained.

As all governments respond to these pressures, economic growth is dampened. Footloose capital, constantly shopping around for the most secure setting, is contributing to what some analysts characterize as a deflationary bias in the world economy. The Bank for International Settlements warned in 1996 that increased global competition and budget cuts, combined with wage flexibility, might lead to global recession.[12]

The world's major economic powers could do themselves and the rest of the world a huge favor by collectively putting more emphasis on growth and employment. All economic classes and nearly all nations would benefit. The shift would mean, for example, that the U.S. Federal Reserve Board would be less inclined to raise interest rates at any hint of possible inflation.

But no individual nation can shift its macroeconomic priorities on its own. International cooperation is required.

Labor Market Flexibility

Some argue that the cure for unemployment is increased "labor market flexibility" – letting minimum wages slip into irrelevance, or deliberately weakening labor unions. As evidence, they point to 30 million new jobs in the United States since 1980. Or to the experience of Taiwan and South Korea. Their relatively unfettered labor markets attracted apparel manufacturing 25 years ago. These jobs have since moved to China and Indonesia as better jobs have become available in South Korea and Taiwan.

Labor market flexibility is not without costs, however. For 15 years, labor markets have become more flexible all over the world. The results include declining wages for low-skilled workers in the United States and the United Kingdom; sharp increases in European unemployment; growing numbers of working poor people; increased income inequality in most industrial countries and Latin America; and increased job-related anxiety almost everywhere (see "Employment Problems...," pp. 26-27).[13]

In many developing countries, where labor markets are least regulated, wages remain extremely low, hours long and workplace conditions abominable. Workers enjoy little bargaining power.

So international cooperation is also needed to establish and maintain basic labor standards (see Chapter 3, pp. 41-42).

Public Finance: Another Casualty of Global Competition

Healthy public finances are necessary to deal with human and social needs, and to make an economy more productive through education, a sound legal system and good infrastructure. Yet global competition is pushing many governments to reduce taxes in order to attract private investment that can now easily move to lower-tax environments.

In fact, both national and local governments often not only waive taxes to attract investors. They offer additional incentives and subsidies, including "union-free" export zones and lax environmental regulations. Such policies create jobs, but at a high social and ecological cost.

In the United States, corporate taxes have dropped from 30 percent of revenues in 1960 to 3 percent in 1995. Governments make up some of the difference by taxing personal incomes. Compared to firms, people are less able or willing to move to lower-tax environments. In the European Union, the overall tax rate on labor grew 20 percent between 1980 and 1993. In contrast, proceeds from capital gains taxes declined 10 percent.

But heavier payroll taxes mean that businesses are less likely to create jobs or pay better wages. More workers and their families need training and retraining, support during periods of unemployment, and safety nets to prevent hunger and poverty.

Governments are also reducing spending, especially spending that helps low-income people. The United States has embarked on a program of sharply reduced welfare benefits premised on moving recipients into employment. But plans to date include neither adequate training nor adequate complementary programs such as assured child or health care. Millions of additional low-skilled workers searching for work seem almost certain to depress low-skilled wages even further.[14] However, as Northwestern University economist Rebecca Blank argues, without social policies to address the human consequences of economic change,

> countries will face very real long-term consequences, such as increases in the size of their underground economies, increasing crime, drug use, family fragmentation and increasing civic disconnection and disorder – frequent outcomes when a share of the population is excluded from mainstream labor markets.[15]

Other Policy Frustrations

A long list of other policy concerns has taken on new complexity as globalization proceeds, while national governments remain the principal policy-setting venue. For example, many forms of environmental degradation cross national boundaries. Antitrust enforcement is difficult when firms' activities overlap several jurisdictions. Consumers and producers of high-quality goods do not want unfair competition from substandard or dangerous products. Workers don't want to compete with child labor in South Asia, or with workers who cannot organize or bargain collectively in Central America.

So more coordination of economic and social policies among governments is a necessary complement to globalized markets.

The Group of 8 (the major industrial powers), the Organization for Economic Cooperation and Development (OECD, which includes governments from the industrial countries and some high-income developing countries), the international financial institutions (Chapter 6), and U.N. fora can all contribute to international policy coordination. A widespread consensus exists on the need to reach common standards, as evidenced by the series of nine major United Nations conferences since 1990, on children, the environment, nutrition, human rights, population, social development, women, habitation and food security.

Citizens and civil society organizations need to press for international cooperation and standards. Environmental, religious, labor and other organizations of civil society are developing their own international networks, parallel to global markets. Hundreds, even thousands, of civil society organizations have taken part in recent U.N. conferences. International coordination of advocacy for World Bank reform is also a clear example (see Chapter 6, p. 73).

Globalization and Politics

The collapse of communism has had profound effects on global political life. Almost every government and viable political party today professes allegiance to market economics. Even the remaining self-proclaimed communist regimes – in China, Cuba, Vietnam and North Korea – eagerly seek foreign investment. Socialist governments in the industrial world have cut welfare programs as sharply as their conservative rivals.

The weakening of alternative political platforms has contributed to the political power of money. In the United States, where television-driven political campaigns absorb enormous sums, both major political parties depend heavily on political action committees and other wealthy special interest groups. A political finance scandal caused the French Socialists to lose the presidency. In East and Southeast Asia, economic growth has spawned indigenous transnational companies that have tried to translate wealth into political influence at home and abroad. Corrupt fundraising led to the prosecution of business and political leaders in South Korea. Asian companies with business interests in China and the United States have sought to influence U.S. policy and election outcomes.

Effective Governments

[D]evelopment requires an *effective state*, one that encourages and complements the activities of private businesses and individuals. An effective state is vital for the provision of the goods and services – and rules and institutions – that allow markets to flourish and people to lead healthier, happier lives. Without it, sustainable development, both economic and social, is impossible. Experience shows that the state is central to economic and social development, not as a direct provider of growth, but as its partner, catalyst and facilitator.

[E]ffective states [have] common features – the ways in which government has set rules that more broadly underpin private transactions and civil society, and how the state has played by the rules itself, acting reliably and predictably and checking corruption.

Note: Excerpted from The World Bank, *World Development Report 1997: The State in a Changing World* (New York: Oxford University Press, 1997).

In the Democratic Republic of the Congo (known until recently as Zaire), President Laurent Kabila, a one-time Marxist, is offering foreign firms attractive deals to exploit his country's mineral wealth.

This political triumph of markets and wealth too often makes the voices of hungry and poor people easy for policy makers to ignore. It is little wonder that fighting hunger is seldom a top public policy priority, or that budget cutters eagerly go after anti-hunger programs. Some governments, such as that of Eritrea, pay attention to popular aspirations and put poverty reduction high on their agendas. Among industrial countries, the Scandinavian nations continue to support strong social policies and to enjoy low rates of poverty and inequality.

Mexico stands at the other extreme. Institutionalized corruption, fraudulent elections and policies that benefit local billionaires while increasing hunger have led to violent rebellions.

Threats to Community & Culture

A world market is not a world community. But globalization powerfully affects culture, social norms and institutions. Hardly a country lacks a McDonald's restaurant these days, and Michael Jackson T-shirts appear in the remotest of villages. The norms of the global economy are those of liberalized trade, which may not jibe with national social conventions. Wheat bread has often displaced rice as a staple, and with it, much of the "culture of rice." U.S. national consensus in favor of "dolphin friendly tuna" becomes an unfair practice under global trade rules.[16]

Globalization has positive aspects as well. The communications revolution contributed to democratization in Poland and made it possible for the whole world to know instantly (by fax, modem and real-time broadcasts) when the Chinese government massacred peaceful protesters in 1989.

But advertising has fostered a globalizing culture of self-gratification and the proliferation of "wants" perceived as "needs." The drive to get more money to acquire more high-tech gadgets has contributed to a weakening of family ties and of a sense of responsibility to vulnerable groups such as children and elderly people, especially through public programs.

People whose "world" is the world economy are less likely to be loyal to their country or local community, engaged in civic life or even committed to their extended family. Location may be seen as a business decision, with little thought to the effects on the quality of life or social fabric.

Religious congregations also get caught up in a commercial mindset. Thirty years ago, critic Peter Berger pointed out that "religious institutions become marketing agencies and the religious traditions become consumer commodities." Congregations develop new programs to enhance their comparative advantage in gaining a larger market share of members who are consumers of religion:

> This means that religion can more easily be marketed if it can be shown to be 'relevant' to private life than if it is advertised as entailing specific applications to the large public institutions.... This ... helps explain why the churches have had relatively little influence on the economic and political views of even their own members, while continuing to be cherished by the latter in their existence as private individuals.[17]

Religious institutions offer uplifting worship, education for children, personal counseling, all kinds of small group experiences and a convenient parking lot. Most of their founders urged justice, righteousness and attention to the needs of vulnerable people.

Most congregations collect canned food for hungry people. But they do not speak much about social justice or ways that public institutions are needed, alongside private volunteerism and charity, to solve public problems. Faithful and effective Bread for the World activists join together across congregational and denominational lines because a joint effort is needed in politics, but also because their views and values are sometimes lonely in the places where they worship.

Conclusion

In the relatively closed economies of the past, some balance between states and markets could be achieved at the national level. Today, the economy is increasingly international, while policy-making remains mostly national. It is more difficult to provide the environment for markets to work as they should – and to translate their benefits into human well-being.

In order to make the most out of globalization, it is necessary to coordinate policies among nations to foster full employment and other social goals. People of all socioeconomic backgrounds concerned about social justice can forge local, national and global alliances to renew genuinely democratic politics and secure the enactment of global policies that harness market imperatives to meeting human needs. Such coalitions must include hungry and poor people at their center. Revitalizing religious and ethical values is also an important part of this project.

Dr. Marc J. Cohen, senior research associate at Bread for the World Institute, is editor of *Hunger in a Global Economy*.
Don Reeves is economic policy analyst at BFW Institute.

CHAPTER 3

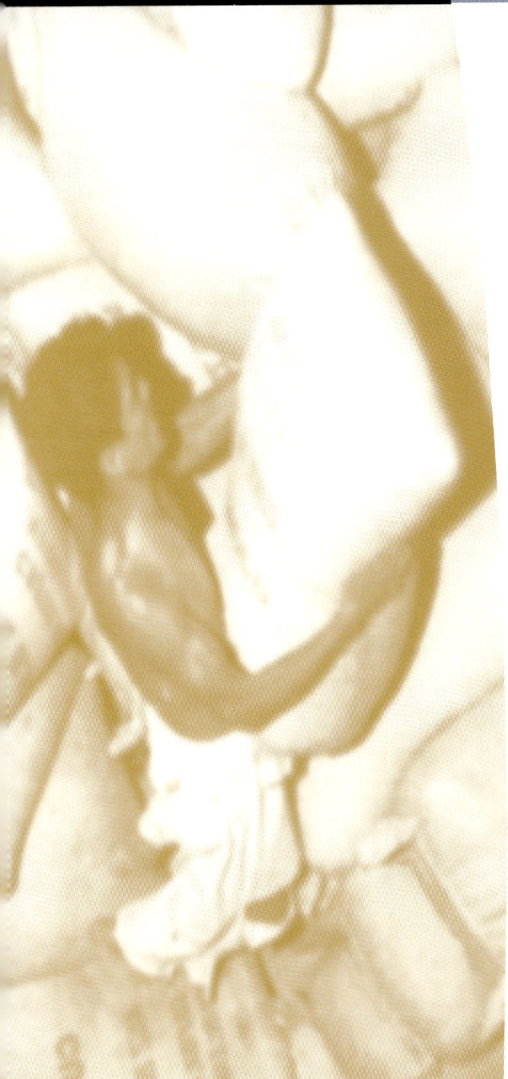

Trade, Poverty Reduction & Economic Opportunity

By Don Reeves

Promote international trade – with safeguards for labor rights, the environment and food security.

For breakfast this morning, I enjoyed orange juice from Florida, tea from South Asia, and a banana from Central America on cereal manufactured in Michigan from grains grown somewhere in the Midwest or Plains states. After breakfast, I put on clothes sewn in the Dominican Republic, Guatemala, Bangladesh and Zimbabwe. My new sneakers were assembled in China, in contrast to the five-year-old pair – same brand and model – which were sewn in Korea.

Nothing in today's breakfast or wardrobe was made in my Maryland suburb of Washington, DC. Only my raincoat was assembled within the state of Maryland, and that factory just closed.

We are all traders, exchanging our time, skills and investments for the income we in turn trade for the things we need or desire. Virtually everything for which we trade crosses at least one political boundary, under greater or lesser regulation. Trade within the United States is relatively unfettered. But an increasing share of our daily provisions also crosses national boundaries, with a myriad of varying rules.

As consumers, we have access through markets to an ever greater variety of goods and services, and their real cost (after inflation adjustments) continues to decline. Trade provides employment for people far removed from us. Apparel imports into the United States, Europe and other industrial countries account for 11 million jobs in developing countries.

But even a cursory look reveals that the benefits from increasing trade are not equitably distributed. Michael Jordan receives more for his endorsement of Nike shoes than the 22,000 women in Indonesia who assemble them. The ratio between the wages of line workers in Fortune 500 manufacturing plants and CEOs in the same companies has widened from 52 to 104 since 1973.

Market-oriented trade is dynamic. Competition, innovation and change are inevitable, and can be a blessing or a curse, or both, depending on how human lives and the environment are affected.

So, even as I eat and dress, I reflect on the conditions under which poor young women have sewn my clothing. Or on the life of the people who used to sew my shoes in Korea, or before that, in Massachusetts, and the changes in their lives as they have moved to better jobs, poorer ones or none at all.

This chapter argues that international trade can contribute to progress against poverty and hunger. It examines developing- and industrial-country issues and then outlines national policies that can help direct benefits from trade toward more secure livelihoods for all. The chapter then describes recent trade agreements, notably GATT and NAFTA. It concludes with a section on how we as consumers can influence corporations directly.

Figure 3.2 **Growing Importance of Trade**

Selected Economies, 1970-1995

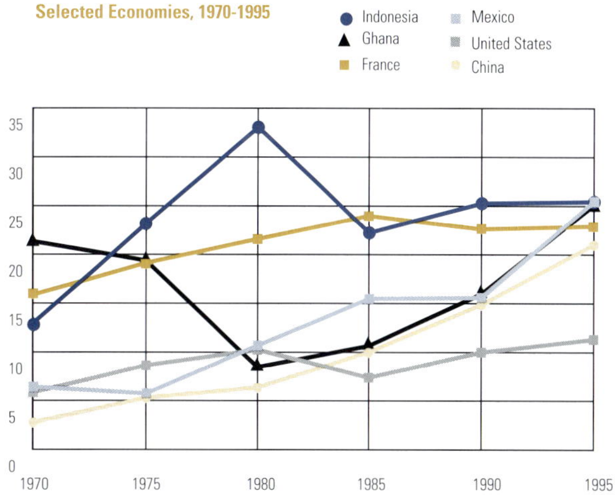

Source: The World Bank.

Trends in International Trade

Except for a downturn in the early 1980s, the volume of trade in both goods and services has grown steadily since 1970 (see Figure 3.1).

International trade has grown faster than overall economic growth in most countries. Exports, measured as a proportion of the total of goods and services produced in a nation (GDP), range from 9 percent in Japan and 11 percent in the United States up to more than 70 percent for Belgium and Ireland among industrial countries. They have grown steadily since 1970. Exports have grown even faster among upper-middle-income developing countries, particularly in East Asia (see Figure 3.2).

On the other hand, exports have not grown in many of the poorest nations. Trade has declined as a proportion of GDP in 44 of 93 developing countries over the past decade, most notably in sub-Saharan Africa, part of the Middle East, and several South Asia countries.

Trade among industrial countries is not growing as fast, but its volume is still larger than that among developing countries or between developing and industrial (see Figure 3.3).

Figure 3.1 **Value of World Trade**

1980-1995

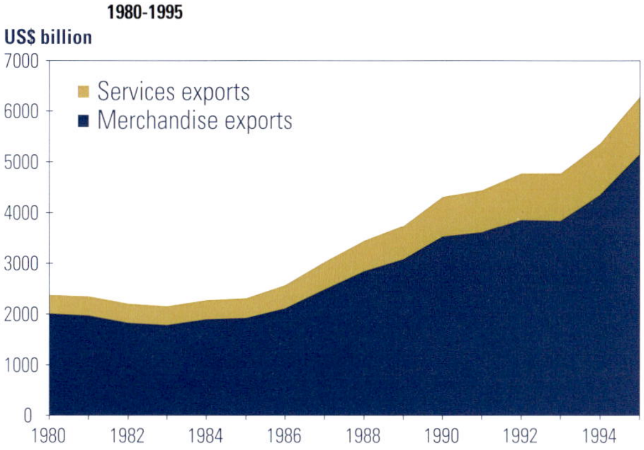

Source: The World Bank.

Terms of Trade

The overall terms of trade have increasingly favored the industrial over developing countries. Real prices (adjusted for inflation) for traditional developing-country exports – unprocessed agricultural crops; mineral ores and petroleum; tropical drinks (coffee, tea, cocoa) and oilseeds – are lower during the 1990s than they were in the 1980s.

Meanwhile, prices have risen for the ever more sophisticated and high-tech products and services exported from the industrial to the developed countries – aircraft, industrial machinery and machine tools; new computer and communications technologies.

Trade in labor-intensive manufactures – apparel, electronic assembly – partially offsets the imbalance, as more of this production moves to developing countries.

Effects of Increasing Trade

Gains and Losses

The hope for gain drives trade. Trade often results in more choice, better quality and lower prices. Economists' classic free trade model assumes many buyers and sellers, all well informed. But, of course, trade is never entirely free; nor are the parties equally

Figure 3.3

Importance of Trade, 1995

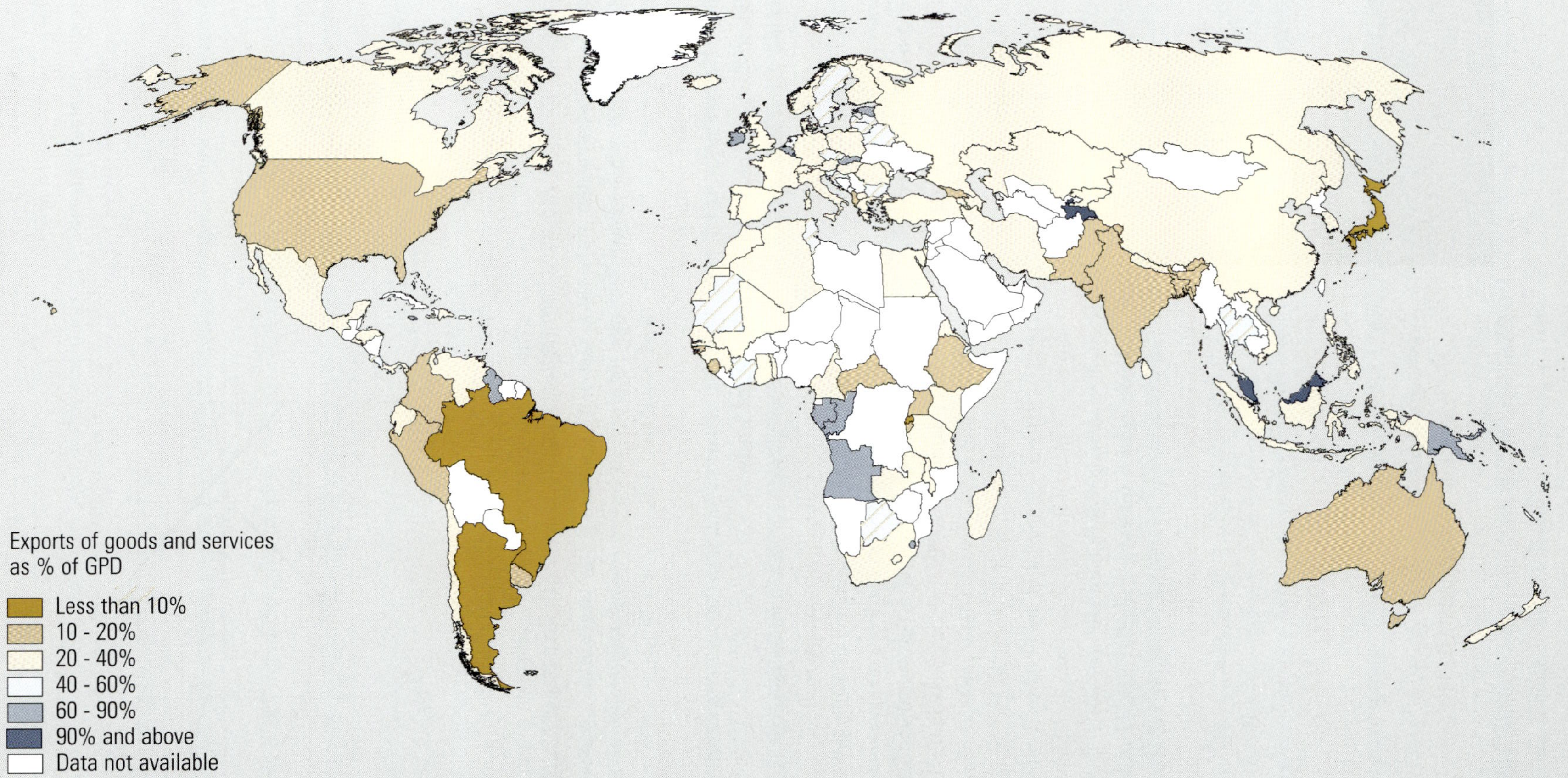

Source: The World Bank.

The Arms Bazaar: Global Trade in Weapons

by Lora Lumpe

As the 20th century races to a close, it already stands out as the most productive *and* destructive century on record. No other comes close to it in terms of social progress – in education, health and wealth provided. Yet no other century equals the 20th in civil violence, the number of conflicts waged, the hordes of refugees created, the millions of people killed in wars and the vast military expenditures.

With the end of the 45-year-old Cold War and, at the same time, the end of the U.S.- and Soviet-sponsored conflicts in the developing world, overall military expenditure has decreased. Global military spending in 1994 continued a downward trend begun in 1987. As a proportion of the world gross national product, total military spending fell below 3 percent for the first time since 1960.

In 1995, even without a superpower adversary, the United States still spent nearly $37 billion – half of its government-sponsored research budget – on weapons development.

Despite this good news, governments of the world still devoted over $700 billion to their militaries in 1994. Much of the overall reduction, moreover, was the result of a sharp decline in military spending by Eastern Europe and the former Soviet republics. Because the economies of these countries had practically collapsed, even this greatly reduced expenditure represented a heavy economic burden.

In 1995, even without a superpower adversary, the United States still spent nearly $37 billion – half of its government-sponsored research budget – on weapons development.

With the end of East-West hostilities, civil wars (such as those in Afghanistan, Angola, Liberia and Somalia) and regional wars became the principal new rationale for the major powers to maintain a massive military capacity. Ironically, trade in weapons sustained these conflicts. The global arms market – still $18 billion in sales in 1994 – was a modest but significant part of the $5.1 trillion global trading system.

The United States and its closest allies in Europe now appear to be engaged in an arms development and production race that has more to do with maintaining current levels of production than meeting any actual threat.

The world's largest arms exporter is the United States. In 1994 it exported more weaponry than all other countries of the world combined. Its arms exports worldwide between 1990 and 1996 amounted to an astounding $110.8 billion. The six Persian Gulf nations – Saudi Arabia, Kuwait, Qatar, Bahrain, the United Arab Emirates and Oman – are its best customers. They already have huge stocks of weapons and spend more of their budgets on defense than any nation outside the region.

Saudi Arabia, the world's largest consumer of U.S. arms, spends between 30 percent and 35 percent of its entire budget on defense. At the same time, rapid population growth and lower oil prices have compelled the Saudi government to cut subsidies for electricity, housing and education. So, while the stated purpose of these huge arms purchases is political stability, they may actually be sowing the seeds of a new, more dangerous instability.[1]

The Soviet Union's arms exports in the 1970s and 1980s were ideologically motivated and therefore heavily subsidized. By 1994, a sharp drop in sales by Russia contributed to the overall decline in global arms exports. More recently, however, in a bid to turn economic losses at home into opportunities abroad, arms manufacturers from Russia and other former Soviet republics are selling low-priced but increasingly sophisticated weapons in the Gulf.[2]

The Cold War arms race has given way to an arms bazaar, more commercially driven than ever.

Lora Lumpe is director of the Arms Sales Monitoring Project of the Federation of American Scientists.

Notes: 1) John Lancaster, "U.S. Presses to Put More Arms in Gulf States' Bulging Arsenals," *Washington Post*, April 4, 1997. 2) Ibid.

Table 3.1 **Gains and Losses from Increased Trade**

Possible Gains to Reinforce	**Possible Losses to Guard Against**
Increased economic growth, from net gains in efficiency and "comparative advantage"	Greater inequality and inequity from (continued) dominance by powerful actors
More choices, better quality, lower prices for consumers	Losses in job security, erosion of job quality, from extreme competitiveness
New jobs in poor countries as they take advantage of their most abundant resource – low cost labor	Erosion of workers' rights; playing workers off against each other across national boundaries
Greater interdependence, growing trust, reduced misunderstandings	Dependence on foreign decisions; loss of self-reliance; possible trigger for political instability
Greater food security against localized disasters	Food insecurity from greater export cropping
Rise in economic well-being, especially of poor people	Human rights traded off for profits, or from desperation
Potential for higher environmental standards	Environmental losses for short-term gains
Potential for greater international equity and political democracy	Loss of power by governments and civil society organizations
Overcome stagnation of isolated economies, especially those dominated by local elites	Erosion of local and community identity and values
Access by poor nations to rich country markets	Commercial domination of cultural values; mass consumerism
Greater income from trade – to help those adversely impacted, and to improve the lives of those who do not benefit directly	Market volatility for primary products
Competitiveness, requiring continual investment in human resources – education, health care	Transmission of volatility from market recessions or political decisions in dominant countries

powerful or well-informed. The balance between costs and benefits must be weighed carefully. Almost every party in a market wants to build in some safeguards, and in every society, some goods and services are deemed too important to leave to markets.

Responsible trade, as used here, strikes a middle ground. It seeks the efficiencies possible through freer trade, but would also include complementary measures to promote broad-based economic growth and more secure livelihoods for poor and hungry people.

On the whole, for most products and services, even imperfect markets seem to work better than administered markets. Virtually every government has now committed to some variation of a market-based economic system. All but a few have staked their future on being part of the global market system.

Trading nations expect new revenues. Developing countries traditionally have exported natural resource products (gold, diamonds, wood, oil) or crops that could be grown in a distinctive climate (spices, tropical fruits, coffee, tea, cocoa, sugar). In recent years, attention has focused on labor-intensive manufactures or crops (apparel, electronics, out-of-season vegetables) and even the labor-intensive aspects of the knowledge industry (writing computer programs and data entry). Low labor costs are the greatest comparative advantage of poor economies. More jobs and income are their greatest hope.

The Northern countries hope that part of the new wealth in the South will lead to increased purchases of products and services at which the North excels (high-tech, capital and knowledge intensive) (see "The Arms Bazaar," p. 35).

Table 3.1 lists a dozen possible gains from increasing international trade, and a dozen possible losses or risks to be guarded against.

Perhaps the greatest benefit of openness to trade is its bracing effect on the domestic economy. International competition forges businesses that provide good value to local customers, too. In response to international competition, the whole economy becomes more disciplined, flexible and dynamic.

Trade, Poverty Reduction and Inequality

Most countries that have opened their economies to global markets (trade, international financing) have reduced hunger and poverty more than those that have not. Economic growth rates have generally climbed as developing countries adopt policies that make them competitive in the global economy. Those nations not taking such steps are definitely falling behind (see Figures 3.4, 3.5).

Economic growth generally leads to a reduction in poverty; its decline produces increased poverty. But the exceptions are numerous enough, and some of the frequent side effects serious enough, to dispel easy or unqualified endorsement of open trade. Poverty has fallen rapidly in some fast-growing economies (Korea, Indonesia, China), but hasn't changed much in others, particularly where inequality is high (Brazil, Oman). And some of the fast-growing economies have promoted exports while restricting imports and foreign investment (Japan, Korea).

Poverty rates have come down more slowly in countries with slower economic growth. Poverty and hunger increased as economies declined in most of sub-Saharan Africa throughout the 1980s and early 1990s. Likewise, economic decline has increased poverty in the former Communist states in Eastern Europe, Central Asia and Vietnam during at least the early stages of their transition to market-based economies.

Economic growth is a necessary, but not sufficient, condition for reducing poverty and hunger. Its distribution is also critical.

Because poverty is experienced in households and by individuals, detailed and accurate information at that level is critical. The World Bank recently commissioned a review of 109 household surveys, covering 64 time-comparisons between 1987 and 1993 in 46 developing and transition economies.[1] The surveys showed that:

- Poverty rates have fallen as average incomes have risen, and risen as average incomes have fallen;
- Poverty rates have not declined anywhere in the absence of economic growth (see Figure 3.6);
- In developing countries, inequality increased as often as it decreased as average incomes rose; and
- In transition economies (former communist states in Eastern Europe and Central Asia), during 1987-1993, inequality consistently increased at the same time as average incomes fell (see Figure 3.7).

Other recent studies confirm these findings. Openness to trade and policies that strengthen competitiveness generally increase economic growth, but do not consistently reduce poverty because of very differing distribution of gains. Relative equality or inequality is more nearly correlated with long-term national income on patterns than with trade gains. Equitable distribu-

Figure 3.4 **Trade and Hunger**

Selected Countries, 1970s to 1980s

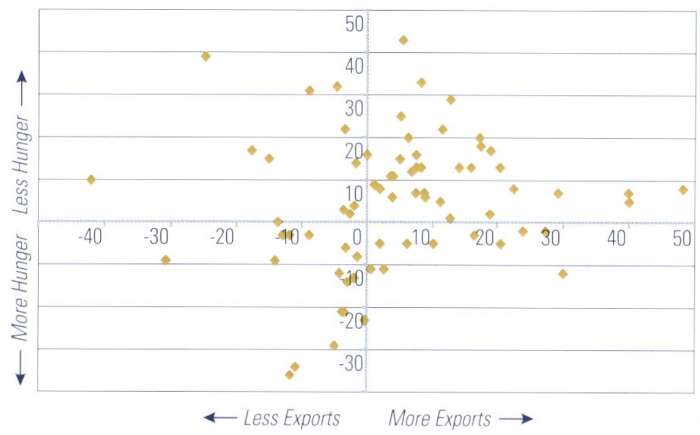

Trade = Exports/GDP in 1990-92 minus Exports/GDP in 1970-72.
Hunger = % Population hungry in 1990-92 minus % Population hungry in 1969-71.
Source: The World Bank.

Figure 3.5 **Trade and Economic Growth**

Selected Countries, 1970 -1995

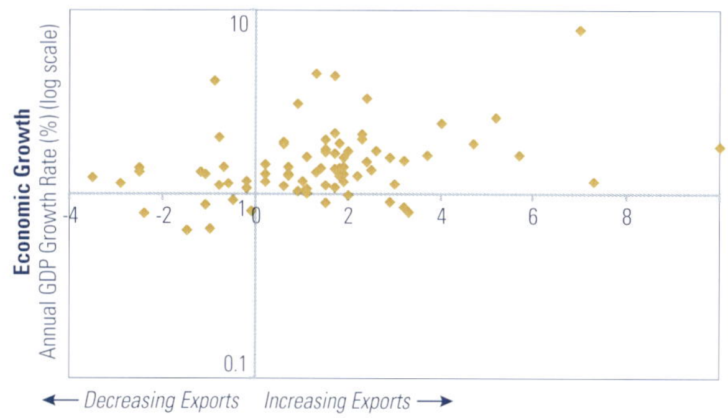

Trade = Exports/GDP in 1995//Exports/GDP in 1970
Source: The World Bank.

tion of income depends less on increased trade than it does on other policies.[2]

Recent research also shows that relative equality in distribution of national incomes increases the likelihood that economic growth and other trade gains can be sustained.[3] Widespread participation in political as well as economic activities reduces the likelihood of enacting bad policies and permits their earlier correction.

Trade and Secure Livelihoods in Developing Countries

Can increasing trade contribute to more secure livelihoods for poor people in poor countries? Clearly, it has in some instances. Will it always, or automatically, do so? Clearly not.

Dramatic reductions in poverty have occurred in South Korea, Taiwan and Malaysia, as they have moved from low- to upper middle-income status by World Bank classifications.[4] Indonesia, Thailand and, more recently, China appear to be on the same trajectory.

In each of these countries, the benefits of growth have been widely shared. Poverty rates are very low in the first group and dropping rapidly in the second. Typical workers in Korea or Taiwan nearly rival their counterparts in many industrial countries in skills, tasks, productivity and pay. Working conditions and worker rights do not measure up to internationally recognized standards in many respects, but an increasing proportion of people are secure in their capacity to meet basic physical needs, and their children are being educated.

But the story also has a sordid side. In 3,500 maquiladoras (foreign-owned assembly plants in tax-favored export zones) along the U.S.-Mexican border and throughout Central America; in many factories in Vietnam, Cambodia and the Philippines; and even in sweatshops in London and Los Angeles, young women workers daily suffer indignities, poor working conditions, sexual harassment and unreasonably low wages, even as measured by prevailing standards in their country. They often live in social and environmental squalor. Attempts at union organizing are squashed, often with government consent. Labor laws may go unenforced.

In African diamond mines and on sugar cane plantations throughout Latin America, workers toil under conditions not much different from those of their grandparents a century ago.

Child Labor

One of the most troubling aspects of international trade in labor-intensive goods is the degree to which they are made by pre- or early-teenaged children. Their submissiveness and nimble fingers have been prized in assembling clothing in Bangladesh, soccer balls in Pakistan and hand-knotted carpets in India. They grow and pick winter vegetables in Guatemala and summer vegetables in California.

Too often, the conditions of their employment include long hours, tedious work, unsafe or unhealthful living and working conditions, and little or no pay, sometimes even bonded servant status. These children are cheated out of much of their childhood. They lose

Figure 3.6 **Economic Growth and Poverty Rates**

Developing and Transition Countries, 1987-1993

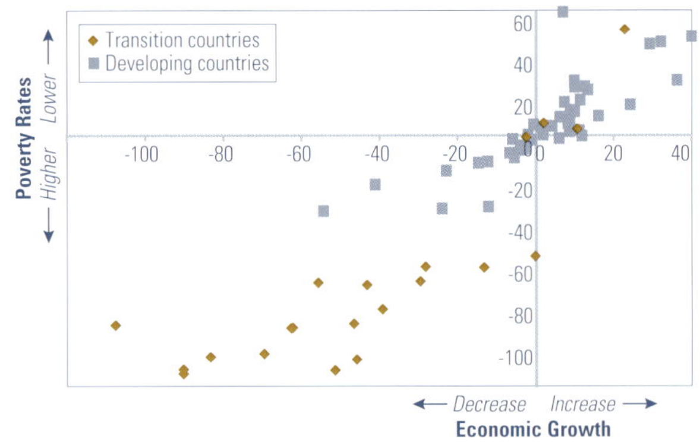

Poverty Rates = Change in % of people poor x -100.
Economic Growth = log of change in average household consumption x 100.
Source: The World Bank.

Figure 3.7 **Economic Growth and Inequality**

Developing and Transition Countries, 1987-1993

Change in Inequality = Gini index x -100
Economic Growth = log of change in average household consumption x 100
Source: The World Bank.

their chance to learn and develop. Some are physically impaired for life.

The International Labor Organization (ILO) estimated in 1996 that at least 120 million children between ages 5 to 14 were "fully at work." Work is a significant secondary activity for about the same number.[5]

Miserable as this situation is, especially from a Northern perspective, policy decisions have to be seen in light of the reality of presently available alternatives. Helen Rahman is founder of Shoishab Bangladesh, an organization devoted to basic human rights for disadvantaged children and working women, especially child domestic workers and street children. She points out that garment manufacturing has created an alternative for girls whose prospects are otherwise limited to early marriage, virtually indentured domestic work, begging, thievery or prostitution. Even meager wages in export-oriented manufactures permit these young women to contribute to the desperate needs of their families, and with it to gain personal dignity and self-esteem.

Simply banning imports made with child labor is strongly opposed by many developing-country governments and civil society organizations (CSOs). Only 46 countries have ratified the International Labor Organization's (ILO) Convention No. 138, which would prohibit employment of children under 15 years of age.

A sense of co-responsibility now marks most industrial-country efforts to reduce exploitative child labor in industrial countries. U.S. Senator Tom Harkin's proposed Child Labor Deterrence Act, for example, would prohibit the importation of mined or manufactured goods produced abroad with child labor. It would also grant $10 million each year to the ILO's ILEP program (the International Program on Elimination of Child Labor). ILEP helps increase educational opportunities for formerly working children and offers stipends to their families in lieu of lost wages.

This concept of co-responsibility is already embodied in several voluntary programs. In early 1997, a diverse coalition announced a pact to eliminate child labor in the soccer ball industry in the Sialkot District of Pakistan by the end of 1998. The Sialkot District produces nearly 75 percent of the world's hand-stitched soccer balls. The coalition includes the World Federation of the Sporting Goods Industry, the Soccer Industry Council of America, the Sporting Goods Manufacturing Association, and 55 sporting goods manufacturers, together with ILO, UNICEF, Save the Children (UK) and the Sialkot (Pakistan) Chamber of Commerce. The coalition has established a $1 million fund to hire independent monitors for ball-manufacturing operations. The coalition also supports educational efforts for the children, and expects to offer the jobs to other members of the families of displaced child workers.[6]

In many respects, this effort was patterned after the earlier Rugmark campaign in Europe. A Rugmark label is permitted for importers who can certify that their hand-stitched rugs do not involve bonded child laborers. Modest license fees are forwarded to UNICEF to create educational opportunities for the children released from the looms.

Under a 1995 agreement involving ILO, UNICEF, the International Confederation of Free Trade Unions, and the Bangladesh Association of Garment Manufacturers and Exporters, efforts are proceeding to keep Bangladeshi children out of garment factories and in school. The ILO's initial census of underage workers identified 12,000 young women workers, of whom 10,000 are now enrolled in 315 new schools. Their families are receiving a stipend that nearly equals their former wages.

Some observers, including Helen Rahman, claim a much larger number of young women have been crowded out of the industry. Manufacturers no longer risk their businesses by employing young women, she says.

Helen Rahman's critical observations on international schemes to ban child labor underscore the complexity of the problem. Above all, they underscore the necessity of continuous, on-the-ground engagement with people affected by a problem in any attempted resolution.

Trade and Employment in Industrial Countries

Although transnational corporations may experience huge gains from trade, benefits to the general populace are mostly modest and shared widely – a dollar or two saved on a shirt or blouse, a few hundred on an automobile. But the adjustments fall heavily on a smaller group – workers laid off; a community saying goodbye to an important employer. Those who lose a job because a plant relocates to Mexico are generally more visible and vocal than those whose plant builds a few hundred extra refrigerators for export there.

Estimates of the proportion of all jobs lost in industrial countries because of increasing trade vary from as low as 9 percent to as high as 40 percent, with a cluster of analysts estimating 20 percent to 25 percent.[7] It is difficult to separate trade job losses from those with other causes such as technical innovations and declining demand for a product (see Chapter 2, pp. 26-27).

Migration

The same forces that move goods and jobs also shift people. Perceptions of greater opportunity – real, hoped for or imagined – entice people to leave their homes to go to a new place. Many move to a nearby city; most stay within their own country. Shortly after the turn of the century, urban residents worldwide will outnumber rural residents for the first time in history.[8]

Global trade in manufactured goods tends to attract workers to port cities or export-oriented free trade zones near transportation centers. With continual improvements in communications technologies, however, service-oriented centers can be more dispersed. Bangalore, India, for example, has become a global center for labor-intensive computer programming. Forecasters have scaled back their estimates of the growth of mega-cities (more than 10 million people in a metropolitan area). We consciously omit discussion of the immense social changes inherent in urbanization. An in-depth look at huge migrations due to war or political repression can be found in *Hunger 1993: Uprooted People* and *Countries in Crisis: Hunger 1996*.[9]

U.S workers, such as UPS package deliverers who struck in 1997 over job security and pension issues, have made gains because of freedom to organize and bargain collectively.

1997/The Washington Post

Global communication has increased awareness of huge disparities of opportunity across national boundaries, and narrowed the perception, if not always the reality, of national and cultural differences. Real costs of travel keep dropping. A number of nations have created guest-worker programs. International migration for work and business opportunities continues to increase – some officially sanctioned; much not. Safety net and retirement programs of industrial countries are very attractive to people in places where they do not exist. Books on how to emigrate to the United States to take advantage of its safety net programs have circulated in several developing countries.

Immigrants' employment varies widely. About 500,000 highly educated professionals, mostly engineers and doctors, left India for the United States between 1972 and 1985.[10] Visiting graduate students often find professional opportunities in their host country more attractive than those at home. These immigrants represent a "brain" and resource drain. Many immigrants, particularly Asians, establish small businesses in the United States; their entrepreneurship may also represent a significant loss to their original communities.

Remittances by guest workers to their home countries, estimated at $55 billion for 1995, give further clues to their employment. Saudi Arabia leads the list of host countries from which workers send remittances home, followed by the United States, Germany, Switzerland, France and other oil-rich Middle Eastern states. India leads the recipient countries, followed by Egypt, Mexico, Portugal, Turkey, Greece and Brazil. Smaller Latin American countries and non-oil Middle East countries receive more than proportionate remittances.[11]

Formal guest worker programs tend to be concentrated in low- and semi-skilled jobs less attractive to citizens – fruit and vegetable production in the United States; work on oil rigs in the Middle East. Undocumented workers, especially low-skilled, often find their way to service industries where language facility is not required.

Resistance to immigration, particularly in the United States, has two foci. Low-skilled workers want greater protection from competition for their jobs and the related downward pressure on wages. Many taxpayers resent providing social services for recent immigrant workers and especially their dependent relatives.

On the other hand, immigrants building their households are a net stimulus to the economy. Stable, aging populations in Europe – and predictably in Japan and the United States – are creating actual shortages of younger workers to support them in their own old age.

Most U.S. analysts agree that the threats to lower-skilled workers are real although modest, particularly in the short range, but that immigration at the present scale is a net benefit to the nation as a whole.

National Employment Policies

In both developing and industrial countries, governments can adopt policies to help channel the benefits of trade into secure livelihoods for all.

All countries, rich and poor, must adopt sound fiscal and monetary policies (see Chapter 2, p. 28). Industrial countries carry special responsibility in this regard because they are so dominant in the global economy. If their economies sink into recession or heat into inflation, weaker economies suffer too.

As discussed in Chapter 2, greater cooperation in macroeconomic management could allow somewhat higher rates of growth and employment.

Both industrial- and developing-country governments can use minimum wage and tax policies to encourage able people to work and employers to provide good jobs. Industrial nations can assure compensation that enables secure livelihoods.

All nations need to establish and enforce equitable, progressive tax systems to support adequate social services, and to help redress steep inequalities in wage and family incomes.

Both industrial and developing countries should give highest priority to investment in human resources – education, health care, job training and re-training. Wealthy nations should make these investments their highest priority for development aid.

Governments should provide education and legal protection to help overcome discrimination against women and disadvantaged ethnic groups.

Both industrial and developing nations should assure maximum feasible participation in policy-making and implementation by communities, civil society, businesses, worker organizations and poor people. This will ensure that varied interests are addressed, help avoid mistakes, contribute to necessary corrections early on, and ensure ownership of some inevitably difficult and painful choices. Governments should also limit undue influence by well-funded special interest groups.

The most troublesome economic policy issues turn out not to be trade issues per se, but the questions about whether to open economic opportunity to disadvantaged groups.

Worker Rights

Worker rights and worker compensation raise thorny cross-border problems. Low-cost labor is a poor country's greatest asset; it is the greatest threat to industrial-country workers. Vast wage differences from country to country are also a powerful stimulus for migration, particularly if accompanied by high unemployment. Progress toward more and better jobs is the surest antidote to waves of economic refugees.

From a moral perspective, those who work should be able to meet the basic needs of their families, as "a global minimum wage" has been defined. The industrial countries have the capacity to assure this level of compensation, and should. But the pool of workers in poor nations willing to work for much less is so large that a global minimum wage, even at its much lower level, is out of reach in the short term.

An individual employer cannot pay much more than "prevailing wages" and stay in business. So, in their efforts to maximize job opportunities, government leaders from poor countries are not willing to put minimum wages on any labor negotiating agenda, lest it gain credence and their non-compliance be used as an excuse to keep their exports out of richer countries. These leaders are joined in this opposition by many transnational corporations quite willing to take advantage of very low wages.

Other core labor rights issues – freedom to organize and bargain collectively; freedom from harassment and discrimination; freedom from forced labor or exploitative child labor; assurance of safe work places – are only slightly more amenable as negotiating points. Again, poor nations' leaders fear that such standards would be used by importing nations as barriers to their exports. So, even though the Organization for Economic Cooperation and Development (OECD – an association for policy coordination among 29 industrial and high-income developing nations) suggests that negotiating standards for improved work place conditions would not be prohibitively expensive, early formal negotiations seem unlikely.

Improved workplace conditions are not terribly expensive to put into place. Some advocates insist they are cost-effective in improved morale and productivity. A number of Northern companies have voluntarily adopted standards for themselves and their contractors that might have been topics for labor negotiations. Many of these programs have involved third parties (e.g., ILO, UNICEF). Some have involved an informal workers' council, but none to date has resulted from formal one-on-one negotiations between a manufacturer and a Southern workers' organization. Even so, the accumulated experience may bear fruit in more formal negotiations at a future date.

Northern workers, meanwhile, resent having to compete with low-paid workers in poor working conditions, and continue to press for improved worker rights in every available forum.

Trade Negotiations

Many trade-related issues can be dealt with by national decisions and policies. But international trade also requires rules accepted by all parties.

Even the most market-oriented economies surround markets with rules to protect the public interest – to assure product and work place safety and honesty in advertising, for example, or to restrain monopolies. The rules vary from nation to nation, depending on their culture and experience.

So, even if all parties are convinced that trade is basically good, negotiations face a welter of national standards and resistance to inevitable adjustments perceived to flow from new agreements. In some ways, it is amazing that any international trade agreement gets signed.

On the other hand, it does not work to forge ahead and trade without some sort of agreement. Businesses want a level playing field to compete in expanding markets, guarantees of intellectual property rights and stable currencies. Poor nations seek freer access to industrial country markets for their products, or protection for their fledgling industries. Workers want protection against unsafe or repressive conditions. Environmentalists and consumer advocates desire enforceable rules that protect the public interest.

Trade agreements, to be achieved in the first place and honored in practice, need to be reached by consensus. They must have something in them for everyone – which means that they usually fully satisfy no one. Marginal agreements may be better than no agreements, if only because they provide an opportunity to keep talking about troublesome issues, and to capture and build on what can be agreed.

The General Agreement on Tariffs and Trade (GATT)

Many world leaders felt that economic chaos following World War I, including trade protection measures adopted during the 1930s, contributed to World War II. Those gathered at the Bretton Woods Conference in 1944 envisioned an International Trade Organization, but it never came to pass. In its stead, 23 nations agreed in 1947 to take voluntary steps to reduce trade barriers between the "contracting parties" to the General Agreement on Tariffs and Trade (GATT).

The four basic operating GATT principles are that:

- Any protection should be in the form of tariffs (taxes on imports) rather than import quotas or other non-tariff barriers;
- Any tariff reduction by one contracting party on another's imports should be matched, as a matter of reciprocity;
- Each contracting party should extend its most favorable terms to every other contracting party without discrimination (Most Favored Nation – MFN – treatment); and
- Contracting parties should meet periodically to negotiate further tariff reductions.

Since 1949, GATT members have gathered in eight negotiating rounds, including the most recent Uruguay Round (named for the initial meeting place) from 1986 through 1993. New nations joined each round. The final GATT agreement was signed by 123 nations. Tariffs came down over the period, from an average 35 percent in 1947 to 5 percent at the end of the seventh round in 1979.

GATT was, for the most part, run by, and for the benefit of, industrial countries. Tariffs were most consistently reduced on the manufactured products they traded with each other, and for which developing countries were at a disadvantage. In 1965, GATT adopted rules that allowed "special and differential treatment" for developing countries.

After 1969, the European Community, Japan and the United States introduced their respective schemes for Generalized Systems of Preferences (GSP) – lists of manufactured or semi-manufactured goods that would be accepted as imports from developing countries with lower, or no, tariffs. But these were often hedged about with quotas and other non-tariff barriers, limiting the imports of preferential goods to 11 – 18 percent of the total imports from GSP-eligible countries in 1984. Some categories of products of special interest to Southern countries were exempted in whole or in part from GATT requirements – textiles, footwear, agriculture, steel and electronics. Several of these categories are where developing countries are most competitive.

The Uruguay Round of GATT (GATT 1994)

Over the seven years of the Uruguay Round of GATT negotiations, the member nations generally met the goals laid out at the first meeting in 1986:[12]

- To reduce most existing tariffs on industrial products by an average of 40 percent over five years, with a longer adjustment period for most developing countries, and even greater flexibility for the poorest countries;
- To convert anti-dumping laws and export subsidies to open tariffs; alternatively to permit governments to levy compensating duties in response to these non-tariff barriers, which have become a favorite tool against imports from both rich and poor countries;
- To extend GATT principles to trade in intellectual property such as patents, and services such as banking and insurance, nearly all to the benefit of industrial countries;
- To extend GATT principles to agriculture (see Chapter 4);
- To phase out, over 10 years, import quotas under the multi-fibre agreement that industrial countries had used to limit clothing and textile imports from developing countries; and
- To strengthen GATT as an organization, particularly by creating stronger, more timely dispute settlement procedures.

The World Trade Organization (WTO)

Late in the Uruguay Round, the general intent to strengthen GATT turned into the plan to create the World Trade Organization (WTO), which replaced the less formal, contractual GATT in January 1995. Three aspects of the new WTO stand out:

- WTO members agree to accept all WTO rules as a single package and change national laws to conform, whereas under GATT they were bound only by those provisions they accepted;
- WTO's dispute resolution process is much stronger – the rulings by WTO panels of experts, including assessment of penalties, will be effective unless opposed by all nations, as opposed to each nation's right to refuse rulings from GATT panels; and
- The WTO is a continuing body; many issues will be resolved in biennial meetings of trade ministers, or on an interim basis by some 30 continuing WTO bodies, rather than waiting several years for another large negotiating round.

The main structure of the WTO is the Ministerial Conference, which meets at least once each two years, and has full authority to interpret or amend the Uruguay Round Agreements. The principal interim body is the General Council, made up of representatives of all members, which also discharges the responsibilities of the Dispute Settlement Body and the Trade Policy Review Body. A dozen councils oversee the enforcement of the main agreements reached in GATT 1994 and since. A series of committees oversee administrative matters and special topics.

All told, WTO bodies met in more than 3,500 sessions during 1995 and 1996 to refine and activate the new rules. More than 70 disputes have been brought for resolution. The majority settled were resolved before the appointment of an expert panel or early during their deliberations. Nations have honored the panels' decisions in those few that have progressed that far, building confidence in the procedures. An additional 30 countries have applied for WTO membership, including China and most of the former Soviet republics.[13]

Five issues on the WTO's growing agenda are especially important to sustainable development and secure livelihoods for poor people (see also Chapter 4).

First, the effects of the WTO accords on the poorest countries need to be monitored. Several analysts forecast that the poorest countries, especially in Africa, seem unlikely to gain from freer trade. Questions to be asked are: Does increased trade actually benefit the poorest countries and, if so, are such benefits broadly distributed? Do poor countries actually gain greater access to industrial country markets for labor intensive or processed goods? Are the poorest nations able to take any advantage of longer adjustment periods in adopting WTO standards? Should such exceptions be extended? These questions seem especially appropriate for the WTO Committee on Trade and Development.

Second, the WTO and member states should establish regular processes for consultation with NGOs (non-governmental organizations). WTO is already more transparent in several regards than was GATT – some documents are de-restricted on a routine basis, albeit often delayed; many of these are available on WTO's web site (<www.wto.org>). But access and opportunity for participation is entirely at the discretion of the secretariat. NGO advisory councils might be set up in relation to the Committee on Trade and Development and the Committee on Sustainable Development. NGOs might be granted standing in dispute resolution procedures. WTO might encourage member states to talk with NGOs, or appoint them to their WTO delegations, as a few already do. Some NGOs represent the interests of low-income people more consistently than almost any government.

Third, environmental concerns need a permanent place on the WTO agenda. The Committee on Trade and the Environment was tacked onto GATT 1994 at the last minute, but does not yet have a clear mandate or agenda. The best hope for environmental sustainability lies in international agreements, since pollution crosses national boundaries. Environmental standards should be linked to trade agreements. At the same time, Southern countries are extremely sensitive to environmental standards being "forced" on them by Northern neighbors, and rightly fear their use to exclude their exports.

Fourth, labor standards are a trade issue, and should be included in trade negotiations. WTO ministers at Singapore in 1996 agreed to the first half of this proposition, but Southern and business interests blocked putting the issue on WTO's agenda. Southern governments and some Southern NGOs expect that labor standards would be used to keep their products out of industrial markets, pointing to current efforts to reduce imports made with child labor as a case in point. Perhaps even more than on environmental issues, Northern countries will need to complement legitimate concerns with constructive assistance before agreement can be reached on common labor standards (see pp. 38-39, 45 on child labor and corporate citizenship).

Fifth, the WTO intends to lead, "when appropriate," a negotiation on trade and investment, working with the World Bank. The initial framing of the issues is progressing on a Multilateral Agreement on Investing (MAI) at the Organization for Economic Cooperation and Development (OECD). Since the OECD is made up primarily of the industrial countries, some observers question whether the interests of the poorer countries will be considered adequately (see Chapter 5, pp. 63-64).

NAFTA and Other Regional Trade Agreements

In 1996, the WTO established a new Committee on Regional Trade Agreements, of which there were then 32. These agreements are very diverse. The European Union, for example, is a lot more than a trade agreement. It also gives people freedom to move from one country to another, establishes common standards for social policy and will lead to a common currency.

APEC (Asia Pacific Economic Cooperation) began as a forum, but has recently announced its intention to move toward a free trade zone among virtually all the countries touching the Pacific Ocean by 2020. Trade among these partners already exceeds that crossing the Atlantic. The Economic Community of West African States (ECOWAS) and the Southern Africa Development Coordination Conference (SADCC) represent efforts in these respective areas to develop a little bit of clout.

The North American Free Trade Agreement (NAFTA) is perhaps the most closely watched of recent regional trade pacts. It took effect in 1994. The United States' and Canada's interest in Mexico lay in increased investments and exports there. Mexico's government wanted easier access and preference over other (Asian) competitors in the huge U.S. and Canadian markets. They also wanted to "lock in" the policies associated with their shift toward a more open economy dating from 1983.

After three years, the effects of NAFTA are difficult to sort out from those of continuing earlier policies and from the collapse of the Mexican peso in late 1994 – the latter largely a consequence of mismanagement and apparent malfeasance. New maquiladora plants have sprung up at about the same pace as before NAFTA, some along the border, and a few more in the interior. Mexican exports into the United States and Canada have grown faster than the reverse. New jobs in Mexico have increased, but not nearly fast enough to absorb the huge numbers of new workers, unemployed and displaced farmers. So the pressure to emigrate is more intense than ever.

The United States has lost jobs to Mexico on a net basis, but not enough to constitute the "huge sucking sound" forecast by Ross Perot. At this early point, judgments about the success or failure of NAFTA are more likely to reflect the point of view of the observer than a cumulation of facts.

Only slightly more assessment is possible regarding the two novel features of NAFTA – the side agreements on labor rights and the environment. The environmental cleanup along the U.S.-Mexican border and loans through the North American Development Bank have languished. Both were promised as part of the Cooperative Environmental Agreement.

On the other hand, labor rights advocates initially held out little hope for NACLA, the North American Cooperative Labor Agreement. But each of the three nations has filed one or more labor complaints, and had one or more filed against it. Labor practices have not been revolutionized, but labor observers have commented on the positive "sunshine" effect of having a trilateral group available to investigate claims of poor labor practices.

At minimum, these experiments in cooperation on environmental and labor rights practices will inform attempts to expand NAFTA into a Free Trade Agreement for the Americas.

Corporate Citizenship & Citizen Action

Corporations, the most common form of business organization, are subject to strict requirements for financial reporting to their stockholders. But corporate behavior also affects others: workers, who have varying degrees of protection in different nations; customers, who have limited protection through labeling and disclosure requirements; communities, who are often dramatically affected by corporate decisions, to locate or re-locate, for example; and the public for environmental impacts. No formal accounting is presently required to these other stakeholders. They may be affected greatly by company decisions in which they have no voice.

The Stakeholder Alliance is proposing that corporations should report to these other stakeholders, voluntarily to start with, but eventually on a formal, uniform basis.[14] Most businessmen and women acknowledge their responsibility for good corporate citizenship, but feel that it can best be achieved on a voluntary basis. They point out that markets already incorporate judgment about their corporate behavior. They argue that formal accounting requirements to a range of stakeholders would be too burdensome.

Partly in response to consumer and public interests, many businesses have voluntarily adopted codes of conduct or standards. About 800 businesses of all sizes are members of Business for Social Responsibility, for example. Its mission is "to help its members achieve long-term success by implementing policies and practices that honor high ethical standards and meet their responsibilities to all who are impacted by their decisions."

Fifty-three businesses have adopted the CERES principles for environmentally responsible performance. They voluntarily submit to external review of their compliance.

The Council on Economic Priorities ranks nearly 200 companies on eight criteria related to work place, community and environment.[15]

In addition to the child-labor oriented activities described above, nine of the largest U.S. apparel manufacturers have joined with labor and consumer representatives and the U.S. Department of Labor in the White House Apparel Industry Partnership announced by President Clinton in early 1997. Each company has committed itself to a minimum code of conduct for worker standards for itself and all its suppliers, and has agreed to independent monitoring of compliance.

Consumers can influence corporations through selective purchases and asking the right questions. Concerned citizens also have an increasing range of products available through "fair trade" channels in Europe (e.g., TransFair) and the United States. These suppliers typically purchase directly from small producer cooperatives in developing countries. Many are run as an adjunct to private development programs, such as Oxfam, Save the Children, Church of the Brethren or the Mennonite Central Committee. These fair traders provide an outlet for their overseas partners, and their sales also help create awareness of the NGOs' development missions.

Other fair trade ventures have developed into for-profit businesses, although the social justice aura is part of what they sell. Equal Exchange, for example, offers a line of gourmet and organic coffees purchased from 12 farmer cooperatives in eight countries in Latin America and Africa. The fair trade principles followed by Equal Exchange include: a minimum price to the farmers regardless of coffee markets; advance credits for crop production; a premium for organically grown coffee; and a worker cooperative form of business for Equal Exchange itself. The message of "justice" and more secure livelihoods for small coffee growers is prominently included in all its promotional activities.

Conclusion

The nations where poverty rates and hunger have dropped the fastest over recent decades have nearly all increased their global trade over the same period. But not all trading nations have seen less hunger. In some, the benefits of increased trade are not shared broadly.

Governments should promote international trade – with safeguards for labor rights, the environment and food security. Other policies also matter – fiscal and monetary policies; taxes; public investment, especially in human resources; rights for disadvantaged groups. To help ensure the best combination of policies for nations and in international trade agreements, and to ensure broad ownership, all parties must participate in making the decisions, particularly poor people.

Don Reeves is economic policy analyst at Bread for the World Institute.

Agricultural Trade & Food Security

By Renée Marlin-Bennett

Foster food security through more liberal agricultural trade coupled with sound agricultural policies and safety nets.

Agriculture is the sector of international trade that has the most direct effect on food security. It is the source of both food and livelihood for most poor people. It is essential to sustainable development. Agriculture accounts for 60 percent of employment in developing countries and is the largest part of the economy in most poor countries. It is an important source of savings for investment throughout the economy. Developing country agriculture is heavily affected by global trade and agricultural trade rules.

In 1994, the Uruguay Round of Multilateral Trade Negotiations culminated in a new General Agreement on Tariffs and Trade (GATT) (see Chapter 3, pp. 42-44). This was the first multilateral trade agreement fully to incorporate agriculture. The Agreement on Agriculture included in GATT 1994[1] addresses some of the thorniest issues of post-World War II agricultural and food trade: access to markets, domestic support and export subsidies, animal and plant health measures and effects of the global agricultural market on the poorest countries.

As advocates of *responsible trade*, we applaud the efficiencies possible through freer trade, but urge complementary measures to help ensure equity and reduce hunger (see Chapter 3, pp. 41-45). Governments can foster food security through more liberal agricultural trade coupled with sound agricultural policies and safety nets.

Is Liberalization a Good Idea for Increasing Food Security?

Trade liberalization promises efficiency, the greatest amount of goods and services produced for the least resources. But food security depends on equity as well as efficiency. Who owns land? Who earns how much? What proportion of the population earns a given percentage of the country's income? How will non-economic factors alter supply and demand? Liberalization simply does not address these essential questions.

Liberalization can benefit farmers in developing countries. For example, if the United States scaled back its system of sugar import quotas, this would increase the market for developing countries that export sugar. But who wins and who loses is always complex: liberalized sugar trade might help developing country farmers and farm workers, as well as U.S. candy and soft drink firms, but it would hurt U.S. corn farmers by reducing demand for corn-based sweeteners.

Liberalization will also benefit developing country farmers who must compete against subsidized imports within their own national economies, and exporters who have found it difficult to compete globally with subsidized or otherwise supported U.S. and European Union (EU) exports. Subsidized EU sugar exports, for example, have long depressed world prices and limited developing country exporters' global market share, notwithstanding EU guaranteed imports from developing countries.[2]

Where government policies have made some foods more expensive, liberalization can decrease prices and help consumers. But less government intervention can also increase price fluctuations, making planning more difficult both for importers and exporters. These fluctuations will strike hardest in poor countries already facing serious food insecurity. In other instances, governments have kept food prices artificially low. Liberalization is likely to raise these prices, causing problems for consumers.

While liberalization generally improves economic efficiency and thus stimulates economic growth, liberalization also forces change. Poor countries and poor people are often ill-equipped to cope with, and adapt to, change.

So, while trade liberalization can help overcome hunger, it is never the whole solution.

Food Self-Reliance

International trade can be rough on poor people. They can least afford price fluctuations and cannot predict – or sometimes even understand – price changes in global markets. Poor farmers with labor intensive operations may be particularly vulnerable to lower income when more efficient production from developed countries or new technologies drive prices down.

In this setting, one option is for developing countries to attempt to become self-sufficient in agricultural production, limiting their imports and setting up food reserves. Self-sufficiency means that farmers produce first and, if necessary, solely for local consumption. Advocates of a self-sufficient strategy, who emphasize the dangers of globalization for weaker states, often fail to recognize the benefits of a global economy. But at the other extreme, a strategy of producing almost solely for export is risky as well. Poor food-importing countries face fluctuating international market prices which they cannot affect or control.

A better strategy is food self-reliance, in which countries boost yields, employing sustainable and efficient farming practices, and diversify their agricultural production, some for export and some for domestic consumption. Earnings from exports can help with increased imports when domestic production falls short (see "It's Not Just the Economy...," p. 48).

India, for example, has moved from a "basket case" dependent on massive external food aid in the 1960s to a net exporter of grain some years during the 1980s and 1990s. It has the potential to become a major rice exporter in the next decade. Expanded grain output in irrigated areas has boosted incomes enormously.

India should, however, maintain investment in dryland agriculture as well. Dryland farming, the basis of livelihood for most of India's low-income people, has received relatively little government attention or help.[3]

Tunisians fight desertification – just one of hundreds of barriers to increased agricultural production that many countries must overcome.

FAO

It's Not **Just** the Economy. . .

Costa Rica and Kenya show how politics and society can shape the relationship between trade and food security. Since 1980, the Central American nation of Costa Rica has rapidly expanded production of fruits, vegetables, ornamental plants and flowers for export, mainly to the United States. By 1994, these "non-traditional" products accounted for 42 percent of the country's export earnings, and helped pay for food imports. Non-traditional export agriculture created jobs (especially for women), boosted rural incomes and improved rural living standards. Between 1969-1971 and 1990-1992, the proportion of chronically undernourished Costa Ricans fell by half, from 25 percent to 12 percent.[1]

In Kenya in East Africa, however, reliance on trade for food security has not proved successful. Agriculture and related activities form the backbone of the country's economy, accounting for about 80 percent of all jobs, 60 percent of gross domestic product and 45 percent of government revenues. Beginning in the late 1980s, the government, under pressure from the World Bank and International Monetary Fund, agreed to liberalize trade and foreign exchange policy, loosen price controls, reduce food subsidies, cut government spending and privatize public enterprises.

The policy changes benefitted export producers of such commodities as tea and horticultural crops, dominated by large-scale Kenyan farmers and transnational corporations.

But the small farmers who account for most local food production (corn, beans, millet and sorghum) and urban poor people have not fared well. Over 46 percent of rural households and 30 percent of those in the cities live in poverty. Small farmers sell their crops at low prices at harvest time, when supplies are plentiful, in order to pay off their debts and because they lack storage facilities. They later buy food on the market when prices are higher. Rural poor people spend 67 percent of their incomes on food. Between 1969-1971 and 1990-1992, the proportion of chronically undernourished people increased from 33 percent to 46 percent (more than 11 million people).

Volatile prices for crops and rising input costs, combined with recurrent droughts, have driven down production and caused a rise in rural poverty during the first half of the 1990s. Industrial countries' subsidized exports of wheat and corn have further undermined rural livelihoods. Today, despite the importance of agriculture in its economy, the Food and Agriculture Organization considers Kenya a Low-Income Food Deficit Country.[2]

Export agriculture had dramatically different results in Costa Rica and Kenya. In Costa Rica, many smallholder farmers produce the export crops. In Kenya, the export crops are plantation crops.

Differing social policies and commitment to democratic governance also help explain the different social outcomes to export-oriented approaches to food security. Costa Rica has a long history of substantial investment in public education, health care, social insurance, public works employment, land reform and relatively equitable income distribution patterns. In addition to holding periodic elections, the country has enjoyed open political debate and freedom to organize. This has contributed to the governmental commitment to secure livelihoods for its citizens.[3]

Kenya has not made equity a high priority. Rural children and girls have much lower school enrollment rates than urban children and boys. The country devoted 17 percent of government spending to education in 1992, compared to 21 percent for Costa Rica. While defense spending equalled just 5 percent of combined health and education expenditures in Costa Rica (which does not maintain a standing army), military spending in Kenya was equivalent to 24 percent of health and education spending. Kenya has experienced one-party rule since independence, and President Daniel Arap Moi's rule has grown increasingly authoritarian.[4]

Notes: 1) Kathleen M. Horkan, *The Benefits and Costs of Nontraditional Agricultural Export Promotion in Costa Rica* (Washington: U.S. Agency for International Development Research and Reference Services Project, 1996); FAO, *Mapping Undernutrition* (Rome: FAO, 1996). 2) Ibid.; <www.fao.org>; ACTIONAID, *Hunger and the Global Agenda: Who Wins? . . . Who Loses? . . . Who Cares?* (London: ACTIONAID, 1996). 3) Jean Drèze and Amartya Sen, *Hunger and Public Action* (Oxford: Clarendon Press, 1989). 4) United Nations Development Programme, *Human Development Report 1996* (New York: Oxford University Press, 1996); World Bank Human Resources and Poverty Division, Africa Technical Department, "Taking Action for Poverty Reduction in Sub-Saharan Africa," *Report* No. 15575-AFR, May 1, 1996.

Other Agricultural Policy Issues

If developing country leaders fail to address inequities or corruption in their own societies, then no trade policy could possibly achieve food security.

Developing country leaders must remove any vestiges of practices, such as state-run marketing boards or taxing agricultural exports, that shortchange farmers. They must develop agricultural development programs that help farmers adjust to price and production fluctuations.

For the long run, agricultural development must be sustainable. Producers must pay attention to soil and water conservation. Sustainable fishing practices are likewise essential.

Finally, war obviously and dramatically impinges on food security. In Burundi and Rwanda, as cruel ethnic violence has eased, food production remains below pre-conflict levels, with a third of the respective populations needing food assistance.[4]

GATT 1994 Agreement on Agriculture

The GATT 1994 Agreement on Agriculture requires member states to decrease protection on agricultural products through "tarrification," the conversion of quotas and other non-tariff barriers to tariffs. Tariffs are considered preferable because they are "transparent," that is, all parties know from the stated rate exactly what the level of protection is. The agreement further requires states gradually to reduce tariffs on agricultural products by an average of 34 percent for developed countries and 24 percent for developing countries. Developed countries have six years to accomplish this; developing countries are granted 10 years. The agreement exempts the poorest developing countries, which are not required to reduce their tariffs. It also mandates additional tariff reductions in some cases of severely limited market access.

The second major goal of the agreement is to end price distortions in international markets created by countries' support of their own farmers and subsidies on agricultural exports. When governments subsidize agricultural production and exports, they drive world market prices down. The agreement requires members to calculate the value of all support for domestic agriculture that significantly affects trade. States must reduce this figure by a percentage that depends on the level of development (20 percent for developed, 13.3 percent for developing, 0 for least developed countries).

Member states have agreed to reduce both the value and the quantity of subsidized exports over six years for developed countries and 10 years for developing countries. Again, the provisions exempt the poorest countries. "Green box policies," or government support to farming that has only a minimal effect on trade – such as agricultural research and disease control programs – are not restricted.

The third area addresses a loophole in prior agreements. Governments have found it easy to devise animal and plant health regulations that do more to block imports than to protect food safety. The new rules seek to harmonize laws and limit the use of such regulations as non-tariff barriers.

The Agreement on Agriculture should result in significant efficiencies and growth. Reduced subsidies to agriculture in the industrial countries will make farming more profitable for hundreds of millions of poor families in rural areas in the developing countries.

On the other hand, reductions in farm support will result in smaller government-held grain stocks, causing prices to fluctuate more and making less grain available for food aid or reduced price sales to developing countries. Reduced subsidies will initially increase prices for some commodities, hurting consumers. To address some of these issues, GATT 1994 member states agreed on the Decision on Measures Concerning the Possible Negative Effects of the Reform Programme on Least-Developed and Net Food-Importing Developing Countries, commonly referred to as the Marrakesh Decision.[5]

The Marrakesh Decision

At the signing of GATT 1994 in Marrakesh, Morocco, member states recognized that the least developed and net food-importing countries[6] could face increased hunger because of higher food prices and market instability. The Marrakesh Decision promises to provide a safety net, in the form of compensation from developed countries to these impoverished states, if GATT 1994 implementation causes negative effects. On the face of it, this is a rather firm promise.

The problem is: how do you know if a particular increase in food insecurity is due to GATT or to other factors? In practice, it is extremely difficult to distinguish among multiple causes of food insecurity and apportion blame. The decision does not specify, moreover, how much worse a country's situation has to become – and by what criteria the worsening should be judged a result of GATT 1994 – before developed countries have to provide compensation.

No consensus currently exists on whether the poorest net food-importing countries are being harmed by GATT 1994. The Food and Agriculture Organization of the United Nations (FAO) says yes; the International Monetary Fund (IMF) says no.[7]

The Marrakesh Decision identifies several forms of assistance: food aid, loans from the international financial institutions (the IMF and World Bank; see Chapter 6), bilateral export credits, and technical and financial aid to agriculture in the affected countries.

Food aid is an obvious safety net: if a country cannot afford to purchase the food its people need, developed countries ought to provide food. With GATT 1994, however, developed country governments are decreasing purchases of surplus commodities from their farmers. Less stockpiled food is available to use as food aid and, with pressure on industrial country budgets, fewer funds allocated to food aid purchases.

International financial institutions can provide loans to countries suffering from temporary balance of payments problems arising from higher costs of imported food. The IMF has a special fund (the Compensatory Financing Facility) for such loans. But the IMF has to agree to use it, and a borrowing country has to accept increased indebtedness and IMF conditions.

Tobacco processing pays Bangladeshi women a modest wage.

F. McDougall/WFP

The Marrakesh Decision also envisions export credits and technical and financial aid to increase agricultural productivity. But aid to agriculture is a declining share of shrinking industrial country spending on development assistance. For example, aid to agriculture provided by the U.S. Agency for International Development fell 50 percent between fiscal years 1992 and 1994.[8]

The Marrakesh Decision was responsible. But the industrial countries have so far done little to provide, or even plan for, the assistance it promised.[9]

New Intellectual Property Rules

GATT 1994 also greatly strengthens international intellectual property rights rules.[10] In the agriculture sector, this means that the big agribusiness firms have more protection for the improved crop strains and technologies that they have developed.

This will have some good effects for poor farmers. Patents encourage technological progress by providing incentives for innovation: those who devote their time, money and effort to develop a more productive or disease-resistant plant variety are rewarded with a time-limited monopoly. If patents are respected, the holder is more willing to export the innovation, making it more widely available to increase productivity and food security.

Patented seed varieties, however, often require adjustments and increase farming risks, particularly for poor farmers. Even though more productive and profitable, new seeds are expensive, usually require fresh knowledge and different management, and often require additional purchased inputs such as fertilizer and pesticides. Poor farmers, especially women, often do not have access to credit, and are frequently overlooked in the distribution of new knowledge. With larger cash expenses, the risks of crop failure multiply. Relatively wealthy farmers have a decided advantage.

The developing world has no lack of ingenuity, but people there hold fewer patents. Even if an innovative developing country farmer knows how to acquire and enforce a patent, she is unlikely to have adequate resources to do so.

Transnational corporations pushed hard for the new intellectual property rules in GATT 1994. Agribusiness will benefit from them much more than poor farmers.

From an environmental perspective, the more productive and profitable new varieties tend to crowd out traditional varieties. The latter, an invaluable source of

Planting Tobacco, Growing Hunger[1] | *by Lily Philipose*

In the red and white barns on John Fritz's farm just outside Lexington, Kentucky, tobacco stems hang to dry, six layers high, slowly turning from green to brown. Half of Kentucky's tobacco production is exported, either directly or in cigarettes, and farmers like John Fritz have enjoyed protected production quotas and guaranteed high prices. Tobacco, the most controversial cash crop grown in the United States, has been at the center of a public debate about devastating health consequences and the issue of regulation.

Global trade in tobacco also affects growers in the developing world, some of whom devote far larger proportions of their farmland to tobacco than the one-twentieth that the typical Kentucky farmer is allowed.[2]

Developing countries' need to earn foreign exchange often leads them to promote cash crops at the expense of food security. In Sierra Leone, where agriculture is the main source of livelihood for 65 percent of the population, the government's 20-year policy of supporting cash crops like tobacco has resulted in a drastic decline in rice self-sufficiency.

In 1992, nearly 16,000 Sierra Leonean farmers were under contract to the Rokel Leaf Tobacco Development Company, which is 60 percent owned by a subsidiary of British American Tobacco. The contracting system, where farmers received subsidized inputs to grow the crop, meant that more and more farmers devoted their labor and land to tobacco, undermining local food production.

Rokel itself has acknowledged that tobacco cultivation has had adverse environmental effects in some parts of the country. In the Bombali District in the north, the once forested land is now bare and rocky as a result of shifting cultivation and exhaustion of the land. Deforestation has been exacerbated by the large quantities of firewood needed for tobacco curing. The end result is infertile land, incapable of supporting any crops.

Long periods of tobacco growing and shifting cultivation practices, together with the declining fertility of the land as well as poor market access and storage facilities, have contributed to hunger in Sierra Leone. While tobacco farms flourish, on average, a farm family in Sella Limba Chiefdom in northern Sierra Leone produces only enough food for eight months of the year.

Dr. Lily Philipose is a Bread for the World Institute intern.

Notes: 1) Adapted from ACTIONAID, *Hunger and the Global Agenda: Who Wins?... Who Loses?... Who Cares?* (London: ACTIONAID, 1996), pp. 4-6. 2) "Fuming on the Farm," *The Economist*, October 12, 1996.

germ plasm for further gains in productivity or protection against new pests, have evolved from decades of patient observation and selection by countless farmers. But they are owned by no one in particular. They may be lost altogether, unless a plan is set up to assure their preservation. Global seed companies have their own seed banks, and have easy access to the public seed banks established by the United Nations and the Consultative Group on International Agricultural Research (CGIAR), the network of international agricultural research centers that helped launch the "green revolution." But the risks of "genetic erosion" are real.[11]

Until very recently, the industrial countries were cutting back funding for CGIAR. Some of its centers have now turned their attention to the needs of poor and dryland farmers and to environmental issues. Despite their record of success in boosting productivity and increased relevance to the needs of poor farmers, these public sources of agricultural knowledge had to reduce their budgets and programs. Adequate and stable funding for CGIAR would be a logical complement to the new protections for agribusinesses' intellectual property.

Responsible Industrial-Country Policies

The industrial countries should live up to the Marrakesh Decision and also restore funding for international agricultural research. These steps would be responsible complements to the impact of GATT 1994 on agriculture.

When Peasants Grow **Narcotics** | *by Lily Philipose*

In the tangled jungle of southeastern Colombia, peasants strip the oval leaves off coca bushes, dump them in plastic-lined pits, douse them with kerosene and water and stomp on them barefoot to make a paste. Altemar Restrepo, one of these peasants, has worked for four of his 25 years in a jungle laboratory, where the kerosene-soaked leaves lie in wooden maturation pens.

Every week the laboratory produces more than 75 pounds of coca, which is refined elsewhere into powdered cocaine. Before taking up this work, Restrepo had earned his living cutting sugar cane. Standing beside a heap of coca leaves, his skin glistening with sweat, Restrepo explains: "We do this because you can't raise cattle or corn in this region. There's no water, and transport is too expensive." As a cane-cutter, he said, he was lucky to earn $35 a week. For processing coca leaves he receives $10 to $15 a day, plus food and a dormitory cot.[1]

Altemar Restrepo's simple words of explanation show how the lack of options is a powerful incentive to grow drugs. Viable alternatives are difficult to find because of the range of advantages drug cultivation offers low-income farmers from Afghanistan to Burma and Bolivia. Both opium poppies and coca are hardy plants that reward poor soils with rich multiple harvests. Small-scale production is enough to maintain a single-family household, and since cropping is labor-intensive, provides an important source of employment. Start-up costs are low, and drug traffickers often extend much-needed credit to laborers. Opium and coca are non-perishable, low-bulk crops; they can easily be stored and transported, even in remote areas. Demand for the crops is high, so farmers know they can rely on a steady market.

Farmers grow drug crops because it is their only means of achieving a secure livelihood. But they earn no more than a small fraction of the final market value of their product. Worldwide revenues of the drug industry in the early 1990s were estimated at $500 billion.[2] Prices spiral upward as opium poppies or coca leaves are turned into heroin or cocaine, passing through the hands of those who process, package, transport, smuggle and sell the drugs. The finished product will have travelled up a staircase of illegal activities that ultimately links Restrepo with the misery of a drug-ridden street in Brooklyn.

Of the short-term economic incentives that attract growers to drug cultivation, price is perhaps the most compelling. In Bolivia, for example – where the per capita gross national product (GNP) is $770 a year – an acre of coca yields about $475 annually. Selling crops like bananas and grapefruit will bring in $35 to $250 – assuming buyers, of course.[3]

In Mexico, after the adoption of the North American Free Trade Agreement (NAFTA), the liberalization of agriculture and the cutting of government subsidies in rural areas has many small farmers worried about their economic security. They may turn to growing illegal crops like marijuana as a household survival strategy. The U.S. Drug Enforcement Agency concluded that "increased illicit drug production will probably be a direct result of the discontinuation of subsistence crop subsidies."[4]

When rich lending countries knock on the doors of developing nations for loan repayment, countries with debt-burdened economies may look to illegal drugs as a source of quick revenue. The domestic belt-tightening that ensues in order to meet foreign debt repayments directly leads to sharply reduced social services and rising unemployment. This, in turn, only entrenches the drug industry more firmly in society as a source of jobs and income.

A workable solution to the problem of drug cultivation is boosting the strength of the formal economy in the drug-growing countries. A comprehensive program of economic development can provide real alternatives to poor farmers. It can offer a relatively secure, legal means of earning a living to people for whom poverty or lack of productive options are the chief motivations for growing drugs.

The only successful example of a large-scale reduction in illicit drug cultivation in recent years took place in Thailand. This was the result of rapid economic growth together with a government strategy that invested not only in seeds and fertilizers but also schools, roads, infrastructure and market access for farmers. The

– continued next page

Hmong hill-tribe, one of the chief growers of opium poppies, now actually makes more money and has a more secure livelihood by growing fruit.[5]

The resilience of the drug industry is a matter of simple economics. Like sweatshop industries, it taps an enormous supply of cheap labor, generates great profit for a few and is assured of a large consumer base. Ultimately, the most potent weapon against drug production is people-centered development.

Dr. Lily Philipose is an intern at Bread for the World Institute.

Notes: 1) Christopher S. Wren, "Keeping Cocaine Resilient: Low Cost and High Profit," *New York Times*, March 4, 1997. 2) Rasul Shams, "The Drugs Economy and Anti-Drug Policy in Developing Countries," *Intereconomics 27* (May/June 1992): 139. 3) Mathea Falco, "U.S. Drug Policy: Addicted to Failure," *Foreign Policy* No. 102 (Spring 1996): 126; 4) Peter Andreas, "U.S.-Mexico: Open Markets, Closed Border," *Foreign Policy* 103 (Summer 1996): 59. 5) Falco, 126; *Narcotics and Development* (Washington: Panos Institute, 1993), 12.

Within the United States, a broad coalition of agricultural and agribusiness interests are showing new interest in expanding both trade and aid in agriculture. They recognize that broad-based economic development and increasing productivity in developing countries are more likely to help than hurt exporters in developed countries – including agricultural exporters.[12] A report from the National Center for Food and Agricultural Policy states:

> Economic success abroad is good for agriculture in the U.S. Even when U.S. foreign assistance efforts are directed toward increasing *agricultural production* in poor countries, the larger results can still be complementary with the interest of the farm sector in the U.S.[13]

The Rome Declaration on World Food Security and World Food Summit Plan of Action (see Chapter 1, pp. 16-17) lay out good first steps toward a structure in which nations can increase their food security through responsible trade policies. The documents also strongly support sustainable agricultural and rural development. But statements and plans do not guarantee results.

International aid should seek to redress the situation of women farmers. They produce up to 80 percent of domestically grown food in sub-Saharan Africa and significant amounts in other developing regions. They often suffer from biased laws, policies and customs. In many places, women are limited in their ability to own land, gain access to irrigation water, receive loans and education, and benefit from agricultural extension and other services. Foreign assistance, with the involvement of nongovernmental organizations, can help change these patterns.[14]

International policies can also make or break food security. Developed countries must guarantee food aid in cases of extreme food shortages or when countries do not have the funds available (from export earnings or international financial institutions). Responsible trade requires multilateral cooperation to establish and maintain essential grain reserves; in this way, wealthier countries can compensate poorer ones for increased risks from liberalization by providing a safety net. Joseph instructed the Egyptians to save food during fat years for use during the lean. His advice remains sound for the governments of today's global community.

The Need for Advocacy

People in industrial countries can make trade more responsible by lobbying against laws, policies and practices that discriminate against developing-country exports and for aid programs that encourage sustainable development and food security:

- Basic research to improve productivity, especially for peasant and dryland farmers;
- Development assistance to support dissemination of research results, especially that which enhances the role of women in marketing and profiting from their products and encourages sustainable agricultural practices; and
- Technical assistance to developing countries to train local people to process agricultural products in ways to make them acceptable and safe for consumers, thereby encouraging higher value exports.

Grassroots support for responsible trade and sustainable agricultural development can encourage the world's political leaders to act. People who raise their voices on behalf of those who are hungry can help increase food security.

Dr. Renée Marlin-Bennett is an associate professor of international relations and director of the Division of International Politics and Foreign Policy, School of International Service, American University. She thanks Monica Wells for research assistance.

CHAPTER 5

International Investment

By Edward J. Chesky

This chapter examines the basic elements of international investment – how it works, who benefits, who doesn't and what might be done about it. Today, virtually every government, including the remaining communist regimes, eagerly seeks foreign investment.

Market economics is at once innovative and cruel, awful and awesome. It introduces new products and technologies, and creates new opportunities, new jobs and higher productivity. It also often leads to downsizing, plant closures and devastated communities. But responsible investment benefits business, workers, consumers and the environment.

Transnational companies are investing over $200 billion annually in the developing world, contributing to vastly improved living standards in a number of countries. How does this affect hunger and poverty? And, what role do public policies and citizen action have in ameliorating inequities, and increasing opportunities, for those harmed or "left out"?

Encourage responsible investing through policies that are good for businesses, workers and consumers.

Looking Back

In 1945, after the Great Depression and World War II, most of Europe and much of Asia lay in ruins, hungry and deeply poor. The leaders of the victorious Allies pledged not to return to the economic nationalism, high trade barriers, depression and unemployment of the 1930s, and to begin by rebuilding the war-torn world. Beyond altruism, the United States realized that it could not prosper unless the nations of Europe and Asia once again became markets for U.S. products and partners in making the market economy function.

Private sector investors were initially unable and unwilling to undertake the large transfers of funds needed to rebuild war-torn factories and jump-start devastated economies. To address these needs, new financial institutions were created – the World Bank and the International Monetary Fund (see Chapter 6). In the beginning, however, these were not sufficient, and the United States initiated its own Marshall Plan. From 1947 through 1952, the U.S. government invested a total of $13 billion in European reconstruction. This cooperative venture proved critical to economic recovery in Europe and sustained prosperity in the United States.

Development Aid

Following the successes of the Marshall Plan, a similar rationale was adopted for aid to developing countries. Since 1961, the United States has provided billions of dollars of assistance, including some to almost every developing nation, through the U.S. Agency for International Development (USAID). These programs, paralleled by those of other nations, international financial institutions and United Nations agencies, have focused on basic infrastructure (roads, ports, electric power and telecommunications, and some basic industries), agriculture, health and education, and on factories, banks and other economic enterprises in the 150 or so recipient countries. Nongovernmental organizations (NGOs) made project level contributions, with particular concern for women, children and the environment.

Forty years of development aid have yielded mixed results. Famine and rampant disease have largely vanished from most nations; hundreds of millions of children are in schools that did not exist before. But strategic considerations have had more influence on aid programs to many countries than humanitarian or development concerns until quite recently.

Since the end of the Cold War, major aid institutions such as the World Bank, the U.N. Development Programme and the USAID have gone through very promising reforms. But the industrial nations, led by the United States, have reduced development aid, especially programs for poor countries and for poor people within countries.

Commercial Bank Lending: Boom and Bust

In the mid-1970s, commercial banks in industrial countries found themselves flush with oil revenues as prices rose. Developing countries borrowed to cover skyrocketing food and fuel import costs. With funds available at low interest, they also sought loans to initiate sometimes ill-advised development projects. By the late 1970s, industrial country central banks pushed up interest rates to control inflation. This made the debt burdens of many

Figure 5.1 **Net Foreign Resource Flows to Developing Countries 1990-1996**

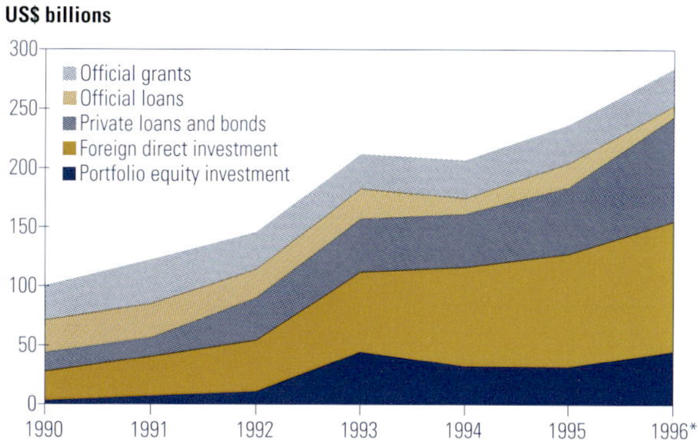

Source: The World Bank.

* Preliminary

developing countries unmanageable, creating the "debt crisis" of the early 1980s (see Chapter 6, pp. 77-78). Commercial banks cut back suddenly and dramatically in their lending to developing countries.

The New Era of Private Investments

In the 1990s, private investment in developing and transition economies has expanded again, now led by *foreign direct investment* (FDI, i.e., full or joint direct ownership of a company).

Net private capital flows to developing countries soared from $43 billion in 1990 to $184 billion in 1995, including $95 billion in FDI, $61 billion in *foreign portfolio investment* (foreign purchases of stocks and bonds) and $28 billion in *foreign bank and trade-related lending* (see Figure 5.1).[1] In 1995, aid and lending from governments and international organizations totaled $69 billion – less than two-fifths the value of private capital flows.

The discussion which follows focuses primarily on FDI, the largest current channel of private foreign investment. It is also the most permanent and the most sensitive to the local investment climate that shapes a country's domestic economy.

In contrast, stock purchases are subject to swings in investor confidence, and may be withdrawn quickly. Bank loans and purchases of company bonds represent an intermediate commitment; such loans cannot be sold as easily as stock shares, but neither do they represent as deep a commitment as direct ownership. Many of the points of the

Table 5.1 **Foreign Direct Investment Flows, 1995 ($ billion)**

	FDI Inflows ($ billion)	FDI Outflows ($ billion)	GDI/GDP (Percent)	FDI/GDI (Percent)	FDI/Pop (US $)
Developed Countries	203.2	270.5	..	3.3	235
European Union	111.9	132.3	..	4.8	302
United States	60.2	95.5	11	4.8	229
Australia	13.1	5.4	23	6.4	728
Canada	11.2	4.8	19	4.8	373
Other Developed	6.8	32.5	..	0.6	37
Transition Economies	12.1	0.3	..	0.9	58
Hungary	3.5	•	23	13.9	350
Poland	2.5	•	17	13.5	64
Czech Republic	2.5	0.1	25	9.1	250
Russian Federation	2.0	•	25	0.1	14
Developing Countries	99.7	47.0	..	7.5	21
China	37.5	3.5	40	24.5	31
Mexico	7.0	0.6	15	10.4	76
Malaysia	5.8	2.6	41	16.1	290
Singapore	5.3	2.8	33	23.5	1767
Brazil	4.9	1.4	22	3.0	31
Indonesia	4.5	•	38	3.6	23
Argentina	3.9	•	18	9.6	111
Chile	3.0	0.6	27	19.9	214
Bermuda	2.9	•	..	..	..
Thailand	2.3	3.1	43	1.1	40
Hong Kong	2.0	25.0	35	8.2	333
India	1.8	•	25	1.1	2
Korea (Republic of)	1.5	3.0	37	0.6	33
Philippines	1.5	•	23	9.6	22
Taiwan	1.5	3.8	..	3.5	..
Sub-Saharan Africa	2.9	0.5	..	11.3	5
Nigeria	1.3	0.5	..	50.5	12

• Less than $50 million

Source: U.N. Conference on Trade and Development; The World Bank.

following discussion, however, are applicable to bank loans, bond and stock investments as well as FDI.

Overview of FDI[2]

Total annual FDI flows more than tripled from the mid-1980s to 1995, when they reached $318 billion. Funds transferred between richer industrial countries accounted for nearly two-thirds of this sum. But FDI flows to developing countries grew fivefold over the decade – from $18 billion in 1986 to $111 billion in 1996, far outstripping total foreign aid of all kinds.

In 1995, two-thirds of FDI originated from just five countries – the United States ($95 billion), the United Kingdom ($38 billion), Germany ($35 billion), Japan ($21 billion) and France ($18 billion). The Netherlands, Sweden, Switzerland, Belgium, Luxembourg, Australia and Canada were also sources for sizeable FDI among industrial countries.

Significant FDI funds originate in several developing countries, notably the fast-growing economies in East and Southeast Asia. Of $47 billion total FDI from developing countries, more than half came from Hong Kong ($25 billion), followed by Taiwan, China, Korea, Singapore and Malaysia.

For the most part, FDI seeks secure locations for profitable investments, most notably the industrial nations themselves. Of the $100 billion that went to developing countries, 80 percent went only to a dozen countries in East and Southeast Asia and Latin America which, with the exception of China, the World Bank classifies as Middle Income, or even High Income. At the opposite extreme, 47 of the poorest countries, primarily in Africa, altogether received barely 1 percent. FDI to Central and Eastern Europe has climbed rapidly during the 1990s, reaching $12 billion in 1995 (see Tables 5.1 and 5.2).

East and Southeast Asia

East and Southeast Asia are the fastest growing regions of the world economy. They have attracted an overwhelming share of FDI – $62 billion in 1995, more than 60 percent of the flow to the developing world. China received over half the total FDI in East and Southeast Asia.

Beginning in the 1950s Japan adopted export-led growth as a national policy. South Korea and Taiwan followed suit in the 1960s and 1970s. They also began to open their doors to foreign trade and finance. The city states of Hong Kong and Singapore were even more open, and prospered as world centers of trade, finance and industry.

After this first generation of Asian "Tigers" came a second group of rapidly growing Asian economies: China, Malaysia, Indonesia and Thailand – the so-called second generation Newly Industrializing Countries (NICs). The Philippines and Vietnam have since sought to emulate their neighbors' pattern of export-led industrialization facilitated by high levels of foreign investment.

Recently, the region's economies have cooled, and investment may decline somewhat. Flows to China appear to have slowed as labor costs have increased in the booming coastal region. Investors are also uncertain about the consequences of China's takeover of Hong Kong.

South Asia

Although lagging behind East Asia in investment and growth, the nations of South Asia – India, Bangladesh, Pakistan, Sri Lanka and surrounding smaller countries – are increasingly alert to lessons that might be learned from the Asian Tigers. By 1995, FDI reached $2.7 billion, as India began to attract foreign capital. This figure is still only half of FDI flows to tiny Malaysia.

Africa

Sub-Saharan Africa received less than $3 billion in FDI in 1995, with Nigeria and Angola capturing most of that to develop oil and other mineral resources. Foreign investment in Africa has long focused heavily on natural resource exploitation. Much of the region receives little or no private foreign investment.

Natural disasters, war, unrest and weak governments have prevented the development of an attractive investment climate in such countries as Zaire, Somalia, Ethiopia and Mozambique.[3] As foreign assistance levels have declined, a rising share has gone into emergency relief rather than sustainable development activities.

Several recent trends bear watching. Many governments have concluded that they need more private investment to prosper and have begun to attract foreign capital with new investment laws. South Africa is the most developed sub-Saharan African nation, and it may be able to attract significant FDI. A dynamic and growing South African economy would probably foster greater prosperity in neighboring nations.

Latin America & the Caribbean

This region is different from other parts of the developing world. Most nations in the region achieved independence almost two centuries ago. But in the last 50 years they found consistent economic growth difficult to achieve. Agriculture stagnated; population grew rapidly. The only option for many poor people was flight to the grim slums that surround burgeoning mega-cities. In the 1980s, most of the region faced a foreign debt crisis only recently surmounted. Now, unevenly, investment of various kinds has again begun to flow to some nations.

In 1995, Latin America and Caribbean countries received $26 billion, about 25 percent of FDI going to the developing world. More than 70 percent of this investment went to just four countries: Brazil, Mexico, Chile and Argentina.

Table 5.2 **Regional Foreign Direct Investment**
Inflows, 1995

	($ billion)
Latin America and Caribbean	26.6
Africa (including North Africa)	4.7
Central and Eastern Europe	12.1
West Asia	2.5
East and Southeast Asia	62.0
South Asia	2.7
Total	**110.9**

Source: UNCTAD.

In addition to FDI, Latin American nations are also major recipients of foreign portfolio investments and bank loans. Much of the portfolio investment is related to privatization of public companies such as electric power and telecommunications facilities.[4]

Transition Economies

The newly independent states of the former Soviet Union and the ex-communist nations of Central and Eastern Europe, the "transition economies," confront another set of problems as they try to shift to market-based economies. Russia, for example, faces immense difficulties in turning around its economy after 75 years with little experience of market institutions. So far, many of the new companies seem to be dominated by organized crime.

Western governments, international financial institutions and private banks and companies have offered advisers, technical assistance and public funding to assist the transition. They want to support the new and inexperienced governments as they try to foster new businesses and create banks, stock exchanges and other private sector institutions. Most transition economies are privatizing large numbers of government companies.

But partnerships with Western businesses have developed more slowly than expected. Total annual FDI flows to Central and Eastern Europe, though recently growing fairly rapidly, reached only $12 billion in 1995. Of this, $2 billion went to Russia. Three nations where the transition is most advanced, Poland, the Czech Republic and Hungary, received the bulk of the funds, $7.5 billion. The other former communist nations appear to be on a slow road to achieving viable market economies and restoring economic growth.

CARE

Apparel manufacture has been important to economic growth in East Asian countries.

National and Corporate Interests and FDI

FDI in developing countries results from the convergence of two sets of interests. Companies seek new opportunities to expand markets or cut costs, or both. Developing countries want resources, technology, skills and jobs.

While it is often assumed that the initiative for a foreign investment comes from abroad, this is not always the case. Developing country leaders increasingly recognize that transnational corporations (TNCs) can contribute to national development. TNCs bring investment funds and create new jobs. Equally important, they provide training and management skills, new technologies and access to developed country markets. FDI also has spin-off effects. Some industries subcontract parts of their work to local entrepreneurs. As workers in new plants spend their income, they help create other jobs in the community.

So, many government officials around the world are courting TNCs, convinced that they will help provide employment and a better life for their community or nation. It is hard to argue against the jobs and relative prosperity that a new factory or assembly plant may bring to a depressed community in Zimbabwe, Indonesia, Haiti or Mississippi. In some cases, officials may consent to excessive tax breaks or lax labor and environmental regulations. But strong and responsible governments are able to woo foreign investors in ways that also contribute to broad-based development.

Lessons from Asia

Fifty years ago most of Asia was desperately poor. Rapid growth in East Asia (the "economic miracle") involved heavy investment in export-oriented industry and agriculture. It was accompanied by sharp reductions in poverty and broadly improved living standards. FDI has played a role, but is only part of the picture. High levels of domestic savings linked to their productive investment have been even more critical, along with increasingly broad engagement in trade and other aspects of the world economy. An economic climate that encourages domestic savings and investment – low inflation and favorable interest rates – also tends to attract foreign investment. More taxes increased public savings, which the governments invested in infrastructure, agriculture, health care and education. They often sent their best students overseas to attain higher university degrees and skills.

East Asian countries began by developing textile and apparel manufacture for export, followed by gradual movement into consumer electrical appliances, electronics, computers and telecommunications equipment – from simple assembly to the manufacture and development of the most sophisticated products.

Japan and Korea (and to a lesser extent, Taiwan) developed various kinds of heavy industry – steel, shipbuilding, heavy machinery and automobiles – often with government sponsorship and guidance. Each of these industries generally became export-oriented and competitive in quality and price. They quickly challenged products from the United States and Europe.

Asian governments had differing policies on admission of foreign investment. Generally, the governments assumed a major role in stimulating local savings and investment, directing economic growth, and fostering new industry and exports. In Taiwan and Korea, foreign investment was tightly controlled, guided and limited. Each Asian nation was different, with varying natural resource endowments, infrastructure, skills and needs. But all the rapidly developing Asian nations recognized the need to go abroad for modern equipment, expertise, patents and other aspects of the western and Japanese industry, although often adapted to local needs, capabilities and market potential.

The fruit was rapid growth with relatively fair distribution of benefits. On the other hand, most countries in the region have limited democracy or authoritarian political systems, and growth often had high environmental costs. For example, Taiwan now suffers extremely high levels of air, water and soil pollution.

Among the most important economic issues today is whether the development patterns that evolved in East Asia in recent decades will work in South Asia, Africa, and Latin America and the Caribbean. Are there new markets and continuing demand for similar or new industrial products to provide productive employment for rapidly growing populations in other regions? Do other developing countries have, or can they develop, the physical infrastructure and educational base that the East Asian countries have? Can they achieve the same high domestic savings rates (up to 30 percent of national income)? Can they attract FDI and manage their relationships with TNCs as skillfully as have East Asian nations?

Prospects in Africa

Many sub-Saharan African countries lack the infrastructure to attract investment in manufacturing, or to enable their agriculture to function well. Education and health care are weak, so workers are not well prepared. Savings rates are low, and the income base for either savings or taxation almost negligible. Heavy debt burdens draw down resources that might be tapped for public services (see Chapter 6, pp.77-79).

The steps required to make African countries attractive for foreign investors include conflict resolution; public investment in education and health care, especially for women; support for agriculture and small businesses, again with an emphasis on women as farmers and traders; and improvements in infrastructure.

Since 1994, an increasing number of African economies have registered economic growth. Some governments have sought to practice sound macroeconomic policies and have reduced inflation.[5] Civil society organizations have proliferated throughout the continent, and have eagerly sought to advance participatory, sustainable development. Peace has finally come to Mozambique, Ethiopia and Eritrea.

As African nations become more politically stable and liberalize their economies, opportunities may open up for private foreign investment in infrastructure.

African governments negotiate with foreign businesses from a position of weakness, often without adequate information. They may cede too much or try to drive too hard a bargain. Corrupt officials too often agree to sweetheart deals with foreign companies and pocket part of the proceeds. But the political, economic and social improvements that will attract a significantly higher level of foreign investment would also, in the main, be good for Africa's poor majority.

Industrial-country governments, for their part, have recently given some attention to Africa's development. Boosting trade with, and investment in, the region was a major topic of discussion at the 1997 economic summit of the world's eight richest countries (see "Africa Trade and Investment Policy," p. 60).

Governments Seeking Investors

In recent years, developing country governments, in pursuit of their own economic boom, have formed or strengthened public agencies to promote new investments. They often go abroad or sponsor their companies on official investment missions sent out to publicize new opportunities. Government boards in most developing countries encourage foreign and domestic investment. They often establish investment codes and incentives to make the nation more attractive to foreign ventures, but also protect vital national interests.

Common provisions in investment codes to attract increased foreign funding include: tax rebates and holidays, rights for foreign companies to have majority ownership in joint ventures, guarantees against uncompensated expropriation and the right to remit profits and repatriate capital. Countries may offer incentives to companies that will employ simpler technology and generate more jobs and good working conditions, or hire more local technicians and managers. Investment codes often include provisions to protect existing businesses and agriculture, worker rights and the environment. Policy toward unions varies widely, all the way from strong support to active discouragement. Development of natural resources such as petroleum is a special case. Governments usually establish a formula for sharing costs and proceeds among a local business partner, the government and a foreign company.

Competition is keen among nations seeking a new foreign venture partner. Similarly, U.S. state governments in Tennessee and Ohio in the United States may compete for a new foreign automobile plant (see Chapter 2, p. 29).

Government incentives to foreign investors may be critical at the margin, but a number of other factors come together to form the "investment climate." Some

Africa Trade & Investment Policy | *by BFW Institute*

Full integration of sub-Saharan Africa into the global economy has recently gained a high place on the international economic policy agenda. The 1997 summit of the eight richest industrial country governments (Group of Eight, or G-8) devoted major attention to increased trade with, and investment in, the region. Legislation currently before the U.S. Congress would improve Africa's access to U.S. markets, especially for processed and manufactured goods, and would help private U.S. investment in the region, with an emphasis on infrastructure. The European Union has had an extensive program of preferential market access in place for many years, with African countries among the major beneficiaries.

The U.S. legislative initiative, the Africa Growth and Opportunity Act of 1997, would offer preferential access to the U.S. market, debt forgiveness and new investment guarantees to African countries that lower their trade barriers and increase investment in their own people. The bill has attracted early support from both the Speaker of the House of Representatives, Newt Gingrich, and President Bill Clinton.

Bread for the World and the Washington Office on Africa have convened the Africa Trade Policy Working Group, a coalition of nongovernmental advocates of sustainable development in Africa. The group has supported the bill's provisions creating a U.S.-African Economic Forum, the enhancement of African market access (provided due respect is paid to labor rights) and the allocation of investment promotion funds. The coalition has urged the inclusion of additional provisions focused on an enabling environment for small and micro-enterprises; broad-based, poverty reducing growth; food security and agricultural and rural development; and environmental protection.

A version of the bill may well become law in 1997 or 1998. Bread for the World and its coalition partners are seeking to incorporate concerns about poverty reduction and participation, while supporting efforts to raise the profile of Africa in U.S. international economic policy.

Supporters of sustainable development in Africa have also expressed concern that the bill establishes policy reform, rather than accountable government and participatory processes, as the main condition for benefits.

Advocates and African leaders alike welcomed the attention that the continent's development needs received from the G-8. The G-8 acknowledged the ongoing need for aid, as well as trade and investment. Unfortunately, its meeting made no commitment to reverse declining aid levels. Other concerns:

- Industrial country governments must substantively include African governments, non-governmental organizations and communities in shaping initiatives; and
- Current proposals have a "trickle down" character. Without a stronger focus on poverty and participation, expanded economic relationships may directly benefit only the economic elite of Africa.

of these factors are beyond government control. Developing countries have virtually no influence over global interest rates or the level of global business activity, for example.

Other elements of the investment climate stem from persistent government efforts over a period of time. Several governments have concluded that the best way to expand and modernize their infrastructure (particularly electric power and telecommunications) is to invite experienced outside firms to finance, build and sometimes operate new systems.

Perceptions of government economic policy, the reliability of public administration, political stability and corruption encourage or discourage potential foreign investors. Countries at war are unlikely to attract new money.

The availability of an educated or trainable work force is also important. Some nations (and states in the United States) emphasize docile or non-union labor. Prevailing wage rates are often critical. If a company is interested in selling its products in local or regional markets, then it must consider the standard of living and consumer tastes.[6]

Taking all of these factors and incentives together, it is clear why most foreign investment goes first to stable, developed nations and then to East Asia. Africa, South Asia and parts of the Americas do not generally offer the kind of investment climate that gains major investor attention.

At least one billion people, mainly in fairly remote rural areas in Africa, South Asia and far western China, are largely out of the reach of foreign investors. Foreign funds continue to flow mainly to areas conducive to major industry where there are concentrations of trained or trainable people, and new markets to be served, combined with appropriate natural resources and modern infrastructure. The challenge for governments and foreign aid institutions is to bring up the poorest areas through strategic public investment in education, agriculture and basic infrastructure.

Some nations may have the option to try to be self-sufficient and to seek their own patterns of growth with little or no foreign involvement. But for most countries this seems less and less viable. Most developing country governments have concluded that the best available path to economic growth relies heavily on the private sector, with foreign capital as part of the solution.

Investors Seeking Opportunity

Transnational companies span a wide spectrum, from a U.S. family firm with a single branch in Mexico to major global corporations like British Petroleum, Citibank, Daimler-Benz, Renault, Sony or Microsoft. In 1995, more than 39,000 international companies had more than 270,000 foreign affiliates worldwide. More than 10,000 foreign firm affiliates are located in the United States; Germany has even more. Even tiny Singapore reports more than 10,000 foreign branch operations. Brazil and Mexico have more than 8,000 each. China hosts an astounding 45,000 affiliates, sure testimony to the belief that China, with a population of 1.2 billion, is the major market and export platform of the future. More than 50 nations are home bases to transnationals.[7]

The 100 largest TNCs have the greatest impact upon the growth of global trade and investment. In 1992, these companies (excluding banking and finance firms) owned $3.4 trillion in global assets, with $1.4 trillion invested outside their home countries. They accounted for more than one-third of FDI from their countries of origin, and about the same fraction of international sales.

Total sales of the top 200 TNCs were $7.1 trillion in 1995, with almost 40 percent, $2.7 trillion, by Japanese-based companies, 28 percent by U.S. firms and 10 percent by German. Although TNCs from the advanced developing world, particularly East Asia, are rising rapidly, all but five of the top 200 firms, measured by 1995 sales, were headquartered in the industrial world. Three Korean and two Brazilian companies make the list.[8]

Total direct employment by the top 200 transnationals was estimated at about 18 million workers, less than 1 percent of the total world's work force.[9]

The interaction between large TNCs and the mass media deserves mention. Image is part of what they create and sell wherever they market. Because of direct ownership or the great influence that accompanies large advertising budgets, media may be reluctant to criticize their owners' or advertisers' misbehavior, even in egregious circumstances. But the weight given to image also makes TNCs vulnerable to reporting by often competitive media outlets, and to concerted action by consumers and investors.

Large corporations invest huge sums in advertising and public policy advocacy. European companies can deduct bribes as a legitimate business expense, and U.S. companies have not always been above bribery. The economic resources of large corporations thus give them considerable influence over public policy and public opinion. Such influence is difficult to counter, because even competing corporations are likely to endorse the same economic or tax policies. This contributes to widespread suspicion of the TNCs, especially in developing countries.

But the top 200 companies do not constitute the whole of the global economy. Smaller firms, right down to fledgling businesses with a handful of employees, are crucial. All told, smaller firms supply nearly two-thirds of FDI, account for nearly two-thirds of international trade and generate more than two-thirds of trade-related employment. Small businesses, including international joint ventures, compete vigorously with each other, often supplying components or services to larger firms at lower cost than larger firms themselves can achieve. For many goods or services, they can often compete directly against huge companies. Market competition offers considerable protection against excessive profits or abuse.

Both large and smaller TNCs have generated new jobs, trained workers and managers, introduced new technologies, shared patents and other innovations, increased worker productivity, and contributed to economic growth and rising incomes. On the other hand, well-known horror stories are linked to FDI in developing countries: employing child labor in the manufacture of soccer balls and rugs; condoning appalling working conditions with wages at a few cents an hour; destroying rainforests; corrupting government officials; dumping toxic industrial wastes; exporting agricultural products from food short countries; creating unhealthy shanty towns just across the border from California and Texas in Mexico and even sweatshops in the United States.[10] Also, many people just don't like the idea of foreign investors – richer, culturally different – running important businesses in their community.

Related Issues & Concerns

Labor Standards

International standards to regulate and to assure at least minimally decent working conditions and other protections are currently a "work in progress," and enforcement is mainly up to sometimes weak and corrupt national governments. Each national government must have laws that not only promote and protect the rights of responsible international investors, but also assure that the communities and people most affected are protected from unrestrained action by powerful firms. Free trade unions offer workers some countervailing power to protect their interests (see Chapter 1, pp. 17-18).

Public Investments and Foreign Aid

Some necessary investments do not lend themselves to private investment: basic health care and education, as well as core agricultural research, and physical and social infrastructure. Adequate public investment in these areas is essential to creating an attractive private investment climate. More important, investment in these areas is integral to human health, happiness and a habitable world.

Each of these activities is an especially appropriate target for foreign assistance. But aid levels have declined in the 1990s, and what is available is still not sufficiently targeted (see Chapters 1, 4 and 6, pp. 15, 21, 50, 51, 53, 70-71, 76).

The Informal Sector and Microcredit

Foreign investments seldom directly reach the informal sector, which in many countries constitutes the majority of total economic activity. Small entrepreneurs share in the spin-off activities generated by such investments, however. Using subcontractors often is cheaper, and is almost a standard method for circumventing regulations in manufacturing, for example. Small, unregulated businesses often predominate in the first stages of gathering agricultural raw materials such as copra (dried coconut) or lumber.

Developing-country governments need to move as quickly as possible to provide the support, resources and safeguards needed by farmers and small businesses – without imposing stifling regulations (see "The Informal Sector," pp. 64-65). Microenterprises – very small businesses, often employing only the entrepreneur herself or himself – offer a promising avenue out of extreme poverty for people in both the developing and industrial countries.

Microcredit – business loans as small as $50 – has allowed 8 million poor people, mostly women, to become entrepreneurs. In Bangladesh, the Grameen (rural) Bank, established by Bangladeshi economist Mohammed Yunus in 1976, has provided about half of those loans, reaching about 20 percent of the households in the country. A third of Grameen borrowers have risen from poverty, and another third are close. Grameen emphasizes social as well as business development: borrowers pledge to cultivate and eat green vegetables and to reject the practice of dowry.

Many of the microcredit programs in 43 countries (including the United States) use the Grameen model of lending to small groups, who are then collectively responsible for repayment. Repayment rates for micro-loans exceed 90 percent. ACCION and its Latin American partner organizations are now able to recover completely the administrative costs of some microcredit programs. That makes it possible to tap private investment funds, which far exceed available aid.

Microcredit is not a panacea for all development needs. But it can boost incomes and help develop skills and self-confidence. Women (the overwhelming majority of borrowers) tend to devote more of their new earnings to their children's health, nutrition and education than men. Development NGOs such as Freedom from Hunger have cost-effectively integrated microcredit programs with nutrition, health and other forms of education, using increased incomes to improve children's nutritional status.[11]

In February 1997, government officials, microcredit institutions and anti-poverty advocates gathered in Washington, DC, to "launch a global movement to reach 100 million of the world's poorest families, especially the women of those

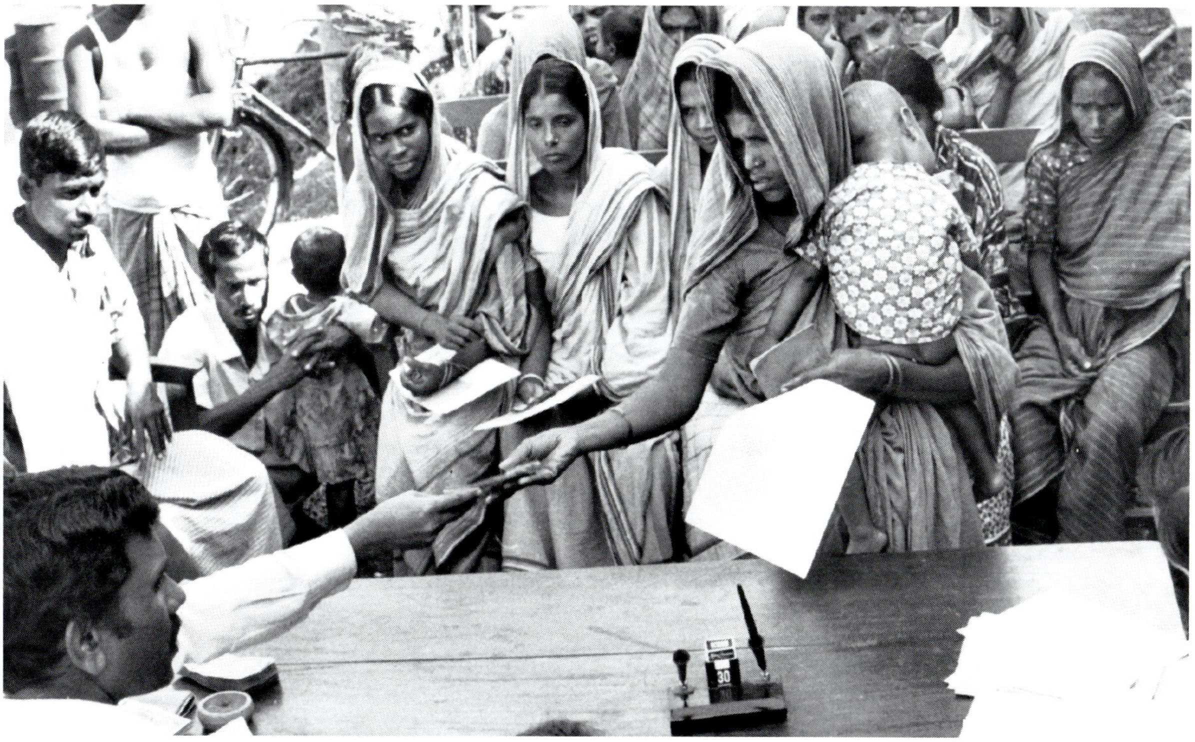

IFAD

Microcredit – business loans as small as $50 – has allowed 8 million poor people, mostly women, to become entrepreneurs. In Bangladesh, the Grameen (rural) Bank, established by Bangladeshi economist Mohammed Yunus in 1976, has provided about half these loans.

families, with credit for self-employment and other financial and business services, by the year 2005." RESULTS Educational Fund organized the gathering. U.S. First Lady Hillary Rodham Clinton called the meeting

> one of the most important that we could have anywhere in the world. . . . Whether we are talking about a rural area in South Asia or an inner city in the United States, microcredit is an invaluable tool in alleviating poverty, promoting self-sufficiency and stimulating economic activity in some of the world's most destitute and disadvantaged communities.[12]

Multilateral Agreement on Investment

Nearly 80 regional and multilateral instruments have been adopted since 1958 to stimulate international investing. More than 700 bilateral investment agreements were signed between 1994 and mid-1996. But each of these is separately negotiated. The concept of a universal multilateral agreement on investment has strong appeal and support from many quarters. But the specifics of such an agreement are hotly disputed.

The 1996 ministerial meeting of the World Trade Organization resolved to negotiate a multilateral agreement in cooperation with the World Bank. The most likely vehicle for negotiation is an agreement currently being developed by the Organisation for Economic Co-operation and Development (OECD), which brings together the governments of 29 industrial and high-income developing countries. The OECD agreement seeks greater predictability, transparency and protection, fewer restrictions and sound investments.

In the first instance, the agreement will only involve high-income countries. They will then encourage developing countries to adhere to its terms.

Many NGOs feel that the process is moving too rapidly. Some are concerned that universal rules for dispute settlement, for example, would further reduce the negotiating strength of poor countries against richer nations and TNCs. It is unclear whether or how the OECD investment agreement will deal with worker rights and labor standards. Some NGOs fear threats to the environment (see Chapter 3, p. 44).

While the need for a multilateral agreement has widespread concurrence, the process must be opened up to include NGOs, developing country governments and the parliaments of the OECD countries.

The **Informal Sector** | *by Lily Philipose & Don Reeves*

A hair stylist of our acquaintance trades haircuts for help with her tax returns from her brother, an accountant. He and his wife, in turn, pay cash to their baby-sitter. Her husband, who has a home-repair business, also works for cash. Both are permanent U.S. residents but have chosen to go around tax rules and regularly send money to relatives in Central America.

Most of us are familiar with exchanges of this sort in what are variously described as *informal, underground, hidden, gray* or *shadow market* activities – beyond the effective reach of taxing or regulatory authorities. The U.S. underground economy has been estimated at $600 billion.[1] The unpaid taxes would more than cover the federal deficit.

People who earn their living in the underground economy avoid taxes and regulations, but also forgo some benefits. The baby-sitter and her husband, for instance, are not accumulating social security credits; failing to report income means they cannot qualify for a mortgage. Undocumented immigrants in the United States are particularly prone to taking jobs that pay less than legal minimum wages, involve unsafe conditions or have little security, such as garment, janitorial, household and farm labor. Recent welfare legislation seems certain to increase the ranks of informal sector workers, since many current welfare recipients lack the skills needed to obtain work in the formal economy.

Informal sector opportunities in industrial countries are very attractive to poor people in much poorer nations. The pull for both legal and illegal immigration seems likely to increase in the near future, especially if people see little hope in their home communities or countries.

In developing and transition countries, the informal sector is a vital, even dominant, source of livelihoods. An estimated 75 percent to 95 percent of wage income in Somalia is never reported to the government. In Zimbabwe and Swaziland, 60 percent of all employment is informal. About 40 percent of Nairobi's population and about 50 percent of Mexico City's live in unauthorized housing. In Russia, as much as 40 percent of production is in the invisible economy.[2]

While the "informal economy" is usually thought of as a problem, and the people within it as lawbreakers (and criminal activities do hide in this shadow area), in reality it includes many hardworking and energetic people. Their illegal activities are strategies for survival. The informal sector includes slums, shantytowns and small businesses, associated with poverty and marginalization. But it also represents people's creative response when formal institutions fail to meet their needs.[3]

Licensing requirements and other regulations designed for substantial businesses make no sense for tiny, bootstrap *– continued next page*

Five Areas for Citizen Action

The flow of FDI and other private investment funds to developing countries seems likely to continue and even increase. As more of the smaller and poorer nations receive and try to deal with these funds, policy decisions in the following five areas will help determine whether the new investments will contribute to more secure lives for hungry and poor people:

- Northern NGOs and civic organizations can support kindred NGOs in developing countries as they contribute to democratic and stable governance, which is good for poor people and attractive to investors;
- Northern NGOs also can help ensure that their own governments and the international financial institutions heed the voices and needs of poor people in setting global rules for international investing;
- Microcredit can boost incomes and help develop skills. It is also an excellent way to target development resources directly to poor people. Yet microcredit currently accounts for just 2 percent of global development aid;
- Governments and international institutions should be encouraged to support internationally recognized labor rights, public health and environmental protection as conditions for foreign investment; and
- Governments should be pressed to agree on a small tax on all currency transactions, to be administered by the International Monetary Fund. International

enterprises. City governments often excessively regulate against street hawking. These practices heighten insecurity for poor entrepreneurs, and also constrict the flow of goods to poor urban consumers.

The fastest growing area of the informal sector is informal settlements or squatter cities, the endpoints of massive rural-urban migration. Tides of migrants surge into cities throughout the developing world, often driven by the difficulty of acquiring land or finding work in the countryside, high infant mortality rates and low wages.

But the migrants find it hard to locate housing, education or regular jobs. So, they illegally occupy land. Marginal neighborhoods, shantytowns and slums spring up. They find informal work – construction day labor, street vending, operating informal transport systems. From Dharavi near Bombay, Asia's largest slum, a 370-acre sprawl of barren, treeless land and rusty shacks, comes some of India's most beautiful artifacts – silver and gold *jari*-work (embroidery), jewelry, pottery, cloth, leather goods.

Typically, official building codes in developing country cities are unrealistic for low-income families. They couldn't possibly afford housing of the standard required by many city regulations.

Historically, the great majority of informal sector workers have been rural – subsistence farmers dependent on unpaid family help, women who do "piece work" at home.[4]

The informal sector shares a long frontier with the formal economy. On one end of international trade – involving such products as rare timber, medicinal plants or copra (dried coconut flesh) – is an enterprising individual who gets the raw material to the roadside, and another who transports it to a central market before it enters any official records. On the other end are those who bring the market commodity to the customer, such as the entrepreneurs who delivered Coca-Cola to villages in the rural Philippines by buffalo sled in the 1950s.

The policy agenda related to the informal sector includes:

- Investing in credit for microenterprises;
- Revamping regulations so that they are realistic and encourage enterprise, but provide some measure of regularization, access to land and credit, and protection from exploitation; and
- Ensuring that basic services (education, health care, water, sanitation) reach *all* children, regardless of their parents' occupations.

Dr. Lily Philipose is an intern and **Don Reeves** is economic policy analyst at BFW Institute.

Notes: 1) The World Bank, *1997 World Development Indicators* (Washington: The World Bank, 1997), Table 4.2. 2) Ed Ayres, "The Expanding Shadow Economy," *Worldwatch*, July/August 1996, 17. 3) Hernando de Soto, *The Other Path* (New York: Harper and Row, 1989). 4) Ayres, 18.

money markets are not only increasingly integrated, but now virtually unregulated. About 90 percent of the approximately $1 trillion in daily currency trading is speculative; 10 percent relates to trade and investment. Too many traders seek profit regardless of the social or environmental consequences. The tax could generate revenues for reducing hunger and poverty and protecting the environment.[13]

Responsible Investing

In addition to influencing public policies, individuals and civic organizations can enhance corporate behavior in their roles as investors. Individuals can choose not to buy shares in companies with whose policies they disagree. Many investors avoid purchasing stocks in companies that manufacture tobacco products or arms, for example, or that operate in countries with poor human rights records. A number of mutual funds screen companies based on criteria of social responsibility (see "Socially Responsible Funds and Money Managers," p. 66).

Corporate financiers may ignore individuals and small mutual funds that decline to buy their stocks. But they are less able to ignore parallel decisions by pension funds, foundations or institutional endowments. The latter are courted by companies anxious to sell their securities, so these funds can have considerable leverage. CALPERS, the California public employees' retirement system, joined many others by divesting from South Africa-related stocks during *apartheid*.

Socially Responsible Funds & Investment Managers

The following funds and money managers sponsored social responsibility shareholder resolutions at 1997 shareholder meetings: Christian Brothers Investment Services; Citizens Trust; Domini Social Equity Fund; Franklin Research and Development; Green Century Funds; Harrington Investments; Informed Investors; Progressive Asset Management; Progressive Securities; the United States Trust Company of Boston; Walnut Street Advisers and the Amalgamated Bank of New York Long View Collective Investment Fund.

The Calvert Social Investment Fund and Pax World Fund offer socially responsible investments. The Interfaith Center on Corporate Responsibility, Investor Responsibility Research Center and Council on Economic Priorities rank corporations based on such criteria as labor relations, advancement of women and environmental practices.[1]

The Ecumenical Development Cooperative Society (EDCS) is an investment fund that allows investors to earn a modest return and help finance sustainable development activities in poor countries and communities. Established by the World Council of Churches, EDCS members (i.e., investors) include local churches and denominations, as well as individuals. In Costa Rica, loans from the society helped Coocafé, a consortium of coffee farmer cooperatives with 1,800 members, to establish a micro-loan fund. Coocafé also receives support from the Friedrich Ebert Foundation in Germany, and exports coffee to industrial countries through "fair trade" organizations, which assure producers a fair price. In 1994, the consortium became EDCS's first project partner to invest funds in the society.[2]

Notes: 1) "Corporate Responsibility Challenges 1997," *The Corporate Examiner* 25:7-8 (February 28, 1997). 2) *EDCS Annual Report* 1995 (Amersfoort, Netherlands: Ecumenical Development Cooperative Society, 1996); information provided by Friedrich Ebert Foundation.

Social responsibility shareholder resolutions at the annual meetings of corporations have often proven an effective way to influence corporate behavior. The Interfaith Center on Corporate Responsibility (ICCR) reported 226 such resolutions prepared for the 1997 annual meetings of nearly 150 companies. Many of these resolutions touched on the companies' responsibilities as international investors, including concern for human and worker rights in China, Latin America, Nigeria, Indonesia, Burma and Northern Ireland.[14] ICCR also represented investor interests in the White House Apparel Industry Partnership (see Chapter 3, p. 45).

Conclusion

International private investment is one of the major factors driving the evolving and increasingly globalized world economy. Tens of thousands of companies have crossed national boundaries in search of greater profits. They carry with them their experience and management skills, along with new technologies and new products. They have helped create millions of new jobs and improve incomes, especially in East and Southeast Asia.

In many instances, international investing has had negative effects – abominable working conditions and wages; environmental abuses; corruption of government officials; jobs lost and lower wages in industrial countries. But perhaps its greatest failure is that several billion people scarcely have been touched. Their circumstances are too harsh and uncertain for foreign investors. Both those ill-affected and those left out need greater voice in shaping their governments' attempts to negotiate good terms with foreign investors.

Governments in both rich and poor countries should adopt policies that will harness international investment capital to the development of human resources and new opportunities for more secure livelihoods. Particularly in the poorest nations, renewed efforts are needed to construct an investment climate both to attract such investments and ensure widespread sharing of the benefits. Governments can encourage responsible investing through policies that are good for business, workers and consumers.

Edward J. Chesky, an economic consultant in Washington, DC, has worked for the U.S. Foreign Service and the Asian Development Bank, and as a trade union educator.

CHAPTER 6

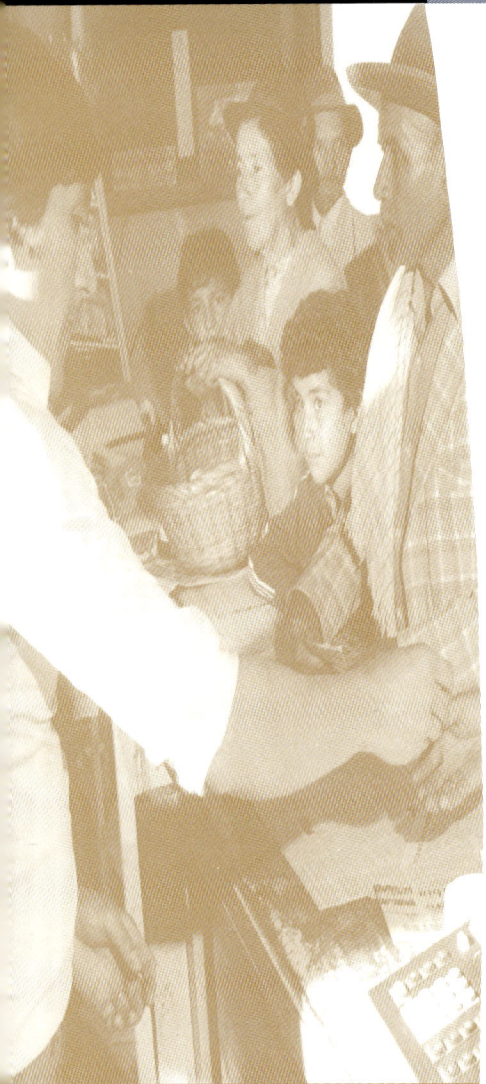

Remaking The World Bank & International Monetary Fund

By Nancy C. Alexander

The poor, the worse-off, the vulnerable groups in our societies... have a *deeply rooted hunger for voice and for finding an effective way of participating fully in the economic and civic lives of the community*....Will the engine of progress become an instrument of vast integration and social enhancement, or, merely a vehicle to benefit the few?... The characteristics of exclusion, of marginalization, of deprivation, should be left behind as shortcomings of the past.

E. Aninat, Chilean Finance Minister, Chair, 1996 Annual Meeting of the World Bank and IMF (emphasis added)

While markets create managerial discipline and induce efficacy through the exercise of "choice," governments are principally disciplined through the exercise of "voice." *Albert O. Hirschman*[1]

Focus the World Bank and other international financial institutions on reducing poverty, and make them accountable to the low-income communities they affect.

The International Financial Institutions (IFIs) – the World Bank and International Monetary Fund (IMF) – were established at Bretton Woods, New Hampshire, in 1944. Initially, the goals of the IMF and World Bank were to provide a stable monetary system and to help rebuild Europe. Their founders – 44 nations with strong leadership from the United States and United Kingdom – saw the IFIs as interventions necessary to prevent the trade protectionism that contributed to the Great Depression and World War II.

Over time, the IFIs focused increasingly on developing countries, always under the assumption that international trade and investment are in the best interest of all countries. IFI advice and pressure have had a strong influence on how the developing countries have responded to the growth of international trade and investment.

Today, the IMF includes 181 nations, and the World Bank, 180. Many of them face very difficult development challenges. Practically everywhere the gaps between rich and poor have grown, within nations and across borders. Per capita incomes are stagnant or declining in more than 100 nations, most of them new since the IFIs' founding.[2] People now living in poverty almost match the earth's population in 1945.

The IFIs have a mixed record as architects and engineers of the global economy. IFI resources have reached needy countries unable to attract private capital. The World Bank invests substantial sums in health, education and infrastructure – important areas for sustainable development that seldom attract private investors. The IMF has provided parallel short-term financial support to ease balance of payments emergencies and stabilize the global economy. If the World Bank and IMF did not exist, equivalent institutions would need to be invented.

But the persistence of poverty for so many stems partly from failures of IFI policy and practice. Some large, top-down World Bank projects, for example, have been dismal failures, creating more victims than beneficiaries. The IMF is too closed and secretive. Its policies are often not properly tailored to local conditions, needs and realities.

IFI prescriptions for economic reform are often not carried out, or lead to disappointing economic results, especially in low-income countries. Even when growth occurs, it often fails to "trickle down" to poor people. Reform efforts should focus the World Bank and other international financial institutions on reducing poverty, and make them accountable to the low-income communities they affect.

Many activists in developing countries want a say in how IFI resources can be used more effectively. At the same time, some of these activists, especially in Africa, fear that excessive criticism of the World Bank by activists in industrial countries could jeopardize vital resource flows that may be imperfect but are still needed.

This chapter describes the role of the IFIs as part of the family of international organizations. It shows how the IFIs could become more responsible by increasing their focus on poverty reduction and by early and regular participation in IFI decision-making by those most affected – particularly hungry and poor people. Such participation can establish checks and balances among the market, government and civil society. Participation can help promote sustainable development, especially the reduction of hunger and poverty in environmentally sound ways; development done with, rather than for or to, people. For this reform agenda to succeed, stronger leadership and financial participation by donor governments such as the United States are required.

Bill Whitaker

IFI decisions have a profound impact on African social and economic development.

The IFIs at a Glance

The IFIs are specialized United Nations (U.N.) agencies. But the industrial countries largely control the IFIs and have kept them independent of the U.N. system. Attempts to hold the IFIs accountable to the U.N. Economic and Social Council have failed consistently.

Power in the IFIs

In contrast to the one-nation, one-vote decision making used in most U.N. bodies,[3] voting power in the

IFIs relates to the number of shares a nation owns. The five major shareholders – the United States, Japan, Germany, France and the United Kingdom – provide leadership for the institutions. They each have their own seat on 24-member Boards of Executive Directors of the World Bank and IMF and control about 39 percent of the votes. In the IMF, China, Russia and Saudi Arabia also have their own seats. The United States alone has 15.08 percent of the votes in the bank and 17.78 percent in the fund. Due to this weighted voting, the industrial countries generally prefer the IFIs to other U.N. agencies, where they have less control. Traditionally, the chief executives of the World Bank and the IMF are people from the United States and Europe, respectively.

The other 170-odd member governments elect 19 executive directors on each board. More than 40 countries in sub-Saharan Africa elect two executive directors, with 6.9 percent of the votes in the bank and 3.8 percent in the fund. China and India (which together have about 45 percent of the world's population) control 6 percent of votes. Given their weak voting position in the IFIs, developing country governments seek allies among the wealthy countries to influence decisions.

IMF

The IMF does not fund development projects. It promotes international monetary cooperation, and assists countries to overcome short-term balance-of-payments difficulties. All member governments contribute resources (a "quota") to the IMF, commensurate with their size and importance in the world economy. In 1996, countries that needed financing drew $18 billion from the IMF.

Each IMF member state voluntarily agrees to allow its currency to be exchanged, to participate in fund surveillance over its monetary and financial policies, and cooperate with the fund in pursuing policies to promote growth and stability.

The IMF surveys each economy and provides financial advice to industrial and developing countries alike. But because industrial countries have not drawn on IMF resources in recent years, they are freer than developing countries to ignore the IMF's advice.

The IMF attaches conditions to its transactions intended to improve the balance of payments and growth prospects. Governments agree to spend within their means and take "structural adjustment" measures to hike production and exports. The adjustment measures are normally called "free market reforms," e.g., economic deregulation and privatization.

The World Bank Group

The World Bank deals with long-term development challenges such as creating physical infrastructure (roads, dams, power plants and factories). It is also the largest international source of social sector financing (education, health, family planning and nutrition).

The World Bank lends funds to governments, provides economic advice and technical assistance, and serves as a catalyst for private investment. Annually, the bank extends an average of 250 loans, averaging approximately $100 million apiece.

At one time, other U.N. agencies took the lead internationally in post-conflict reconstruction, promoting sustainable development, and providing technical assistance and social investment. Today, the World Bank provides considerable leadership in these areas, and funding is shifting from U.N. grants to World Bank loans.

The World Bank has two principal branches:

- *International Bank for Reconstruction and Development (IBRD).* This non-concessional, or "hard loan," window lends at market interest rates, repayable over 15 to 20 years. It committed $14.5 billion in fiscal year 1996. IBRD operations are financed by borrowing on world capital markets.

  The bank can maintain a triple-A credit rating regardless of the quality of its loans, because member country governments guarantee loan repayment.[4]

- *International Development Association (IDA).* Post-colonial nations lacked creditworthiness. They tried unsuccessfully to establish a bank within the U.N. Economic and Social Council with a large concessional (i.e., grant) component. In 1960, industrial country governments agreed to establish IDA as the "soft loan" window of the World Bank.

  IDA credits to borrowing governments have a 10-year grace period and are repaid over 35 to 40 years at 0.75 percent interest. In fiscal 1996, IDA committed $6.9 billion. It is the largest source of concessional lending to Africa. Fiscal 1996 commitments to Africa totaled $2.7 billion for 53 projects.

  IDA is financed primarily by contributions from donor governments. Other donor nations have agreed to put up $3 for each $1 the United States provides. But this arrangement is under severe strain because of U.S. arrears of nearly $1 billion.

IDA-borrowing countries have an average annual per capita income of less than $400. Countries receiving direct grants from the United States foreign aid program have an average per capita income of more than $4,000 per year.

The World Bank has two affiliates:

- *The International Finance Corporation (IFC)* mobilizes capital, including its own, to invest in, or loan to, commercial enterprises. Its investments grew an average of 17 percent annually from 1986 to 1996, when they reached $3.2 billion.
- *The Multilateral Investment Guarantee Agency (MIGA)* insures private businesses against non-commercial risks, especially war and expropriation.

IMF/World Bank Structural Adjustment Programs (SAPs)

Until the early 1980s, the World Bank and IMF had relatively few dealings with one another, even though their headquarters are on opposite sides of the same street in Washington. Then the debt crisis (see Chapter 5, p. 55) left many developing country governments on the brink of default on their commercial bank debts, jeopardizing the stability of the international financial system. Growing realization of the importance of macroeconomic policies led the World Bank to stress "structural adjustment" prescriptions similar to those of the IMF. These prescriptions moved the bank from focusing on individual projects to dysfunctional national economies. Among other things, the new focus sought to stabilize economies by setting exchange rates that would make exports globally competitive, balancing budgets and generating foreign exchange. By fiscal 1996, 21 percent of World Bank lending and all IMF transactions directly or indirectly supported structural adjustment.

SAPs have two aspects: restraint of aggregate demand (consumption) and expansion of supply (production). The IMF specializes in measures to achieve demand restraint, which helps tame inflation and improve the balance of payments. Such measures include cutting government spending, raising taxes, and promoting savings and monetary discipline. The World Bank specializes in boosting supply efficiency through trade liberalization, privatization and the efficient use of government resources.

Although SAPs sometimes succeed in reducing subsidies for rich people, heavy burdens usually fall upon poor and marginalized people. Leaner government budgets generally mean reductions in social services and food subsidies; higher interest rates can drive down employment and increase business costs; wages can decline; devalued currencies can price imported medicines, fertilizers and other goods out of reach. While those who produce export crops sometimes do well, those growing food for domestic consumption often suffer.

These effects of SAPs have led to considerable criticism. In the mid-1980s, the World Bank began to design "safety nets" to help vulnerable people survive SAPs. Almost a decade later, numerous African countries, especially the poorest ones, still experience a weak correlation between adjustment and growth; a negative correlation between adjustment and investment; and lower rates of agricultural production.

Many Latin American and, especially, Asian nations have had impressive growth rates. Some analysts attribute these countries' growth to governments' adherence to SAPs. Others argue that growth more often resulted from maintaining strong state intervention in markets, contrary to the thrust of SAPs. Regardless, Asia's growth has had high environmental, social and human rights costs.

IFAD

The 1974 World Food Conference established a third and much smaller IFI, the International Fund for Agricultural Development (IFAD). It has a successful record of providing credit for rural development activities that reduce hunger and poverty such as microcredit initiatives. Often, IFAD co-finances operations with other donors, including the World Bank. Its power structure is different from those of the other IFIs. It receives substantial financial support from members of the Organization of Petroleum Exporting Countries, and they have a significant role in decision making. Despite IFAD's strong track record, industrial-country governments are tight-fisted in providing funding.

The Regional Development Banks

Over the years, smaller regional development banks were established in each geographical region. They are not considered IFIs, but together with the World Bank, make up the system of multilateral development banks (MDBs). Most have both hard and soft loan windows, as well as private sector lending facilities.

The regional banks include the African Development Bank in Abidjan, Côte d'Ivoire; the Asian Development Bank in Manila, Philippines; the European Bank for Reconstruction and Development in London, United Kingdom; the Caribbean Development Bank in Bridgetown, Barbados; and the Inter-American Development Bank in Washington, D.C. These regional banks lend approximately $13.5 billion per year.

Debt

The IFIs and the regional development banks should take more leadership in reducing developing country debt. In 1996, World Bank gross disbursements totaled $19 billion, but low-income countries' heavy debt service burdens to the World Bank resulted in a net transfer of only $2.2 billion. The IMF's net transfer totaled $7.8 billion; over the past decade the flows have usually been negative. Developing countries owe the IMF and World Bank $251 billion; repayments constitute nearly half of the poorest developing countries' debt service.

In 1996, the IFIs and other creditor institutions launched the Highly Indebted Poor Countries' (HIPC) debt initiative (see "Poor Country Debt," pp. 77-79).

IFI policies often raise the price of fuel and other basic necessities in developing countries. Bill Whitaker

This is a welcome, but modest, step forward. Eligibility should be expanded and the depth of relief enhanced.

Governments, Markets & Civil Society in Borrowing Countries

To support a sustainable future, balance is required among the interests of three sectors with overlapping realms: markets, civil society and governments.

IFI Clients are Governments

The IFIs have dealt almost exclusively with borrowing governments – specifically, finance ministries – and often from the position of master rather than partner. Some interpretations of the IFIs' charters would preclude them from promoting political agendas involving popular participation, democracy and human rights. Ignoring such matters, however, is itself a political agenda that, too often, has added legitimacy to authoritarian regimes.

Even in open societies, the IFI-client government relationship can short-circuit consultation between governments and civil society. As Tetteh Hormeku-Ajei, a Ghanaian associated with Third World Network, puts it:

> ...Until now, the bank has only reinforced the non-consultative style of policy-making by most African governments. Its closed-door style of negotiating exclusively with governments has reassured authoritarian rulers in giving little weight to non-governmental viewpoints.

Popular participation in economic decision-making is a key to establishing the right checks and balances among market, government and civil society actors. Democratic countries seldom experience famine.[5] Lack of democratic participation contributes to deep hunger, poverty and rebellion. History is replete with examples – from the American Revolution's rejection of Britain's policy of "taxation without representation" to the protest of peasants in Chiapas, Mexico, against "trickle down" growth that deepened their deprivation.

IFIs and Markets

A stated purpose of the IFIs is to instruct governments how to open up to market forces. IFI adjustment policies and World Bank procurement practices should provide more support to local firms in developing countries than to transnational corporations.

Many citizen groups are uneasy about the current predominance of market ideology among government policy-makers. They object to trade agreements that place limits on how much welfare or environmental protection a nation can maintain. In the United States, some citizen groups have challenged "fast track" trade legislation that limits the input of ordinary people and their elected representatives by disallowing amendments.

Historically, governments have had more power to control their economies. Borders mattered more. Citizens feel that their votes also used to matter more. The IFIs need to orient governments to markets in ways that support local decision-making and sustainable development.

The Rise of Civil Society

Over the past decade, democratization movements and new communication technologies have given tremendous impetus to popular sustainable development campaigns. Social justice and environmental movements have changed dynamics in regional and international arenas, including regional pacts such as the North American Free Trade Agreement, the outcomes of U.N. conferences and operations of the World Bank. Reform efforts have had little impact so far on the IMF, which stresses the importance of openness and transparency to its members, but rarely practices what it preaches.

A decade ago, the World Bank had no contact with civil society and almost no capacity to address environmental issues. Today, largely because of pressure from environmentalists, the bank has civil society liaison officers at its headquarters and resident missions around the world. Its sizable environmental staff can assess environmental impacts of proposed loans.

People can exercise their voice through civil society groups, including grassroots and nongovernmental organizations (NGOs) – community groups, labor unions, women's groups, religious organizations, cooperatives and business and professional organizations. It is more likely that groups directly affected by a World Bank-supported project (the stakeholders) will be beneficiaries rather than victims if they have a say in project decisions.

If borrowing governments agree to new policies to include broad consultation with relevant ministries and parliamentary bodies or organizations of civil society (CSOs), they may avoid charges of governing without popular consent. They may also gain widespread ownership and support, and increase the likelihood of successful projects.

The World Bank should encourage governments to adopt participatory approaches to lending operations and adapt its own project cycle to make this possible. The bank defines participation as a process wherein "stakeholders influence and share control over development initiatives and the decisions and resources which affect them."[6] Experience shows that stakeholder participation is critical to success in poverty reduction and environmental protection.[7] In fiscal 1995, bank-supported agriculture and education projects without NGO involvement were more likely to have problems meeting their development objectives than those with NGO participation.

IFI Power and Influence

Two Classes of Borrowers

World Bank leverage is often inversely related to the economic strength of a borrowing country. Countries able to obtain private capital do not need an intermediary such as the World Bank. Global private capital flows to developing countries have surged from $44 billion in 1990 to an estimated $244 billion in 1996, fueling high growth rates in a handful of Asian and Latin American countries. Eighty percent of this capital went to just 12 countries (see preceding chapter, pp. 55-57). Some of these countries also draw on World Bank and IMF loans.

In glaring contrast are nations unable to attract private capital and marginalized by globalization. Concentrated in Africa, they often depend heavily on public, or "official" flows, which include grants, loans, and debt relief from wealthier governments and the IFIs.

Seal of Approval

The IFIs' approval or disapproval of a member government's economic policies and performance influences that country's ability to secure private capital. Those that adhere to IFI economic reform prescriptions receive a financial seal of approval, which helps ensure their capacity to borrow from commercial banks, attract private investors and qualify for bilateral official flows. The IMF records of each member's economic performance, for example, are a basis for decisions by other investors.

The World Bank's stated social and environmental policies are relatively enlightened and sometimes looked

Figure 6.1 **World Bank* Procurement of Goods and Services from Private Enterprises,** Fiscal Year 1996

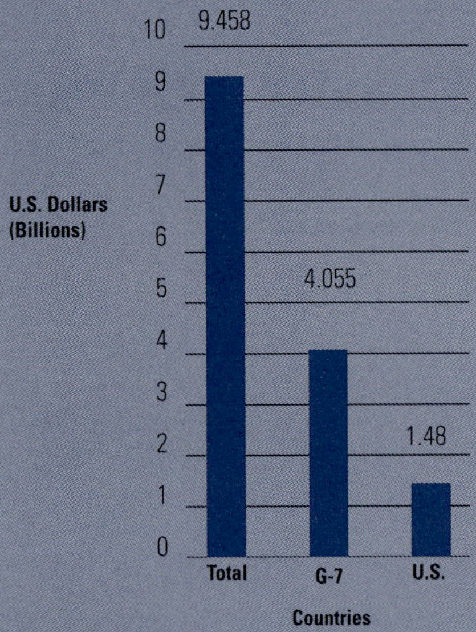

* IBRD and IDA combined / Source: The World Bank.

to by corporations as models of "best practices," even though the bank's own performance often lags far behind.

Status of Preferred Creditor

The IFIs also derive power from their status as preferred creditors – meaning that governments must service IFI debts ahead of those held by other creditors.

Creating Business Opportunities

World Bank-supported projects have provided lucrative contracts for industrial country firms. These contracts are springboards for ongoing trade and investment (see Figure 6.1).

Reforming the IFIs

The IFIs are here to stay. They have helped modernize many economies. But they sometimes create big debt burdens for borrowing governments without much to show for them.

Reforms are crucial, therefore, to ensure that they help governments support sustainable development. But this requires a serious commitment by the IFIs to poverty reduction. During 1998, as negotiations occur on a new agreement governing IDA policies and funding, citizens can work with their governments to shape the outcome.

IFI Commitment to Poverty Reduction

On the whole, World Bank attempts to put into operation its overarching goal of poverty reduction have been weak. In 1995, an evaluation showed that just 10 percent of World Bank projects launched several years earlier contained poverty reduction components, and many of these projects failed to achieve their poverty goals.

Surveys of borrowing government officials reveal a high level of dissatisfaction with the bank's lack of focus on poverty and equity issues. One survey of African officials found that some borrowers were unaware that the bank's purpose is poverty reduction. Thus, the World Bank needs a far more systematic approach to these issues.

The IFIs should have explicit poverty reduction objectives in *country-wide lending priorities* described in the World Bank's Country Assistance Strategies and the IMF's Policy Framework Papers.

Every IFI loan or transaction should also detail how it will reduce poverty in environmentally sound ways. Investments in nutrition, health, education and population should increase, as should programs that will facilitate poor people's access to productive assets such as land, water and credit.

SAPs and growth programs must include a social benefit, or at least a safety net. In 1995, the bank evaluated 238 growth programs begun several years earlier. Only six had substantial social or safety net components.

The bank's *evaluation system* is flawed insofar as it focuses on the poverty impact of small social components that are add-ons to bigger investments. It should be revamped to assess how all investments (industry, infrastructure, agriculture) benefit poor people and generate jobs while protecting the environment.

Lend to Governments Committed to Reducing Poverty

Currently, the World Bank stresses lending to countries that adopt sound macroeconomic policies. Often, borrowing governments are those with the least need for IFI resources. Instead, the bank should give priority in lending to governments, such as Eritrea's, which listen to their people, involve them in development activities and demonstrate a commitment to reducing poverty.

Watching The World Bank

Bread for the World Institute's Development Bank Watchers' Project began in 1994. Its goal is to help empower organizations of civil society (CSOs) and strengthen their networks in order to reduce hunger and poverty by changing the policies and practices of donors (especially the World Bank Group) and borrowing governments. In particular, the project works to open them to participation, especially by low-income and marginalized communities.

The project seeks to reduce hunger and poverty by: providing information to equip and empower civil society organizations in developing countries to participate in shaping the policies and projects of their government and donors; working with Bread for the World members throughout the United States to influence the U.S. government to make the development banks more effective instruments of poverty reduction; and directly influencing the management of the institutions to make participation and the reduction of poverty and hunger overriding priorities. This project is financed by the Ford Foundation.

Bread for the World is a separate, grassroots lobbying organization. In 1997, Bread for the World members urged World Bank officials, the U.S. Treasury and members of Congress to make the World Bank more supportive of local participation in development decisions. Specifically, Bread for the World proposed that the World Bank make democratic participation, especially by low-income communities, routine for all its loans.

In July 1997, the bank's management adopted this policy. Now the challenge will be to see that it is routinely practiced.

Involve Poor People in Development Activities

Parliaments and organizations of civil society should discuss and have input into the IFIs' economic reform and project investment priorities. The bank and IMF have confidential documents that outline these priorities within a one- to three-year time horizon.

In consultation with NGOs and grassroots groups, the IFIs should conduct *social assessments* of each operation or transaction. These should identify the affected people's projected benefits and losses. In the case of the World Bank, the assessments should begin by involving affected communities in project identification, design and implementation.

The World Bank's project cycle often requires rapid implementation that precludes stakeholder participation. The cycle should be revamped to provide the necessary flexibility.

IFIs and member governments should collaborate with organizations of civil society to design structural adjustment programs that primarily benefit poor people, for instance by creating jobs and increasing access to resources while protecting the environment. Also, the IFIs should reverse the trend that shows SAPs exacerbating inequality, imposing heavy burdens on women and despoiling the environment.

Governance

The IFIs' governance must become open, accountable and transparent, providing a model for borrowing governments (see "Participation and Good Governance," p. 76). As public institutions, they should accelerate timely disclosure (especially within borrowing countries) of information about operations and transactions.

The IMF should urge its members to make public their IMF advisory document, which analyzes monetary and fiscal health and the strengths and weaknesses of economic management. The fund should also make public the "Policy Framework Papers" that lay out the rationale and priorities for SAPs in countries with active IMF programs.

The World Bank should make public its Country Assistance Strategies (CASs). The CAS outlines the rationale and priorities for bank lending. The bank should also make an early draft of each CAS public, so that citizens can provide input into the final document.

The same standards for information disclosure and filing complaints should apply to World Bank-supported public and private sector operations. Presently, the bank has an inspection panel that, when permitted by the board, investigates complaints brought by parties affected by bank-supported operations who allege that the bank has violated its own policies. The panel should be

Participation & Good Governance: A World Bank View

Transparency enables people affected by development plans to know the options available to them. *Accountability* of government structures and officials to local organizations (for example, civil councils and village committees) reinforces macrolevel accountability. *Due process* of public hearings and other local-level consultations ensures that people affected by development activities can voice their concern, debate alternatives and negotiate compensation. Finally, the effective *voice* of local people, particularly the poor, can be increased by policy reforms at the national level that allow greater freedom to join nongovernmental organizations, trade unions and other bodies to understand better and influence decisions that affect them.[1]

Note: The World Bank, *Governance: The World Bank's Experience* (Washington: The World Bank, 1994), 42-43.

able to investigate claims without prior board approval, and its jurisdiction should extend to IFC and MIGA.

Treat Member Governments Equally

Unlike the World Bank, the IMF has responsibility for advising *all* member governments, including those of industrial countries. Ideally, this could help overcome double standards – such as industrial country governments' unwillingness to live by the free trade policies that they and the IFIs preach to developing countries. Wealthy nations often subsidize agricultural exports and impose barriers to developing country imports. According to the Organization for Economic Cooperation and Development, these policies cost developing countries more in export revenues than they receive in aid.[8]

The IFIs should speak out about economic mismanagement, protectionism and unsustainable consumption among donors as ardently as they do about mismanagement, protectionism and unsustainable population growth among borrowers.

Donors Must Fulfill Their Pledges

Donor countries should fulfill their commitments to the IFIs. Since the United States and other industrial countries have the privileges of global leaders, they should meet their financial responsibilities. The U.S. practice of promising, and then withholding, contributions has thrown donor coordination out of kilter.

Reforms cannot take place without strong donor financial support and principled leadership. Creditor governments, especially the United States, should meet their financial obligations so that they can be credible proponents of IFI reform.

Conclusion

The IFIs do relatively well at channelling resources to poor countries, but need to do better at reaching poor and marginalized people within countries. People, through their civil society organizations, can help build consensus on the needed reforms.

People in the industrial countries support the IFIs with their tax dollars and have a right to say how they want their resources used. However, people in the developing world – who constitute the overwhelming majority of the global populace and are most affected by IFI programs – deserve a greater voice than those in wealthy countries.

A growing number of industrial country anti-hunger, social justice and environmental movements are trying to wield influence with the IFIs in ways accountable to developing country groups, as well as to their own domestic constituencies. Especially for those with access to information technology, collaboration among geographically disparate groups is occurring rapidly (see "Watching the World Bank," p. 75).

Activists can help achieve a responsible balance among the market, governments and organizations of civil society. Balance is needed so that the economy is the servant rather than the master of human communities. Communities need some forms of economic regulation and direction so that they can choose development values, such as food security, equity, safety, education, health, and environmental and natural resources preservation. Such values cannot be advanced by market forces alone.

Nancy C. Alexander manages the Development Bank Watchers' Project at Bread for the World Institute.

Poor Country Debt: Payable in Hunger

by Kathleen A. Selvaggio & Marc J. Cohen

Jane and Stephen Kabonese own 12 acres in southwest Uganda. Stephen suffers from tuberculosis; working mostly by herself, Jane can cultivate only four acres. The family consumes most of what she grows, but Jane sells some peanuts and beans when crops are good. Sometimes she also works for neighbors. Three of the eight Kabonese children died of preventable diseases. Malaria, measles, diarrhea and respiratory infections afflict surviving family members, especially during the dry season, when food supplies dwindle and workloads grow. The nearest health facility is 14 miles away; the family cannot afford the fees. Similarly, they can only pay tuition for one child, and illness has forced him to miss classes.

Debt, Well-Being & Debt Relief in Uganda[1]

Uganda is one of the world's poorest countries, with an annual per capita income of $190, and also one of the most indebted. In 1996-1997, the government owes $184 million on its debt, 10 times what it spends on primary health care and seven times its primary education budget. Until recently, one-third of primary school-aged children were not enrolled. High health service fees keep many poor Ugandans away from clinics.

For the past 11 years, Uganda has faithfully followed economic reforms prescribed by the International Financial Institutions (IFIs). The IFIs, which hold 70 percent of the country's external debt, have urged poor countries to charge fees for basic services such as health and education.

In September 1996, donor country political leaders and the IFIs agreed to a plan that, if further developed and well done, could help break debt's stranglehold over the poorest countries. For the first time, creditors have agreed to reduce – not just refinance or stretch out – debt burdens of 20 poor countries that agree to undergo economic reform. The lenders have agreed to coordinate debt reduction by all creditors in order to reduce total debt to manageable proportions. The IFIs are supposed to judge a country's eligibility not only by fiscal and monetary performance, but also by commitment to poverty reduction. The institutions designated Uganda as the first country to receive debt forgiveness through this plan. Other likely candidates include Bolivia, Burkina Faso, Mozambique and Côte d'Ivoire.

Ugandan President Yoweri Museveni committed much of the expected savings to expanding primary schooling. Education raises productivity, income and gender equality. Research in Uganda showed that four years of primary education for rural people raises crop production by an average of 7 percent. In February 1997, the government began providing free primary education for up to four children per family. Children flooded into schools. In many poor rural areas, school populations doubled or tripled.

But a number of creditor governments, led by the United States, pressed in early 1997 to delay Uganda's debt relief for a year. This could force 1.7 million school children to stay home.

In far too many developing countries, crushing national debt burdens foreclose opportunities for millions of poor families like the Kaboneses. By 1996, developing countries owed $2.2 trillion to foreign creditors. For many, this debt is simply unpayable.

Relieve the debts of poor-country governments committed to reducing poverty, and expand foreign aid programs that help hungry and poor people.

Origins of the Debt Crisis

Colonialism geared the developing world's economies toward agricultural, mineral and other raw material exports. Prices for most raw materials have steadily declined in relation to the cost of manufactured goods. Poor countries that still depend on these exports find themselves increasingly disadvantaged in the global marketplace and often deeper in debt. Declining commodity *– continued next page*

Poor Country Debt (continued)

prices between 1986 and 1990 alone cost Africa $50 billion in export earnings, more than double the funds received in foreign assistance from all nations.

The dramatic rise in interest rates in the late 1970s led to a global recession that depressed demand and commodity prices. In 1982, Mexico, Brazil and other middle-income countries announced that they were about to default on billions of dollars in loans. Frightened banks suddenly stopped new lending to developing countries. By the late 1980s, the crisis had eased for most middle-income countries, as a result of some debt reduction by commercial banks, intervention by the IFIs and export growth. But some of the poorest countries continue to struggle under a heavy unpayable debt burden.

Much of the borrowed money had kept schools, hospitals, buses, trains, power lines and other essential government services running. Some had financed effective development efforts. But other foreign borrowing was wasted on white elephant projects, often designed by aid agencies and involving huge contracts for foreign firms. Also, foreign loans indirectly financed some countries' military build-up. In the 1970s, Zaire borrowed $1 billion to provide power to a copper smelter that never opened. Corrupt officials pocketed some of the money or deposited it in foreign banks.

How Deep is the Debt Problem?

In 1995, the 35 Highly Indebted Poor Countries (HIPCs), 28 of which are in Africa, owed foreign creditors $226 billion. Excluding South Africa and Namibia, sub-Saharan Africa's debt is $199 billion, 20 percent higher than Africa's total annual income and almost four times its yearly export earnings.

To service this debt, African countries forked over $11 billion in 1994 – just half the $22 billion due. Arrears have accumulated to $62 billion, about a third of Africa's total debt. Mozambique added $570 million to its debt stock between 1990 and 1993 because it could not even make 10 percent of scheduled payments.

The problem is not so much the size of the debt as the huge share of income it gobbles up. The United States has the world's largest external debt, $835 billion in 1995. U.S. government interest payments were $232 billion in 1995. These payments work out to $890 per U.S. citizen, no pittance, but equal to only about 3.5 percent of the average citizen's income.

By contrast, Mozambique's foreign debt was only $5.5 billion in 1994. But payments due in 1994 amounted to $361 million, or $23 per person – almost 25 percent of average income.

Since commercial banks have not been willing to risk lending much to very poor countries, these nations owe mainly to other governments (almost one-half of their total debt) and to the IFIs and regional development banks (approximately one-quarter of their debt). Because these institutions insist on being paid first, they take an even greater share of total debt payments.

The result is a build-up of unpaid debts owed to governments and growing diversion of development aid to repay the IFIs. This has led to a bizarre financial merry-go-round. During 1993-1994, for example, the World Bank's lending program provided $2.9 billion to HIPCs. But these countries made $1.9 billion in debt service payments to the bank.

Lenders have optimistically assumed that poor countries would grow their way out of debt. In 1986, the World Bank predicted that by 1995 sub-Saharan Africa would owe only $29 billion. In fact, by 1995, Africa owed seven times that much! Such rosy projections helped justify international creditors' strategy of extending new loans and rescheduling some old ones. But after more than 8,000 debt renegotiations since 1980, sub-Saharan Africa's total debts have nearly tripled.

What is the Human Price?

To repay their debts, governments shift scarce resources from schools, health clinics, roads, the environment and other *– continued next page* sustainable development investments. Oxfam International estimates that if Africa invested annual debt payments in health and education, it would save the lives of 21 million children by the year 2000.

In order to continue receiving IFI loans, poor countries must adopt structural adjustment policies. These lead many governments to reduce spending on health and education, and to impose user fees at schools or clinics. Some encourage a shift away from food production for local consumption toward export crops. Such policies can cause hardship for poor people. These policies, furthermore, have not succeeded in promoting economic growth in most of Africa. Huge debt burdens, meanwhile, discourage private investors, who fear that debt might lead to more taxation or inflation.

If Africa invested annual debt payments in health and education, it would save the lives of 21 million children by the year 2000.

Why Forgive the Debts?

Poor countries' debts not only contribute to hunger, disease and illiteracy, they hurt people in creditor countries as well. Deepening poverty associated with debt contributes to violent conflict, refugee flows and environmental destruction. When countries channel most of their export earnings to debt service, not much remains for imports.

Since creditors can only sell off developing country debts for a fraction of their face value, the price of debt forgiveness is relatively modest. The 1996 debt relief plan will cost an estimated $5 billion to $8 billion. This assistance is critical for poor countries, especially in light of recent steep cuts in aid.

What Should be Done to Solve the Debt Crisis?

Wealthy countries and international financial institutions should relieve the debts of poor-country governments committed to reducing poverty, and expand foreign aid programs that help hungry and poor people. The IFIs and creditor governments should not delay in providing the debt relief promised by their 1996 agreement. Rather, they should expand it to include more poor and indebted countries, increase the amount of eligible debt and reduce debts much sooner than six years hence, as proposed.

Creditors should link debt relief to poverty reduction and democracy, rather than tying it mainly to free-market economic reforms. Debt relief conditionality should benefit, or at least not harm, poor people and the environment. The IMF, through the sale of some of its gold holdings, should contribute to a debt relief trust fund.

Religious and environmental groups in industrial and developing countries, including Bread for the World, are beginning to work on a debt cancellation campaign called "Jubilee 2000." Based on the biblical tradition of forgiving all debts every 50 years, it envisions one-time forgiveness of the backlog of unpayable debt owed by the world's poorest countries. Pope John Paul II, Johannesburg Anglican Archbishop Desmond Tutu and the Archbishop of Canterbury are among the religious leaders who are promoting the idea.

In the wake of the Cold War, the industrial nations have been reducing international aid, especially to low-income countries and to low-income people within countries. These trends should be reversed, and part of the new aid should help underwrite the costs of relieving unpayable debts in the poorest countries.

Kathleen A. Selvaggio, an international policy analyst at Bread for the World, recently visited Uganda with a Bread for the World Institute travel seminar. **Dr. Marc J. Cohen**, senior research associate at Bread for the World Institute, is editor of *Hunger in a Global Economy.*

1. This section draws on Oxfam International, *Debt Relief and Poverty Reduction: New Hope for Uganda* (Washington: Oxfam International, 1996).

CHAPTER 7

Update on: Global Hunger

By Marc J. Cohen

This chapter provides a look at world hunger trends and major recent developments. But hunger is more than dry numbers. It has names and faces:

- Shirley Jupiter, a single mother of eight in a squatter settlement in Georgetown, Guyana, who says, "I am cooking now and I don't know when next I'll cook a proper meal and when I'll be able to live in a proper place;"[1]
- Rudeen Kean, a 28-year-old pedicab driver in Phnom Penh, Cambodia, who works 18 hour days but cannot feed his family adequately;[2]
- Tesfaye and Senait, Ethiopian farmers forced by drought to sell their meager assets to buy food;[3] and
- A "working poor" family in the midwest United States struggling to make ends meet.[4]

Hunger is more than dry numbers. It has names and faces.

Hunger in Developing Countries[5]

This section draws on new data from the Food and Agriculture Organization of the United Nations (FAO) on the extent of developing-country hunger and changes between the periods 1969-1971 and 1990-1992.

Sub-Saharan Africa

As Chapter 1 notes, the numbers and proportion of hungry Africans rose. In 1993, 39 percent of Africans (219 million people) lived in "absolute poverty," with daily incomes below $1. The poverty population and rate increased over 1987. On average, poor Africans earned 85 cents per day. Africa's income distribution is quite unequal; a substantial gap exists between male and female incomes. School enrollment rates are lower, and infant mortality rates higher, than in other regions.

South Asia

The greater Asia-Pacific region is home to three of every five hungry people. In South Asia, high population growth rates caused an increase in the number of hungry people even as the proportion dropped by a third. In 1990, 51 percent of all underweight preschoolers lived in South Asia, although it is home to just 30 percent of the world's children under 5.

The region also has the largest number (515 million) and highest proportion (43 percent) of absolutely poor people; their daily incomes average 87 cents. As in Africa, poor people live mainly in rural areas, where they engage in subsistence agriculture or low-skill wage labor.

Incomes are more equally distributed than in Africa, but gender inequality is a major problem. Women suffer from less education, poorer health, lower life expectancy and heavier work burdens. Female infanticide is common in some areas, and in many households, girls and women eat only after men and boys have had their fill.

East and Southeast Asia

East and Southeast Asia have made dramatic progress against hunger (excepting Cambodia and Vietnam). The hungry proportion of the populace declined by 60 percent, while the number of hungry people fell by 44 percent. The reasons include rapid economic growth, usually export-led, combined with substantial investment in health, education and improved nutrition, and resolution of conflicts in Indochina and the Philippines.

The absolute poverty rate fell from 23 percent in 1987 to 14 percent (26 million people) in 1993. Infant mortality declined and life expectancy improved. Income distribution is more equal than in most other regions. Women participate in the work force at higher rates than in any other region, including the industrial countries.[6]

Latin America and the Caribbean

In Latin America and the Caribbean, the number of chronically undernourished people jumped by over 20 percent, from 53 million in 1969-1971 to 64 million in 1990-1992. Causes include debt, adjustment policies, population growth and extremely high levels of income inequality. In some countries, the richest 20 percent earn 15 times as much as the poorest.

UNRWA

Palestinian refugees pick up food rations in Jordan.

The region has experienced economic revival in the 1990s. During the "lost decade" of the 1980s, living standards declined for many. Extreme inequality, however, helped contribute to a 10 percent jump in the number of people living in absolute poverty (to 110 million, a quarter of the populace) between 1990 and 1993. Sixty percent of the region's children live in poverty. The rural poverty rate, 53 percent, is considerably higher than the urban rate (34 percent). Yet 75 percent of poor people live in urban areas, often in squalid slums, as lack of economic opportunities in the countryside has spurred outmigration.[7]

Maria Antonia Padilla, a single mother of three in Tegucigalpa, Honduras, ekes out a living peddling fruit. She laments, "Poverty is crisis. Beans at 35 *lempiras*, that alone empties the account. Giving a child half an egg because of how much they cost – that too, is poverty...."[8]

Middle East

Hunger declined region-wide in the Middle East, but the proportion of undernourished people rose in Kuwait and remained the same in Iraq and the United Arab Emirates. Also, while the regional incidence of hunger remained stable, the number of chronically undernourished people rose. Environmental problems, such as soil erosion, pose serious constraints to sustainable food security. Access to water is also a significant problem.

The incidence of absolute poverty is relatively low (4 percent in 1993), and income inequality is modest. Poverty rates are higher in rural areas, but migrants to cities are bringing their poverty with them. Small traders, elderly and disabled people, and those in female-headed households are especially vulnerable. Social indicators are often below those of countries with similar per capita income in other regions. Slow economic growth hampers improvements.

U.N. sanctions imposed against Iraq in 1990 exempted food and medicine, but numerous studies indicate that the embargo has contributed to serious shortages. These, in turn, have led to the deaths of several hundred thousand Iraqi infants and children.[9] U.N.-approved oil sales in 1996 and 1997 will finance food imports, but FAO estimates that these will cover only 50 percent of requirements.

Countries in Transition[10]

The transition from centrally-planned to market economies since 1989 has created hardships for many people in Central and Eastern Europe and the newly independent states of the former Soviet Union (NIS). Poverty, unemployment and income inequality have generally increased, and social safety nets have frayed. The regional absolute poverty rate increased from 0.6 percent in 1987 to 3.5 percent in 1993. Unemployed workers and those with little education, elderly people on fixed pensions and female-headed households are especially vulnerable to food and livelihood insecurity. War and civil strife have complicated the transition in Bosnia and several former Soviet republics.

A survey of household income in 27 industrial, transition and high-income developing countries found that Russia had the highest level of both income inequality and poverty in the mid-1990s (Figure 7.1 and Table 7.1).

FAO classifies several poorer transition economies as Low-Income Food Deficit Countries (LIFDCs, see Table 1.2, p. 10). Their poorest citizens live on $5 to $15 per month, unable to afford minimum food requirements. Refugees and internally displaced people, elderly and disabled people, orphans and single-parent households depend on food aid. Low-income city dwellers have eliminated meat, butter and fresh fruit from their diets, and only consume vegetables if they have access to gardens. Rural folk increasingly engage in subsistence farming. There are scattered indications of undernutrition in Georgia, Azerbaijan and Tajikistan.

Figure 7.1 **Income Gap in Industrial and Transition Countries**

1982 - 1995

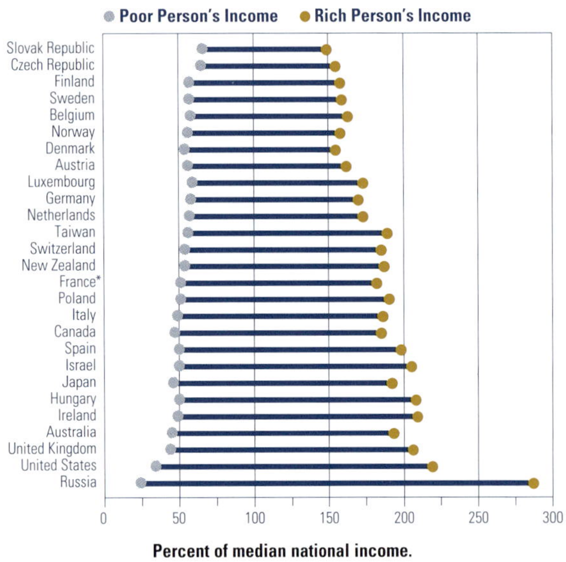

* From household budget surveys.

Source: Bread for the World Institute calculations using the Luxembourg Income Study (LIS) database; Japanese Ministry of Welfare; Organization for Economic Cooperation and Development.

Industrial Countries

United States

According to the Food Research and Action Center, 29 percent of U.S. children under the age of 12 (nearly 14 million) are hungry or at risk of hunger. Even short periods of undernutrition can affect children's behavior, cognitive development and future productivity. Declining purchasing power among low-skilled workers has contributed to food insecurity.

In 1996, an average of 26.6 million people relied on the federal Food Stamp Program each month. Virtually all participants have incomes below the official poverty line (an annual income of $15,569 for a family of four in 1995), and 80 percent of the benefits go to households with children. According to the U.S. Department of Agriculture, food stamps increase the nutritional quality of poor children's diets by 20 percent to 40 percent.

Legislation enacted in 1996 will reduce food stamp benefits by $27.7 billion by 2002. That would buy food to fill a convoy of trucks stretching to the moon and back.

Table 7.1 **Household Poverty, Circa 1990**

Country	Poverty Rate
Australia	19.7
Belgium	7.1
Canada	15.1
Czech Republic	2.1
Denmark	8.2
Finland	9.6
Germany	17.5
Hungary	11.4
Israel	20.0
Italy	9.6
Netherlands	9.3
Norway	8.2
Poland	13.1
Russia	34.3
Spain	16.0
Slovakia	2.2
Sweden	9.1
Taiwan	17.5
United Kingdom	23.0
United States	23.5

Source: LIS. The definition of poverty is those households with income below 50 percent of average after receiving government benefits and paying taxes.

By 1998, families with incomes below half the poverty level will lose an average of $656 per year in benefits. Able-bodied but unemployed and childless people aged 18 to 50 face a food stamp time limit of three of 36 months. Most legal immigrants no longer can receive food stamps.

The United States has higher rates of infant mortality, poverty and income inequality than most other industrial countries. Twenty-one countries have lower infant mortality rates (IMRs) than the United States. Infant deaths are closely linked to nutritional deficiencies among pregnant women. The African American IMR is more than double the white rate.

In 1995, 13.8 percent of the population (36.4 million people) lived in poverty, down from 1994 (14.5 percent) because of sustained economic recovery – but still above the 1989 level (13.1 percent).

Race, family composition, age, national origin and region of residence all bear significantly on U.S. poverty. The Hispanic poverty rate was 30.3 percent, compared to 29.3 percent for African Americans, 14.6 percent for Asia-Pacific Americans and 8.5 percent for non-Hispanic whites. Female-headed households had a 32.4 percent poverty rate. Foreign-born people had a poverty rate of 22.2 percent. Forty percent of all poor people lived in the South, where the poverty rate was 15.7 percent.

The U.S. child poverty rate is twice the average of the other industrial countries. Government assistance lowers the child poverty rate about half as much in the United States as the average for other industrial countries.

In 1995, the official poverty rate for U.S. children under 18 was 20.8 percent, and for children under 6 it was 23.7 percent. Children under 18 accounted for 40 percent of the people in poverty, but only 25 percent of the total population. Of children under 6 living in female-headed households, 61.8 percent were poor.

The Urban Institute expects the 1996 "welfare reform" to push an additional 2.6 million people, including 1.1. million children, into poverty. State-level cutbacks could drive another 2.5 million to 7.5 million people into poverty. The federal policies adopted in 1996 will be phased in through the year 2002. Their initial impact has been moderated by a booming economy and tight labor market.

Despite an increase in the minimum wage in 1996, full-time minimum wage work pays only $9,880 annually, still below the poverty line for a family of two ($10,360).

According to the U.S. Census Bureau, the gap between rich and poor increased between 1975 and 1995. The income share of the poorest 20 percent fell from 4.4 percent to 3.7 percent, while that of the richest 20 percent rose from 43.2 percent to 48.7 percent. The income of the top 5 percent grew from 15.9 percent to 21 percent.

United Kingdom

Among wealthy countries, the United States, the United Kingdom and Sweden experienced the sharpest increases in income inequality in the 1980s, but inequality remains less pronounced in Sweden. Inequality increased especially steeply in the United Kingdom, mainly due to the social policies of former Prime Minister Margaret Thatcher.[11]

By 1992, 20 percent of the U.K. population was poor. During the 1980s, average income rose, but the poorest 10 percent faced falling living standards. Single-parent households, women, disabled people and non-whites are especially vulnerable.

A 1994 study found that more than 1.5 million U.K. families cannot afford an adequate diet. Low-income families face higher rates of illness, shorter life expectancies and higher mortality rates, as well as food insecurity. One welfare mother commented, "I'll cut down myself on food. Sometimes if we're running out

A homeless resident of Washington, D.C. Michael Keating

the back end of the second week and there's not a lot for us to eat, I'll sort of give the kids it first and then see what's left."[12]

Canada[13]

Growing food insecurity has led to a proliferation of food banks in Canada since the early 1980s (Figure 7.2). They now outnumber McDonald's restaurants. In 1994, 8.6 percent of Canadians (2.5 million people) relied on charitable food assistance; in Toronto, the largest city, the figure was 12 percent. A survey in Edmonton found 12.5 percent of all residents food insecure; 28 percent of low-income households were hungry and 34 percent were at risk of hunger.

The United Nations Development Programme ranks Canada highest in the world in human development (based on income, health and education). Food insecurity threatens that rating by contributing to increased low birth weight, anemia, infant death and developmental disabilities.

Figure 7.2 **Growth in Canadian Food Banks, 1981-1995**

Source: *First World Hunger.*

Federal and provincial economic and social policies have abetted inequality, and as in the United States, the federal government has transferred much responsibility for anti-poverty efforts to the provinces. In an effort to achieve greater competitiveness in the global economy, federal and provincial governments of both left and right have pushed for deficit reduction. As in other industrial countries, spending cuts have focused on anti-poverty programs. The rise of food banks represents the privatization of social policy, in contrast to Canada's traditional emphasis on economic and social rights for all.

The federal government does not have an official measure of poverty, but in 1993, the unofficial estimate was 17 percent, including 20 percent of children and 60 percent of people in female-headed households. In 1995, unemployment was 9.6 percent. As in the United States, an increasing number of workers find that their wages are inadequate to assure secure livelihoods. Women workers disproportionately fill insecure jobs with inadequate wages.

European Union

Less information is available about food insecurity in other industrial countries. Food banks have spread in continental Europe, and some 18 million residents of the European Union (EU) are either homeless or extremely poorly housed.

In France, 450,000 people rely on charitable food assistance. Low-income people, particularly school aged children, are vulnerable to food insecurity. The government supports food agencies, and provides direct income supplements to low-income families.[14]

Since 1990, unemployment has averaged 8 percent to 12 percent in Italy, 10 percent to 12 percent in France and 6 percent to 8 percent in Germany. In Spain, the figure is 24 percent. Youth unemployment rates are typically double the overall rate.

Child poverty increased in France, Germany and Ireland during the 1980s. Continental European countries generally have had more expansive social safety nets than Anglo-Saxon countries. But competitiveness considerations have created pressures for reduced government spending in all industrial countries. EU members have agreed to further cuts in government spending to meet fiscal targets related to their adoption of a common currency.[15]

A new study by Eurostat, the EU statistical agency, found a Union-wide poverty rate of 17 percent (57 million people) in 1993 and 20 percent for children under

Figure 7.3

Vitamin A Deficiency - Children Under 5, Developing Countries

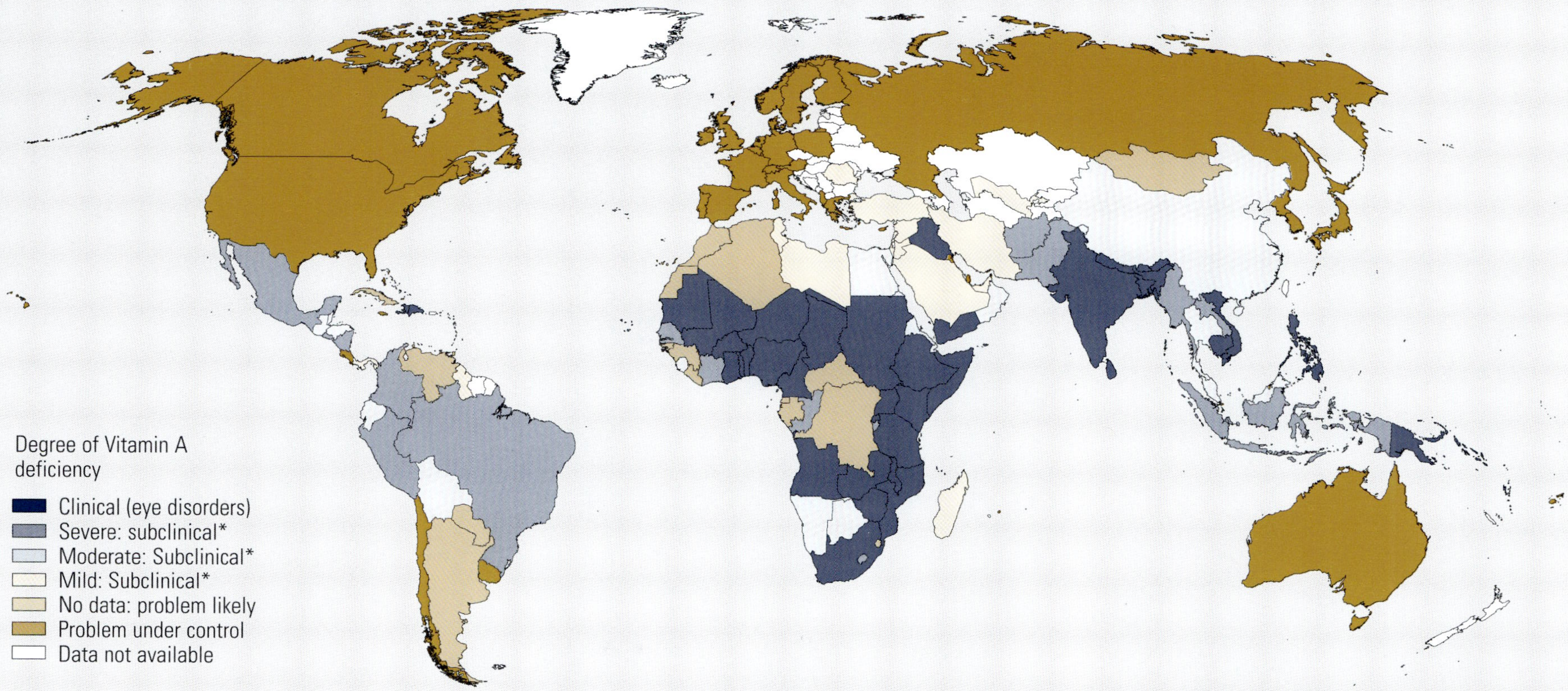

Source: WHO
Note: *At risk. Estimated from surveys conducted 1965-1996.

Table 7.2 **Goiter and Vitamin A Deficiency, 1995**

Region	Population all Ages Suffering from Goiter (millions)	Population Under Age 5 with Vitamin A Deficiency (millions)
Africa	136	1.05
Americas	50	0.06
Southeast Asia	213	1.45
Europe	89	no data
Eastern Mediterranean	116	0.16
Western Pacific	156	0.13
Total	760	2.85

Source: WHO.

16. The incomes of the richest 20 percent were seven times greater than those of the poorest 20 percent. National poverty rates varied from 6 percent in Denmark to 22 percent in both the United Kingdom and Greece, to 26 percent in Portugal. The United Kingdom had the highest child poverty rate, 32 percent.[16]

"Hidden Hunger"

Even when people get all the required calories and protein, they may still suffer from life-threatening conditions because they do not get enough vitamins and minerals. Iodine deficiency disorders, lack of vitamin A and iron-deficiency anemia, often referred to as "hidden hunger," seriously undermine the health and productivity of poor people. Such "micronutrient" malnutrition claims up to 5 percent of national income in some developing countries due to disability and lost lives and productivity.

Insufficient iodine can lead to goiter (an enlargement of the thyroid gland) and mental retardation. It affects people in some European countries as well as in the developing world. In 1995, 760 million people worldwide suffered from goiter. Vitamin A deficiency can cause blindness and even death from infectious diseases. It afflicted nearly 3 million preschool children in 1995, half of them in Southeast Asia (Table 7.2 and Figure 7.3).[17]

Inadequate iron intake is one cause of anemia, which reduces work and school performance and increases susceptibility to disease. Worldwide, 48 percent of pregnant women (80 percent in Southeast Asia and 64 percent in the Eastern Mediterranean) suffer from iron-deficiency anemia. They are at heightened risk of death in childbirth or bearing low-birth-weight babies, who in turn are vulnerable to disease and impaired development. Altogether, anemia affects nearly 2 billion people worldwide.[18]

Relatively inexpensive public health interventions can minimize "hidden hunger": salt iodization; encouraging consumption of vegetables rich in vitamin A or capsules; fortifying sugar and cooking oil with vitamin A; and encouraging pregnant women to take iron sulfate tablets. Bangladesh, with assistance from UNICEF and Kiwanis International, has increased salt iodization from none to 100 percent in just 10 years. "We use iodized salt so that we don't get goiter...," said a mother attending a village health center.[19]

In Indonesia, the world's fourth largest nation, 250,000 community-based health posts provide vitamin A and iron supplements, immunization and other preventive health measures to preschool children. Between 1973 and 1993, undernutrition fell by half, with the health centers accounting for 50 percent of the reduction. Broad-based economic growth also played a significant role.[20]

Countries in Crisis[21]

Violent conflicts and their aftermath, poor weather and the hardships of the transition from central planning led to hunger emergencies in 1996-1997. Table 7.3 shows the populations in need of food and other humanitarian assistance in 22 countries affected by war, civil strife, ethnic violence and post-conflict reconstruction burdens. In all, 22 million people are affected.

Three consecutive years of poor weather, loss of Soviet and Chinese aid and an inefficient food production system put 5 million people at risk of starvation in North Korea. In April 1997, there were reports of serious undernutrition and cannibalism. Donors responded slowly to U.N. appeals for food aid. The United States and South Korea linked assistance to progress on a permanent peace accord, while North Korea conditioned peace talks on more food aid. The country has reportedly sold arms and drugs to finance food purchases.

Natural disasters left millions of people in need of food assistance in 1996-1997. Drought ruined secondary cereal crops in East Africa. A cyclone in Bangladesh left over a million people homeless in May 1997.

Dr. Marc J. Cohen, senior research associate at Bread for the World Institute, is editor of *Hunger in a Global Economy.*
Jashinta D'Costa, BFW Institute consultant, assisted in research for this chapter.

Table 7.3

Hunger in Conflict and Post-Conflict Countries, April 1996

Country	People in Need of Humanitarian Assistance (millions)	Circumstances
Afghanistan	1.5	**Civil War** Internally displaced people, food shortages
Angola	1.0	**Post-Conflict** Internally displaced and war-affected people, demobilized troops; some fighting continues
Armenia	0.3	**Active Conflict** Refugees
Azerbaijan	0.8	**Active Conflict** Internally displaced people
Bosnia	3.1	**Post-Conflict** Low-income and elderly people continue to need assistance
Cambodia	1.1+	**Civil War** Extremely fragile economy and security situation
Ethiopia	1.9	**Post-Conflict** Fragile reconstruction and reconciliation; widespread food insecurity
Georgia	0.3	**Active Conflict** Internally displaced people, people affected by economic transition face food insecurity
Great Lakes Region, Central Africa	Burundi: 0.3 Rwanda: 2.6 Tanzania: 0.4 Uganda: 0.4 Congo (Zaire): 0.5 Total: 4.2	**Active Conflict** Refugees, internally displaced people, food used as a weapon, military intervention, economic sanctions on Burundi
Iraq	2.1	**Active Conflict** International embargo, internal embargoes, internally displaced people
Liberia	0.7	**Post-Conflict** Internally displaced people; shaky security situation
Russia (Northern Caucasus)	0.4	**Post-Conflict** Internally displaced people
Sierra Leone	0.5	**Civil War** Internally displaced people; shaky security situation
Somalia	0.7	**Civil War** People in internally displaced camps
Sri Lanka	0.2	**Civil War** War has disrupted normal economic activity in north
Sudan	2.7	**Civil War** Internally displaced people, food used as a weapon
Tajikistan	0.6	**Post-Conflict** Internally displaced and people affected by economic transition face serious undernutrition

Sources: FAO; United Nations Administrative Committee on Coordination/Subcommittee on Nutrition; U.S. Mission to the United Nations.

Exercise our influence as responsible citizens, consumers, employers, workers and investors to make the world economy work for everyone.

Everybody's Business: Call to Action

By Lily Philipose

Economic growth is necessary to assure that the global economy offers everyone, including hungry people, opportunities to achieve secure livelihoods. Paradoxically, growth based on present patterns of consumption in industrial nations is not environmentally sustainable. And, the scenario of a two-tiered world – overdeveloped and developing, rich and poor forever – is morally unacceptable.

Given the scope of the global economy, where webs spin out in every direction and intersect at barely visible points, it seems audacious to ask the question: What can we do to make the world economy work better for hungry and poor people?

Yet all of us, as responsible citizens, consumers, employers, workers and investors, acting with spirit, energy and urgency, can exercise our influence to help make global commerce pay attention to moral concerns: the welfare of hungry and poor people everywhere, food security, labor standards, human rights, environmental protection and cultural identity. Globalization can contribute to a broadly shared prosperity and still address our moral concerns.

As citizens, we can work actively for government policies that reduce hunger and poverty (see "Plugging Into Activism," opposite page, for practical suggestions on how to get involved).

Policies that encourage work with liveable wages and public investment in health, education and safety nets are good for hungry people. Over time, they are good for business and society as a whole, too.

As members of organizations such as Bread for the World, we can help reform and democratize international financial institutions (IFIs) and win debt relief for the poorest countries. In Africa alone, debt relief could save the lives of about 21 million children by 2000 and provide 90 million girls and women with access to basic education.[1]

Plugging into Activism

As citizens we can:

- Learn about critical policy issues. Bread for the World's website, http://www.bread.org, provides current information, action alerts and links;
- Join Bread for the World and other anti-hunger advocacy groups. U.S. domestic anti-hunger organizations working at the state, national and global levels are listed at http://www.bread.org; and
- Work directly with low-income communities. Volunteer and contribute to a community agency. Seek out one that not only assists poor people, but speaks out on their behalf and builds their capacity for self-reliance.

As consumers we can:

- Use our purchasing power to send the message that business decisions must factor in human needs. The Council on Economic Priorities (CEP) publishes guides to socially responsible shopping, with profiles of over 200 companies, ranking them on policies and practices. Some profiles are also available at http://www.accesspt.com/cep;
- Buy from companies that have joined the White House Apparel Industry Partnership's "No Sweat Initiative," focused on the eradication of sweatshops in the United States and abroad. For more information contact Stop Sweatshops: A Partnership for Responsibility, c/o National Consumers League, 1701 K Street N.W., Suite 1200, Washington, DC 20006; telephone: (202) 835-3323; fax: (202) 835-0747; and
- Support fair trade initiatives such as SERRV International (Sales Exchange for Refugee Rehabilitation Vocations), founded by The Church of the Brethren, and Ten Thousand Villages, run by the Mennonite Central Committee.

As employers we can:

- Follow the lead of Business for Social Responsibility. Their members, representing about 800 businesses of all sizes, are executives who support social justice policies and honor high ethical standards. Call (202) 463-9036 or visit their web site at http://www.bsr.org; and
- Give generously to charitable causes, especially groups that also speak up for people in need or equip them to speak for themselves. InterAction, the nation's largest coalition of relief, development and advocacy groups, lists international development organizations, both religious and secular, at http://www.interaction.org, or call (202) 667-8227.

As workers we can:

- Join/support workers' unions. Contact the American Federation of Labor and Congress of Industrial Organizations at 815 16th Street, N.W., Washington, DC 20006-4145, or call (202) 637-5000; and
- Find out about labor rights issues. The International Labor Rights Fund at (202) 544-7198 or http://www.laborrights.com provides information on child labor, bonded labor and labor rights clauses in international agreements. For basic information on the status of workers and labor standards visit the International Labor Organization at http://www.ilo.org.

As investors we can:

- Challenge companies in which we or our pension funds own stock, to make progress on issues such as: humane working conditions, withdrawing investment that supports repressive regimes and strengthening environmental performance. The Interfaith Center on Corporate Responsibility (ICCR), at 475 Riverside Dr., Room 550, New York, NY 10115, or (212) 870-2295, tracks social responsibility corporate resolutions. The SCREEN link on CEP's web site (see above) includes a special section for responsible investors; and
- Invest through socially conscious investment funds. For a listing of such funds and investment services (with brief profiles, contact names, addresses and telephone numbers) refer to *ICCR's Conscientious Investor's Guide to Socially Responsible Mutual Funds and Investment Services*.

As consumers, we can shape corporate practices by casting our economic vote conscientiously. Buyers who purchase a company's product have a right to know what policies and practices they support with their money. Responsible consumers should ask questions: are company practices polluting air, land and rivers? Do employers show concern about the health and well-being of their workers at home and contracted workers overseas? Are they committed to promoting ethical practices in developing countries and protecting labor rights? Does the company invest in the local community?

The key, says theologian Daniel Finn, will be not so much a transfer of wealth from rich countries but an increase in the daily productivity of ordinary people.

Making informed choices means that as consumers we are not extensions of products. Instead, the things we buy become extensions of ourselves, our values and beliefs.[2]

As employers, we can adopt policies that treat employees, local communities and the environment well.

As workers, we can choose worthwhile jobs. We can also support and join workers' unions committed to seeking worker and consumer participation in policy making at all levels.

As investors, we can give weight to social values in our investment decisions. We can make companies hear our voice by joining shareholder efforts to shape corporate policy.

Simply as human beings – whatever our limitations – we can hope and pray for a better world and act decently toward those around us.

The foregoing chapters have outlined the scope of world hunger in a global economy, the dynamics of international trade and investment and the role of the international financial institutions. The basic question has been how, within the framework of a global economy, we can bring about lasting improvements in human lives. How can we harvest the potential benefits of globalized markets for the good of all people?

The key, says theologian Daniel Finn, will be not so much a transfer of wealth from rich countries but an increase in the daily productivity of ordinary people.[3] The productivity of a farmer in Africa or a carpenter in South Asia can be hampered by various obstacles – a dearth of schooling opportunities, the unavailability of clean water, powerlessness and far-off trade negotiations that can depress the entire economy of some nations.

A 13-year-old boy in a low-income U.S. community faces oddly similar obstacles – an underfunded school besieged with social problems, too many hours on his own while his mother tries to make a living, and far-off decisions to reduce the U.S. government deficit by curtailing food stamps.

Most disadvantaged people manage to cope somehow. Some succeed, through years of intense effort, in overcoming hunger and poverty. A vibrant civil society and laws that seek justice can open market opportunities for such struggling people.

The best hope for hungry and poor people today is improving their own productivity so that they are equipped to support themselves and insist on their rights. We can support them in their self-reliance. We can work for policies that increase our realistic hope for a more just and sustainable world economy.[4]

Dr. Lily Philipose is an intern at Bread for the World Institute.

Appendix

Table 1 Global Hunger – Life and Death Indicators

	Population: Total (millions) 1997	Population: Projected (millions) 2025	Population: Projected growth rate (%) 1995-2000	Population: Projected total fertility rate 1995-2000	Population: % population below age 15 1997	Population: % population urban 1995	Life expectancy at birth 1995-2000: Male	Life expectancy at birth 1995-2000: Female	Infant mortality rate per 1,000 live births 1995	% infants with low birth weight 1990-1994	% 1-year-old children immunized (measles) 1992-1995	Under 5 mortality rate per 1,000 live births: 1960	Under 5 mortality rate per 1,000 live births: 1995	Maternal mortality rate per 100,000 live births 1990	Refugees 1996: Country of origin	Refugees 1996: Country of asylum
Developing Countries	**4,670.3**	**6,818.9**	**1.7**	**3.08**	..	**38**	**62.1**	**65.2**	**67**	**19**	**76**	**216**	**99**	**477**	..	..
Africa (sub-Saharan) **3,496,300e**	**621.6e**	**1,244.1e**	..	..	..	..	..	..	**106**	**16**	**53**	**256**	**175**	**980**	**3,543,200e**	
Angola	11.6	25.5	3.3	6.69	48	32	44.9	48.1	170	19	32	345	292	1,500	220,000	9,300
Benin	5.7	12.3	2.8	5.83	48	31	52.4	57.2	85	..	72	310	142	990	..	11,000
Botswana	1.5	2.6	2.2	4.45	43	28	48.9	51.7	41	8	68	170	52	250	..	..
Burkina Faso	11.1	23.5	2.8	6.57	47	27	45.1	47.0	86	21	55	318	164	930	..	26,000
Burundi	6.4	12.3	2.8	6.28	46	8	45.5	48.8	106	..	50	255	176	1,300	285,000	12,000
Cameroon	13.9	28.5	2.7	5.30	44	45	54.5	57.2	66	13	46	264	106	550	..	1,000
Cape Verde	0.4	0.7	..	3.56	41	54	65.5	67.5	54	..	66	164	73	..	..	..
Central African Republic	3.4	6.0	2.1	4.95	42	39	46.4	51.0	106	15	36	294	165	700	..	36,400
Chad	6.7	12.6	2.8	5.51	43	21	46.3	49.3	94	..	26	325	152	1,500	15,500	100
Comoros	0.7	1.3	..	5.51	46	31	57.0	58.0	85	..	59	248	124	..	..	..
Congo (Brazzaville)	2.7	5.7	2.8	5.87	46	59	48.6	53.4	81	16	70	220	108	890	..	16,000
Côte d'Ivoire	14.3	24.4	2.0	5.10	44	44	50.0	52.2	90	14	57	300	150	810	..	320,000
Djibouti	0.6	1.1	..	5.39	41	83	48.7	52.0	113	..	42	289	158	..	10,000	22,000
Equatorial Guinea	0.4	0.8	..	5.51	43	42	48.4	51.6	113	..	61	316	175	..	..	..
Eritrea	3.4	6.5	3.7	5.34	44	17	49.1	52.1	114	13	45	294	195	1,400	343,100	1,000
Ethiopia	60.1	136.3	3.2	7.00	47	13	48.4	51.6	114	16	43	294	195	1,400	58,000	328,000
Gabon	1.1	2.1	2.8	5.40	39	50	53.8	57.2	89	..	56	287	148	500	..	1,000
Gambia	1.2	2.0	..	5.20	41	26	45.4	48.7	80	..	87	375	110	1,100	..	5,000
Ghana	18.3	36.3	2.8	5.28	44	36	56.2	59.9	76	7	46	213	130	740	10,000	35,000
Guinea	7.6	15.3	1.4	6.61	47	30	46.0	47.0	128	21	69	337	219	1,600	..	650,000
Guinea-Bissau	1.1	1.9	2.0	5.42	42	22	42.4	45.2	134	20	82	336	227	910	..	15,000
Kenya	28.4	50.2	2.2	4.85	45	28	52.3	55.7	61	16	73	202	90	650	..	186,000
Lesotho	2.1	4.0	2.5	4.86	42	23	57.3	59.9	105	11	74	204	154	610	..	..
Liberia	2.5	6.6	8.6	6.33	43	45	50.0	53.0	144	..	68	288	216	560	755,000	100,000
Madagascar	15.8	34.5	3.1	5.65	47	27	57.0	60.0	100	17	60	364	164	490	..	..
Malawi	10.1	20.4	2.5	6.69	47	14	40.3	41.1	138	20	70	365	219	560	..	..
Mali	11.5	24.6	3.0	6.60	47	27	46.4	49.7	117	17	49	400	210	1,200	80,000	15,000
Mauritania	2.4	4.4	2.5	5.03	42	54	51.9	55.1	112	11	53	321	195	930	65,000	15,000
Mauritius	1.1	1.5	1.1	2.28	27	41	68.3	75.0	19	13	85	84	23	120	..	..
Mozambique	18.3	35.4	2.5	6.06	45	34	45.5	48.4	158	20	40	331	275	1,500	..	..
Namibia	1.6	3.0	2.4	4.90	42	37	54.7	56.6	61	16	69	206	78	370	..	1,000
Niger	9.8	22.4	3.3	7.10	49	17	46.9	50.2	191	15	18	320	320	1,200	15,000	27,000
Nigeria	118.4	238.4	2.8	5.97	45	39	50.8	54.0	114	16	40	204	191	1,000	..	8,000
Rwanda	5.9	13.0	7.9	6.00	46	6	40.8	43.4	80	17	50	191	139	1,300	257,000	20,000
Senegal	8.8	16.9	2.7	5.62	44	42	50.3	52.3	70	11	80	303	110	1,200	17,000	51,000
Sierra Leone	4.4	8.2	3.0	6.06	44	36	36.0	39.1	164	11	46	385	284	1,800	350,000	15,000
Somalia	10.2	23.7	3.9	7.00	48	26	47.4	50.6	125	16	45	294	211	1,600	467,100	..
South Africa	43.3	71.6	2.2	3.81	37	51	62.3	68.3	51	..	76	126	67	230	..	22,500
Sudan	27.9	46.9	2.2	4.61	40	25	53.6	56.4	69	15	74	292	115	660	433,700	395,000
Swaziland	0.9	1.7	..	4.46	42	31	57.7	62.3	74	..	93	233	107	..	..	..
Tanzania	31.5	62.4	2.3	5.48	46	24	50.0	52.8	100	14	82	249	160	770	..	335,000
Togo	4.3	8.8	2.7	6.08	46	31	48.8	51.5	80	20	65	264	128	640	30,000	10,000
Uganda	20.8	45.0	2.6	7.10	49	13	40.4	42.3	111	..	79	218	185	1,200	15,000	225,000
Zaire (Congo-Kinshasa)	48.0	105.9	2.6	6.24	48	29	51.3	54.5	119	15	39	286	185	870	116,800	455,000
Zambia	8.5	16.2	2.5	5.49	47	43	42.2	43.7	114	13	69	220	203	940	..	126,000
Zimbabwe	11.7	19.3	2.1	4.68	44	32	47.6	49.4	50	14	74	181	74	570	..	1,000
South Asia **1,736,600e**	**1,346.4e**	**1,971.7e**	..	..	..	..	..	..	**82**	**33**	**73**	**238**	**121**	**607**	**2,916,500e**	
Afghanistan	22.1	45.3	5.3	6.90	41	20	45.0	46.0	165	20	41	360	257	1,700	2,628,550	18,900
Bangladesh	122.0	180.0	1.6	3.14	39	18	58.1	58.2	85	50	79	247	115	850	53,000	40,000
Bhutan	1.9	3.6	2.8	5.89	43	6	51.6	54.9	122	..	85	324	189	1,600	121,800	..
India	960.2	1,330.2	1.6	3.07	34	27	62.1	62.7	76	33	78	236	115	570	13,000	352,200
Maldives	0.3	0.6	..	6.80	46	27	65.7	63.3	55	..	62	258	77	..	..	..
Nepal	22.6	40.6	2.5	4.95	43	14	57.6	57.1	81	..	57	290	114	1,500	..	109,800
Pakistan	143.8	268.9	2.7	5.02	42	35	62.9	65.1	95	25	53	221	137	340	..	1,215,700
Sri Lanka	18.3	23.9	1.0	2.10	28	22	70.9	75.4	15	25	88	130	19	140	100,150	..

Table 1, continued: **Global Hunger – Life and Death Indicators**

	Population: Total (millions) 1997	Population: Projected (millions) 2025	Population: Projected growth rate (%) 1995-2000	Population: Projected total fertility rate 1995-2000	Population: % population below age 15 1997	Population: % population urban 1995	Life expectancy at birth 1995-2000: Male	Life expectancy at birth 1995-2000: Female	Infant mortality rate per 1,000 live births 1995	% infants with low birth weight 1990-1994	% 1-year-old children immunized (measles) 1992-1995	Under 5 mortality rate per 1,000 live births: 1960	Under 5 mortality rate per 1,000 live births: 1995	Maternal mortality rate per 100,000 live births 1990	Refugees 1996: Country of origin	Refugees 1996: Country of asylum
East Asia & the Pacific	**1,830.6**e	**2,404.2**e	**..**	**..**	**..**	**..**	**..**	**..**	**42**	**11**	**88**	**200**	**55**	**214**	**516,700**e	**441,900**e
Brunei	0.3	0.5	..	2.70	33	58	73.4	78.1	8	..	100	87	10	..	..	..
Burma (Myanmar)	46.8	67.6	1.8	3.30	35	26	58.5	61.8	105	16	75	237	150	580	184,300	..
Cambodia	10.5	17.0	2.2	4.50	42	21	52.6	55.4	110	..	75	217	174	900	34,400	..
China	1,243.7	1,480.4	0.9	1.80	26	30	68.2	71.7	38	9	93	209	47	95	128,000	294,100
Fiji	0.8	1.2	..	2.76	33	41	70.6	74.9	21	..	94	97	25	..	..	..
Hong Kong[a]	6.2	6.5	0.8	1.32	19	95	76.1	81.8	5	8	77	52	6	7	..	1,300
Indonesia	203.5	275.2	1.5	2.63	32	35	63.3	67.0	50	14	70	216	75	650	10,000	..
Korea, N.	22.8	30.0	1.6	2.10	27	61	68.9	75.1	23	..	98	120	30	70	..	..
Korea, S.	45.7	52.5	0.9	1.65	22	81	68.8	76.0	8	9	92	124	9	130	..	..
Laos	5.2	10.2	3.1	6.69	45	22	52.0	55.0	91	18	68	233	134	650	..	..
Malaysia	21.0	31.6	2.0	3.24	37	54	69.9	74.3	11	8	81	105	13	80	..	5,200
Mongolia	2.6	4.1	2.1	3.27	38	61	64.3	67.3	57	6	85	185	74	65	..	..
Papua New Guinea	4.5	7.5	2.2	4.65	39	16	57.2	58.7	67	23	63	248	95	930	..	10,000
Philippines	70.7	105.2	2.0	3.62	38	54	66.6	70.2	40	15	86	102	53	280	..	50
Singapore	3.4	4.2	1.5	1.79	23	100	75.1	79.5	5	7	88	40	6	10	..	..
Solomon Islands	0.4	0.8	..	4.98	44	17	69.6	73.9	25	..	68	185	31	..	..	1,000
Thailand	59.2	69.1	0.8	1.74	27	20	66.3	72.3	27	13	90	146	32	200	..	95,850
Vietnam	76.5	110.1	1.8	2.97	36	21	64.9	69.6	34	17	95	219	45	160	288,000	34,400
Latin America and the Caribbean	**491.9**	**689.6**	**1.5**	**2.65**	**..**	**74**	**66.4**	**72.9**	**38**	**10**	**85**	**159**	**47**	**190**	**64,850**e	**77,100**e
Argentina	35.7	47.2	1.3	2.62	28	88	69.6	76.8	24	7	76	68	27	100	..	400
Belize	0.2	0.4	2.5	3.66	41	47	73.4	76.1	32	..	83	104	40	..	..	8,700
Bolivia	7.8	13.1	2.3	4.36	40	61	59.8	63.2	73	12	80	252	105	650	..	550
Brazil	163.1	216.6	1.2	2.17	30	78	63.4	71.2	51	11	88	181	60	220	..	2,200
Chile	14.6	19.5	1.4	2.44	29	84	72.3	78.3	13	5	96	138	15	65	..	200
Colombia	37.1	52.7	1.7	2.69	34	73	68.2	73.7	30	10	84	132	36	100	..	200
Costa Rica	3.6	5.6	2.1	2.95	34	50	74.5	79.2	14	6	94	112	16	60	..	23,150
Cuba	11.1	11.8	0.4	1.55	22	76	74.2	78.0	9	9	100	50	10	95	..	1,650
Dominican Republic	8.1	11.2	1.7	2.80	34	65	68.9	73.1	37	11	85	152	44	110	..	600
Ecuador	11.9	17.8	2.0	3.10	35	58	67.3	72.5	31	13	62	180	40	150	..	200
El Salvador	5.9	9.2	2.2	3.09	36	45	66.5	72.5	34	11	93	210	40	300	12,000	150
Guatemala	11.2	21.7	2.8	4.90	44	41	64.7	69.8	49	14	75	205	67	200	34,650	1,200
Guyana	0.8	1.1	..	2.32	32	36	61.1	67.9	44	..	84	126	59	..	..	..
Haiti	7.4	12.5	1.9	4.60	40	32	52.8	56.0	71	15	31	260	124	1,000	..	..
Honduras	6.0	10.7	2.8	4.30	43	44	67.5	72.3	31	9	90	203	38	220	..	..
Jamaica	2.5	3.4	0.9	2.44	31	54	72.4	76.8	11	10	89	76	13	120	..	..
Mexico	94.3	130.2	1.6	2.75	35	75	69.5	75.5	27	8	90	148	32	110	..	34,450
Nicaragua	4.4	7.6	2.6	3.85	42	63	65.8	70.6	46	15	81	209	60	160	18,200	900
Panama	2.7	3.8	1.6	2.63	33	53	71.8	76.4	18	9	84	104	20	55	..	650
Paraguay	5.1	9.4	2.6	4.17	41	53	67.5	72.0	28	5	75	90	34	160	..	..
Peru	24.4	35.5	1.7	2.98	35	72	65.9	70.9	41	11	98	236	55	280	..	300
Suriname	0.4	0.6	..	2.39	34	50	69.0	74.0	26	..	69	96	32	..	..	..
Trinidad and Tobago	1.3	1.7	0.8	2.10	29	72	71.5	76.2	16	10	84	73	18	90	..	..
Uruguay	3.2	3.7	0.6	2.25	24	90	69.6	76.1	19	8	80	47	21	85	..	..
Venezuela	22.8	34.8	2.0	2.98	35	93	70.0	75.7	20	9	67	70	24	120	..	1,600
Middle East & North Africa	**377.8**e	**627.5**e	**..**	**..**	**..**	**..**	**..**	**..**	**46**	**11**	**86**	**244**	**60**	**323**	**669,600**e	**6,041,150**e
Algeria	29.5	47.3	2.3	3.81	38	56	67.5	70.3	51	9	77	243	61	160	..	114,000
Bahrain	0.6	0.9	..	2.97	31	90	71.1	75.3	17	..	89	203	20	..	..	..
Cyprus	0.8	1.0	..	2.31	25	54	75.4	79.8	9	..	83	36	10	..	..	100
Egypt	64.5	95.8	1.9	3.40	37	45	64.7	67.3	40	10	90	258	51	170	..	46,000
Iran	71.5	128.3	2.2	4.77	44	59	68.5	70.0	35	9	95	233	40	120	46,100	2,020,000
Iraq	21.2	41.6	2.8	5.25	42	75	60.9	63.9	57	15	95	171	71	310	608,500	114,400
Jordan	5.8	11.9	3.3	5.13	43	71	67.7	71.8	21	7	92	149	25	150	..	1,362,500
Kuwait	1.7	2.9	3.0	2.77	37	97	74.1	78.2	12	7	93	128	14	29	..	42,000
Lebanon	3.1	4.4	1.8	2.75	34	87	68.1	71.7	33	10	88	85	40	300	..	355,100
Libya	5.8	12.9	3.3	5.92	45	86	63.9	67.5	52	..	92	269	63	220	..	27,200
Morocco	27.5	39.9	1.8	3.10	35	48	64.8	68.5	61	9	88	215	75	610	80,000d	..
Oman	2.4	6.5	4.2	7.20	47	13	68.9	73.3	20	8	98	300	25	190	..	..
Qatar	0.6	0.8	..	3.77	27	91	70.0	75.4	18	..	86	239	23	..	..	..
Saudi Arabia	19.5	42.4	3.4	5.90	41	80	69.9	73.4	29	7	94	292	34	130	..	257,850
Syria	15.0	26.3	2.5	4.00	43	52	66.7	71.2	30	11	98	201	36	180	..	384,400
Tunisia	9.3	13.5	1.8	2.92	34	57	68.4	70.7	30	8	91	244	37	170	..	300

Table 1, continued: **Global Hunger – Life and Death Indicators**

	Population: Total (millions) 1997	Population: Projected (millions) 2025	Population: Projected growth rate (%) 1995-2000	Population: Projected total fertility rate 1995-2000	Population: % population below age 15 1997	Population: % population urban 1995	Life expectancy at birth 1995-2000: Male	Life expectancy at birth 1995-2000: Female	Infant mortality rate per 1,000 live births 1995	% infants with low birth weight 1990-1994	% 1-year-old children immunized (measles) 1992-1995	Under 5 mortality rate per 1,000 live births: 1960	Under 5 mortality rate per 1,000 live births: 1995	Maternal mortality rate per 100,000 live births 1990	Refugees 1996: Country of origin	Refugees 1996: Country of asylum
Turkey	62.8	85.8	1.6	2.50	30	69	66.5	71.7	44	8	42	217	50	180	15,000	13,000
United Arab Emirates	2.3	3.3	2.0	3.46	30	84	73.9	76.5	16	6	90	240	19	26	..	400
West Bank and Gaza[a]	0.9c	..	..	..	52c	..	..	..	..	..	..	..	..	..	3,718,500f	1,249,300
Yemen	16.3	39.6	3.7	7.60	48	34	57.4	58.4	76	19	40	340	110	1,400	..	54,600
Countries in Transition[b]	**..**	**..**	**..**	**..**	**..**	**..**	**..**	**..**	**33**	**..**	**80**	**..**	**38**	**88**	**1,846,450e**	**1,707,200e**
Albania	3.4	4.3	0.6	2.60	31	37	68.0	74.0	34	7	91	151	40	65	..	..
Armenia	3.6	4.2	0.2	1.70	27	69	67.2	74.0	26	..	95	..	31	50	197,000	150,000
Azerbaijan	7.7	9.7	0.8	2.30	31	56	66.5	74.5	34	..	97	..	50	22	238,000	249,150
Belarus	10.3	9.6	-0.1	1.40	21	71	64.4	74.8	17	..	97	..	20	37	..	10,800
Bosnia and Herzegovina	3.8	4.3	3.9	1.40	21	49	70.5	75.9	15	..	57	155	17	..	1,006,450	..
Bulgaria	8.4	7.5	-0.5	1.45	18	71	67.8	74.9	16	6	93	70	19	27	..	550
Croatia	4.5	4.2	-0.1	1.60	18	64	68.1	76.5	12	..	92	98	14	..	300,000	167,000
Czech Republic	10.2	9.6	-0.1	1.40	18	65	69.8	76.0	9	6	96	..	10	15	..	2,900
Estonia	1.5	1.3	-1.0	1.30	19	73	63.9	75.0	19	..	81	..	22	41	..	..
Georgia	5.4	5.8	-0.1	1.90	23	58	68.5	76.7	22	..	63	..	26	33	105,000	..
Hungary	10.0	8.7	-0.6	1.40	18	65	64.5	73.8	13	9	100	57	14	30	..	5,400
Kazakhstan	16.8	20.0	0.1	2.30	29	60	62.8	72.5	40	..	95	..	47	80	..	14,000
Kyrgyzstan	4.5	6.0	0.4	3.21	36	39	63.4	71.9	45	..	80	..	54	110	..	17,000
Latvia	2.5	2.1	-1.1	1.40	20	73	62.5	74.3	22	..	85	..	26	40	..	..
Lithuania	3.7	3.5	-0.3	1.50	21	72	64.9	76.0	16	..	94	..	19	36	..	..
Macedonia	2.2	2.5	0.7	1.90	24	60	70.3	74.7	26	..	86	177	31	..	..	5,100
Moldova	4.4	4.9	0.1	1.80	25	52	63.5	71.5	30	4	98	..	34	60	..	..
Poland	38.6	40.0	0.1	1.65	22	65	66.7	75.7	14	..	91	70	16	19	..	3,200
Romania	22.6	21.1	-0.2	1.40	20	55	66.0	73.2	23	11	93	82	29	130	..	600
Russia	147.7	131.4	-0.3	1.35	20	76	58.0	71.5	27	..	94	..	30	75	..	484,000
Slovakia	5.4	5.5	0.1	1.50	22	59	67.0	75.8	13	..	99	..	15	..	..	2,000
Slovenia	1.9	1.7	-0.1	1.30	17	64	69.2	77.8	7	..	91	45	8	13	..	10,300
Tajikistan	6.0	9.7	1.9	3.93	41	32	64.2	70.2	61	..	80	..	79	130	215,600	2,200
Turkmenistan	4.2	6.5	1.9	3.58	39	45	61.2	68.0	69	5	66	..	85	55	..	22,000
Ukraine	51.4	46.0	-0.4	1.38	19	70	63.6	74.0	20	..	96	..	24	50	..	8,000
Uzbekistan	23.7	36.5	1.9	3.48	39	41	64.3	70.7	50	..	81	..	62	55	52,000	3,000
Yugoslavia	10.4	10.7	0.5	1.80	21	57	69.8	75.3	20	..	81	120	23	..	..	550,000
Industrial Countries	**1,178.4**	**1,220.3**	**0.3**	**1.59**	**..**	**75**	**70.6**	**78.4**	**7**	**6**	**83**	**37**	**8**	**13**	**..**	**980,500e**
Australia	18.3	23.9	1.1	1.89	21	85	75.4	81.2	7	6	..	24	8	9	..	7,400
Austria	8.2	8.3	0.6	1.42	18	56	73.7	80.1	6	6	60	43	7	10	..	80,000
Belgium	10.2	10.3	0.3	1.62	18	97	73.9	80.6	8	6	70	35	10	10	..	18,200
Canada	29.9	36.4	0.9	1.61	20	77	76.1	81.8	6	6	98	33	8	6	..	26,100
Denmark	5.2	5.3	0.2	1.82	18	85	73.0	78.3	6	6	88	25	7	9	..	24,600
Finland	5.1	5.3	0.3	1.83	19	63	73.0	80.1	4	4	98	28	5	11	..	1,700
France	58.5	60.4	0.3	1.63	19	73	74.6	82.9	7	5	76	34	9	15	..	29,200
Germany	82.2	80.9	0.3	1.30	16	87	73.4	79.9	6	..	75	40	7	22	..	436,400
Greece	10.5	10.1	0.3	1.38	16	65	75.5	80.6	8	6	70	64	10	10	..	5,600
Ireland	3.6	3.7	0.2	1.80	23	58	74.0	79.4	6	4	..	36	7	10	..	1,800
Israel	5.8	8.0	1.9	2.75	29	91	75.7	79.5	7	7	94	39	9	7	..	..
Italy	57.2	51.7	0.0	1.19	15	67	75.1	81.4	7	5	50	50	8	12	..	10,600
Japan	125.6	121.3	0.2	1.48	16	78	76.9	82.9	4	7	68	40	6	18	..	300
Luxembourg	0.4	0.5	..	1.76	18	89	73.1	79.7	8	..	80	41	9	..	..	..
Netherlands	15.7	16.1	0.5	1.55	18	89	75.0	80.6	6	..	95	22	8	12	..	46,200
New Zealand	3.6	4.9	1.1	2.02	23	86	74.7	79.7	7	6	87	26	9	25	..	..
Norway	4.4	4.7	0.4	1.88	20	73	74.8	80.6	6	4	93	23	8	6	..	12,700
Portugal	9.8	9.4	-0.1	1.48	17	36	71.8	78.9	9	5	94	112	11	15	..	200
Spain	39.7	37.5	0.1	1.22	16	76	74.5	81.5	8	4	90	57	9	7	..	7,200
Sweden	8.8	9.5	0.3	1.80	19	83	76.2	80.8	4	5	96	20	5	7	..	60,500
Switzerland	7.3	7.6	0.7	1.46	17	61	75.3	81.8	6	5	..	27	7	6	..	41,700
United Kingdom	58.2	59.5	0.1	1.72	19	89	74.5	79.8	6	7	92	27	7	9	..	40,500
United States	271.6	332.5	0.8	1.96	22	76	73.4	80.1	8	7	89	30	10	12	..	129,600
World	**5,848.7**	**8,039.1**	**1.4**	**2.79**	**..**	**45**	**63.4**	**67.7**	**61**	**18**	**77**	**191**	**90**	**428**	**9,557,300e**	**14,480,750e**

.. Data not available.
a Territory.
b Central and Eastern European countries and the newly independent states of the former Soviet Union.

Table 2 **Food, Nutrition and Education**

	Food supply			Food production per capita	Food expenditures	Iodine deficiency	Adult literacy rate 1994			Educational enrollment (% of relevant age group)					
	Per capita dietary energy supply (DES) (calories/day) 1990-1992	DES annual growth rate 1969-1971 to 1990-1992	Daily per capita calorie supply (% of requirements) 1988-1990	(1989-1991 =100) 1995	(% of household consumption) 1980-1985	total goiter rate in school-age children (%) 1969-1992	Total	Male	Female	Primary school 1993 Total	Primary school 1993 Male	Primary school 1993 Female	Combined primary, secondary and tertiary 1994 Total	Combined primary, secondary and tertiary 1994 Male	Combined primary, secondary and tertiary 1994 Female
Developing Countries	**2,520**	**0.7**	**107**	**96.7**	**41**	**..**	**69.7**	**78.4**	**60.3**	**..**	**..**	**..**	**56**	**60**	**52**
Africa (sub-Saharan)	**2,040**	**-0.2**	**93**	**94.7**	**38**	**16.0**	**..**	**..**	**..**	**72**	**..**	**..**	**..**	**..**	**..**
Angola	1,840	-0.7	80	86.0	..	7.4	42.5	..	..	88	..	..	31	..	..
Benin	2,520	0.7	104	103.5	37	23.7	35.5	46.6	23.0	64	88	44	35	48	23
Botswana	2,320	0.4	97	94.9	25	8.0	68.7	79.3	58.0	116	113x	120x	71	70	72
Burkina Faso	2,140	1.0	94	101.9	..	16.2	18.7	28.8	8.6	38	47x	30x	20	25	15
Burundi	1,950	-0.4	84	82.4	..	42.4	34.6	48.2	21.0	72	76	63	31	35	27
Cameroon	2,040	-0.6	95	94.2	24	26.3	62.1	74.0	49.5	87	..	..	46	51	42
Cape Verde	..	..	..	212.0	..	0.0	69.9	79.4	59.8	114	119	110	64	65	62
Central African Republic	1,720	-1.5	82	95.4	..	63.1	57.2	66.7	43.9	..	92	..	37	47	27
Chad	1,810	-0.9	73	101.3	..	15.0	47.0	60.7	32.7	59	80x	38x	25	35	15
Comoros	..	..	..	91.8	..	20.0	56.7	63.4	49.4	81	96	81	39	42	35
Congo (Brazzaville)	2,210	0.3	103	91.1	37	7.5	73.9	..	..	..	..	..	56	..	..
Côte d'Ivoire	2,460	0.1	111	90.7	39	6.0	39.4	49.4	27.5	69	80	58	39	47	32
Djibouti	..	..	..	70.1	..	0.0	45.0	..	..	36	41	31	20	..	..
Equatorial Guinea	..	..	..	84.1	..	10.0	77.8	88.9	67.3	..	..	..	64	70	59
Eritrea	..	..	..	..	..	..	25.0	..	..	47	52	41	24	..	..
Ethiopia	1,620	-0.3	73	..	49	21.8	34.5	44.5	24.1	23	27x	19x	18	21	14
Gabon	2,490	0.6	104	91.4	..	5.0	62.6	74.1	51.8	134x	132x	136x	60	60	60
Gambia	2,320	0.3	..	82.6	..	20.0	37.2	50.9	22.7	76x	84	61	34	41	27
Ghana	2,090	-0.3	93	130.1	50	9.5	63.4	75.2	51.0	76	83x	70x	44	50	38
Guinea	2,400	0.5	97	105.9	..	18.7	34.8	48.4	20.3	44x	61	30	24	33	15
Guinea-Bissau	..	..	97	101.9	..	19.0	53.9	67.1	40.7	..	..	..	29	38	21
Kenya	1,970	-0.5	89	87.2	38	7.0	77.0	85.2	67.8	91	92	91	55	56	54
Lesotho	2,260	0.6	93	78.5	..	16.2	70.5	80.3	60.9	98	90	105	56	51	60
Liberia	1,780	-1.1	98	..	..	5.5	..	..	..	..	..	..	..	..	..
Madagascar	2,160	-0.6	95	89.4	59	24.1	45.8	..	..	89x	90x	88x	33	..	..
Malawi	1,910	-1.0	88	111.0	30	12.7	55.8	71.7	40.4	80	84x	77x	67	71	63
Mali	2,230	0.4	96	94.9	57	28.5	29.3	36.7	20.2	31	38	24	17	21	13
Mauritania	2,610	1.4	106	86.7	..	0.0	36.9	48.4	25.6	69	76	62	36	42	31
Mauritius	2,780	0.9	128	100.3	24	0.0	82.4	86.8	78.4	106	107	107	61	61	62
Mozambique	1,740	-0.5	77	97.5	..	20.0	39.5	55.8	22.1	60	69	51	25	30	21
Namibia	2,190	0.0	..	93.8	..	34.5	40.0x	..	..	136	134x	138x	84	..	..
Niger	2,190	0.5	95	99.8	..	8.5	13.1	20.5	5.6	29	35x	21x	15	19	11
Nigeria	2,100	-0.6	93	113.8	48	10.0	55.6	66.1	43.8	93	105x	82x	50	55	44
Rwanda	1,860	-0.4	82	71.6	29	49.6	59.2	..	..	50	78x	76x	37	..	..
Senegal	2,310	-0.3	98	100.4	49	11.5	32.1	42.1	21.2	56x	67x	50x	31	37	25
Sierra Leone	1,820	-0.8	83	77.9	56	6.5	30.3	43.7	16.7	..	..	..	28	34	22
Somalia	1,590	-0.6	81	..	..	7.0	..	..	..	..	..	..	..	..	..
South Africa	2,810	0.0	128	76.2	34	2.0	81.4	81.4	81.2	111	111	110	81	80	82
Sudan	2,150	-0.1	87	108.6	60	20.0	44.8	56.4	31.3	50	59	41	31	35	28
Swaziland	2,680	0.7	..	80.4	..	10.0	75.2	76.4	73.3	120	123	116	72	74	70
Tanzania	2,110	0.9	95	85.6	64	37.0	66.8	78.8	54.3	70	71	69	34	35	33
Togo	2,290	0.0	99	87.5	..	22.1	50.4	65.6	34.4	102	122	81	50	62	37
Uganda	2,220	-0.2	93	99.3	..	6.5	61.1	73.2	48.7	91	99	83	34	39	30
Zaire (Congo-Kinshasa)	2,090	-0.1	96	85.7	..	9.0	76.4	..	..	55x	59x	51x	38	..	..
Zambia	2,020	-0.4	87	83.0	36	50.5	76.6	84.4	69.3	104	109	99	48	51	44
Zimbabwe	2,080	-0.2	94	76.0	40	42.3	84.7	90.2	79.0	119	123	114	68	72	64
South Asia	**2,290**	**0.9**	**99**	**..**	**51**	**12.6**	**49.7**	**61.6**	**34.3**	**98**	**..**	**..**	**53**	**60**	**43**
Afghanistan	1,660	-1.3	72	..	..	20.0	..	..	..	31	46	16	..	..	..
Bangladesh	1,990	-0.3	88	89.2	59	11.3	37.3	48.4	24.3	111	128	105	39	45	34
Bhutan	..	..	128	102.0	..	25.0	41.1	..	..	70x	81x	60x	31x	..	..
India	2,330	0.6	101	104.3	52	9.0	51.2	64.5	36.1	105	113	91	56	63	47
Maldives	..	..	..	96.2	..	0.0	93.0	93.1	92.9	134	136	133	71	70	70
Nepal	2,140	0.6	100	92.4	57	44.2	27.0	39.7	12.8	107	129	87	55	68	42
Pakistan	2,340	0.3	99	122.0	37	32.4	37.1	49.0	23.3	65	80	49	38	50	25
Sri Lanka	2,230	-0.1	101	106.5	43	14.4	90.1	93.2	86.9	106	106	105	66	65	68
East Asia & the Pacific	**2,680**	**1.1**	**112**	**..**	**45**	**12.3**	**..**	**..**	**..**	**117**	**..**	**..**	**..**	**..**	**..**
Brunei	..	..	..	98.3	..	2.0	87.9	..	..	107	111	104	70	..	..
Burma (Myanmar)	2,580	1.1	114	127.5	..	18.0	82.7	88.6	76.8	..	..	..	48	48	47

	Food supply			Food production per capita	Food expenditures	Iodine deficiency	Adult literacy rate 1994			Educational enrollment (% of relevant age group)					
	Per capita dietary energy supply (DES) (calories/day) 1990-1992	DES annual growth rate 1969-1971 to 1990-1992	Daily per capita calorie supply (% of requirements) 1988-1990	(1989-1991 =100) 1995	(% of household consumption) 1980-1985	total goiter rate in school-age children (%) 1969-1992	Total	Male	Female	Primary school 1993			Combined primary, secondary and tertiary 1994		
										Total	Male	Female	Total	Male	Female
Cambodia	2,100	-0.8	96	81.3	..	15.0	35.0x	..	..	47x	..	..	58	..	..
China	2,710	1.4	112	113.3	61	9.2	80.9	89.6	70.9	109x	120	116	58	61	55
Fiji	..	..	..	96.9	..	47.0	91.3	93.7	89.2	..	128x	127x	79	80	78
Hong Kong[a]	3,150	0.8	125	57.1	12	..	92.3	96.0	89.1	102	..	..	72	72	73
Indonesia	2,700	1.3	121	112.0	48	27.7	83.2	89.4	77.1	114	116x	112x	62	65	59
Korea, N.	2,930	1.0	121	..	..	14.7	95.0x	..	..	..	..	..	75	..	..
Korea, S.	3,270	0.7	120	111.2	35	0.0	97.9	99.0	96.8	101	100	102	82	86	78
Laos	2,210	0.1	111	102.4	..	25.0	55.8	68.6	42.7	107	123	92	50	58	42
Malaysia	2,830	0.7	120	103.2	23	20.0	83.0	88.2	77.5	93	93	93	62	61	63
Mongolia	2,100	-0.3	97	70.1	..	7.0	82.2	87.9	75.8	..	..	..	52	45	59
Papua New Guinea	2,610	0.9	114	95.2	..	30.0	71.2	79.8	60.7	74	80x	67x	38	41	34
Philippines	2,290	1.2	104	103.7	51	14.7	94.4	94.8	93.9	111	..	..	78	75	80
Singapore	..	..	136	41.0	19	0.0	91.0	95.6	87.2	107	..	..	72	73	71
Solomon Islands	..	..	..	90.8	..	0.0	62.0	..	..	94	102	87	47	..	..
Thailand	2,380	0.4	103	104.0	30	12.2	93.5	95.6	90.7	98	98x	97x	53	53	53
Vietnam	2,200	0.0	103	111.2	..	20.0	93.0	95.7	89.9	111	..	..	55	57	52
Latin America & the Caribbean	**2,740**	**0.0**	**114**	**98.0**	**34**	**14.2**	**86.2**	**87.3**	**84.9**	**110**	**..**	**..**	**69**	**69**	**69**
Argentina	2,950	-0.5	131	103.8	35	8.3	96.0	96.0	96.0	107	108x	107x	77	76	79
Belize	..	..	..	118.2	..	0.0	70.0x	..	..	107	111x	107x	68	..	..
Bolivia	2,030	0.2	84	82.0	33	20.9	82.5	90.4	75.2	..	..	..	66	72	61
Brazil	2,790	0.6	114	106.6	35	14.1	82.7	82.8	82.5	111	..	..	72	72	72
Chile	2,540	-0.2	102	114.5	29	9.0	95.0	95.4	95.0	98	99	98	72	72	71
Colombia	2,630	1.2	106	92.5	29	10.0	91.1	91.1	91.3	119	118	120	70	67	72
Costa Rica	2,870	0.8	121	99.4	33	3.0	94.7	94.6	95.0	105	106	105	68	69	67
Cuba	3,000	0.6	135	61.5	..	10.0	95.4	95.9	94.8	104	104	104	63	61	65
Dominican Republic	2,270	0.6	102	90.8	46	..	81.5	81.2	81.2	97	95	99	68	67	69
Ecuador	2,540	0.8	105	94.2	30	10.0	89.6	91.8	87.8	123	124x	122x	72	73	71
El Salvador	2,530	1.5	102	102.1	33	24.6	70.9	72.8	68.7	79	79	80	55	55	55
Guatemala	2,280	0.4	103	89.5	36	20.4	55.7	62.2	48.3	84	89	78	46	50	42
Guyana	2,350	0.1	..	142.0	..	..	97.9	98.5	97.4	98	98	98	67	66	67
Haiti	1,740	-0.6	89	83.7	..	3.8	44.1	46.9	40.4	..	..	..	29	30	28
Honduras	2,310	0.4	98	88.6	39	8.8	72.0	71.7	71.6	112	111	112	60	59	61
Jamaica	2,580	0.1	114	110.2	36	..	84.4	79.6	88.4	109	109x	108x	65	64	67
Mexico	3,190	0.7	131	101.5	35	15.0	89.2	91.5	86.7	112	114	110	66	67	65
Nicaragua	2,290	-0.2	99	89.0	..	4.3	65.3	64.3	66.0	103	101	105	62	61	63
Panama	2,240	-0.1	98	96.70	38	13.2	90.5	91.2	89.7	105	..	..	70	69	71
Paraguay	2,620	-0.1	116	105.0	30	48.7	91.9	93.2	90.2	112	114	110	62	62	62
Peru	1,880	-1.0	87	110.6	35	35.8	88.3	94.5	82.2	119	..	..	81	84	77
Suriname	2,510	0.6	..	88.6	..	0.0	92.7	..	..	..	..	..	71	..	..
Trinidad and Tobago	2,630	0.3	114	101.3	19	0.0	97.9	98.6	97.2	94	94	94	67	67	67
Uruguay	2,680	-0.5	101	105.7	31	0.0	97.1	96.7	97.3	109	109	108	75	70	80
Venezuela	2,590	0.4	99	106.7	23	10.7	91.0	91.6	90.3	96	95x	97x	68	66	69
Middle East & North Africa	**2,960**	**0.3**	**123**	**..**	**39**	**21.0**	**..**	**..**	**..**	**97**	**..**	**..**	**..**	**..**	**..**
Algeria	2,900	2.2	123	101.7	..	8.5	59.4	71.8	43.5	103	111x	96x	66	70	61
Bahrain	..	..	..	98.2	..	0.0	84.4	87.7	77.6	111	109	112	85	83	87
Cyprus	..	..	..	114.3	..	..	94.0x	94.0x	94.0x	101	101	101	75	75	75
Egypt	3,340	1.4	132	107.4	49	5.2	50.5	62.6	36.7	97	105	89	69	75	63
Iran	2,760	1.4	125	117.7	37	30.0	68.6x	..	..	105	109	101	68	..	..
Iraq	2,270	0.0	128	94.2	..	7.3	56.8	69.5	42.2	91	98x	83x	53	59	46
Jordan	2,900	0.8	110	137.0	35	..	85.5	..	..	94	94x	95x	66	..	..
Kuwait	2,460	-0.3	..	132.9	..	0.0	77.8	80.4	72.6	..	..	..	57	56	57
Lebanon	3,260	1.6	127	105.4	..	15.0	92.0	94.3	89.5	115	117x	114x	75	74	76
Libya	3,290	1.4	140	74.6	..	6.3	75.0	88.9	57.2	110	110	110	91	91	90
Morocco	3,000	1.0	125	70.6	38	20.0	42.1	54.5	27.7	73	85x	60x	46	52	39
Oman	..	..	..	74.7	..	0.0	35.0x	..	..	85	87	82	60	..	..
Qatar	..	..	..	110.7	..	0.0	78.9	78.2	78.3	90	92	87	73	71	74
Saudi Arabia	2,730	1.8	121	80.6	..	0.0	61.8	70.6	47.6	75	78x	73x	56	59	53
Syria	3,220	1.5	126	107.8	..	73.0	69.8	84.8	53.0	105	111	99	64	68	59
Tunisia	3,260	1.7	131	81.0	37	4.3	65.2	77.9	50.4	118	123	113	67	71	64
Turkey	3,510	0.8	127	96.1	40	35.6	81.6	91.7	71.1	103	107x	98x	63	70	55
United Arab Emirates	3,370	0.3	..	129.8	..	0.0	78.6	78.0	77.9	110	112	108	82	80	85
West Bank and Gaza[a]	..	..	..	c	..	..	..	..	..	..	..	..	..	..	..
Yemen	2,160	0.9	..	..	..	32.0	41.1x	..	..	..	..	..	52	..	..

Table 2, continued: **Food, Nutrition and Education**

	Food supply: Per capita dietary energy supply (DES) (calories/day) 1990-1992	Food supply: DES annual growth rate 1969-1971 to 1990-1992	Food supply: Daily per capita calorie supply (% of requirements) 1988-1990	**Food production per capita** (1989-1991 =100) 1995	**Food expenditures** (% of household consumption) 1980-1985	**Iodine deficiency** total goiter rate in school-age children (%) 1969-1992	**Adult literacy rate** 1994: Total	Adult literacy rate 1994: Male	Adult literacy rate 1994: Female	**Educational enrollment** (% of relevant age group): Primary school 1993: Total	Primary school 1993: Male	Primary school 1993: Female	Combined primary, secondary and tertiary 1994: Total	Combined 1994: Male	Combined 1994: Female
Countries in Transition[b]	**3,230**	**-0.5**	**128**	**..**	**..**	**..**	**98.1**	**98.1**	**98.1**	**97**	**..**	**..**	**75**	**73**	**77**
Albania	2,630	0.3	107	132.2	..	40.8	85.0x	85.0x	85.0x	96	95	97	59	59	60
Armenia	..	..	..	..	..	10.0	98.8x	98.8x	98.8x	90	87	93	78	74	83
Azerbaijan	..	..	..	..	..	20.0	96.3x	96.3x	96.3x	89	91	87	72	74	71
Belarus	..	..	..	..	..	21.6	97.9x	97.9x	97.9x	96	96	95	80	79	81
Bosnia and Herzegovina	..	..	..	..	..	10.0	..	..	..	..	..	..	..	..	..
Bulgaria	3,160	-0.5	148	64.5	..	20.0	93.0x	93.0x	93.0x	92	87	84	66	64	69
Croatia	..	..	..	..	..	25.0	97.0	97.0x	97.0x	85	..	..	67	67	68
Czech Republic	..	..	..	..	..	2.5	99.0x	99.0x	99.0x	103	99	100	70	69	70
Estonia	..	..	..	..	..	..	99.0x	99.0x	99.0x	83	84	83	72	69	74
Georgia	..	..	..	..	..	20.0	94.9x	94.9x	94.9x	..	..	..	69	68	69
Hungary	3,560	0.3	137	72.3	25	0.0	99.0x	99.0x	99.0x	95	95	95	67	66	68
Kazakhstan	..	..	..	..	..	20.0	97.5x	97.5x	97.5x	86	86	86	73	71	75
Kyrgyzstan	..	..	..	..	..	20.0	97.0x	97.0x	97.0x	..	..	..	73	71	74
Latvia	..	..	..	..	..	..	99.0x	99.0x	99.0x	83	83	82	67	66	69
Lithuania	..	..	..	..	..	..	98.4x	98.4x	98.4x	92	95	90	70	68	72
Macedonia	..	..	..	..	..	..	94.0x	94.0x	94.0x	87	88	87	60	60	61
Moldova	..	..	..	..	..	..	98.9x	98.9x	98.9x	77	78	77	67	66	68
Poland	3,340	-0.2	131	83.7	29	10.0	99.0x	99.0x	99.0x	98	98	97	79	79	80
Romania	3,160	0.2	116	100.8	..	10.0	96.9x	96.9x	96.9x	95	87x	86x	62	62	62
Russia	..	..	..	..	..	10.0	98.7x	98.7x	98.7x	107	107	107	78	75	82
Slovakia	..	..	..	..	..	..	99.0x	99.0x	99.0x	101	101	101	72	71	73
Slovenia	..	..	..	..	..	15.0	96.0	96.0x	96.0x	97	97	97	74	72	76
Tajikistan	..	..	..	..	..	20.0	96.7	96.7	96.7	89	91	88	69	70	67
Turkmenistan	..	..	..	..	..	20.0	97.7x	97.7x	97.7x	..	..	..	90	90	90
Ukraine	..	..	..	..	..	10.0	98.8x	98.8x	98.8x	87	87	87	76	75	78
Uzbekistan	..	..	..	..	..	18.1	97.2x	97.2x	97.2x	80	80	79	73	75	71
Yugoslavia	..	..	..	..	..	5.0	..	..	..	..	72x	73x	..	..	..
Industrial Countries	**3,410**	**0.5**	**134**	**..**	**14**	**6.3**	**..**	**..**	**..**	**..**	**..**	**..**	**..**	**..**	**..**
Australia	3,180	0.0	124	105.3	13	0.0	99.0	99.0	99.0	108	108	107	79	77	80
Austria	3,530	0.4	133	95.4	16	0.0	99.0	99.0	99.0	103	103	103	87	88	85
Belgium	3,670d	0.6d	149	111.2d	15	5.0	99.0	99.0	99.0	99	99	100x	86	86	86
Canada	3,100	0.1	122	104.6	11	0.0	99.0	99.0	99.0	105	106x	104x	100	100x	100x
Denmark	3,620	0.6	135	104.6	13	5.0	99.0	99.0	99.0	98	97x	98x	89	87	90
Finland	3,030	-0.2	113	91.6	16	0.0	99.0	99.0	99.0	100	100	100	97	92	100
France	3,640	0.4	143	97.0	16	5.0	99.0	99.0	99.0	106	107	105	89	87	91
Germany	3,410	0.3	..	84.6	12	10.0	99.0	99.0	99.0	97	97	98	81	83	79
Greece	3,770	0.8	151	101.1	30	10.0	96.7x	96.7x	96.7x	..	..	..	82	83	80
Ireland	3,790	0.5	157	103.8	22	0.0	99.0	99.0	99.0	103	103x	103x	88	87	89
Israel	3,140	0.1	125	97.3	21	0.0	95.0x	95.0x	95.0x	95	95x	96x	75	74	76
Italy	3,540	0.2	139	99.0	19	20.0	98.1x	98.1x	98.1x	98	98	99	73	72	74
Japan	2,900	0.4	125	93.9	17	0.0	99.0	99.0	99.0	102	102	102	78	79	77
Luxembourg	..	..	..	..	..	0.0	99.0x	99.0x	99.0x	..	..	..	58	57	59
Netherlands	3,170	0.2	114	100.4	13	2.5	99.0	99.0	99.0	97	96x	99x	91	93	88
New Zealand	3,580	0.4	131	104.7	12	0.0	99.0	99.0	99.0	102	102	101	94	91	96
Norway	3,230	0.3	120	98.6	15	0.0	99.0	99.0	99.0	99	99	99	92	92	93
Portugal	3,620	0.9	136	90.3	34	15.0	89.6x	89.6x	89.6x	120	122x	118x	81	77	84
Spain	3,680	1.3	141	84.3	24	10.0	97.1x	97.1	97.1	104	104	105	90	87	94
Sweden	2,960	0.1	111	91.1	13	0.0	99.0	99.0	99.0	100	100	100	82	81	84
Switzerland	3,380	-0.2	130	88.4	17	0.0	99.0	99.0	99.0	101	100	102	76	78	73
United Kingdom	3,280	0.0	130	98.4	12	0.0	99.0	99.0	99.0	112	112x	113x	86	85	86
United States	3,700	0.6	138	104.2	10	0.0	99.0	99.0	99.0	107	107	106	96	93	98
World	**2,720**	**0.5**	**112**	**107.5**	**..**	**..**	**77.1**	**83.5**	**70.8**	**104**	**..**	**..**	**60**	**64**	**57**

.. Data not available.

a Territory.

b Central and Eastern European countries and the newly independent states of the former Soviet Union.

c Gaza, 80; West Bank, 115.

d Luxembourg included.

The number '0' (zero) means zero or less than half the unit shown.

x Data refer to a period other than specified in the column heading, mostly more recent.

Table 3 Regional Prevalence of Anemia, 1997

Region	Children (% affected)		Women 15-59 years (% affected)			Men 15-59 years (% affected)	Elderly 60 years and above (% affected)	Regional and world total	
	0-4 years	5-14 years	Pregnant	Non-pregnant	Total			Population affected (thousands)	% affected
Sub-Saharan Africa	33.1	52.0	46.9	36.6	37.9	28.0e	47.0	233,714	38.8
Americas	17.7	27.3	33.0	22.2	23.3	8.3	14.7	141,742	18.1
Industrialized	4.7	2.7	17.0	10.0	11.0	4.0	12.0	21,712	7.3
Non industrialized	22.9	36.9	39.0	30.0	31.0	11.0	18.0	120,022	24.5
Europe	11.0e	10.0	17.0	10.0	11.0	5.0	12.0	79,797	9.2
Middle East and North Africa	38.3	30.8	63.9	49.0	51.1	32.7	46.9	179,481	38.5
Southeast Asia[a]	52.7	63.9	79.6	57.0	60.0	42.4	59.3	765,161	52.7
Western Pacific[b]	14.1	53.9	37.3	31.5	31.7	33.1	48.2	587,424	36.2
Industrialized	5.0e	5.0e	17.0	10.0	11.0	4.0	12.0	11,307	7.9
Non industrialized	14.7	56.9	38.5	33.8	33.8	36.0	55.0	576,263	38.4
TOTAL	**31.0**	**45.8**	**47.8**	**33.0**	**34.4**	**27.3**	**35.1**	**1,987,319**	**34.3**

a Bangladesh, Bhutan, Burma (Myanmar), India, Indonesia, Maldives, Mongolia, Nepal, North Korea, Sri Lanka and Thailand.

b Australia, Brunei, Cambodia, China, Cook Islands, Fiji, Japan, Kiribati, Laos, Malaysia, Marshall Islands, Micronesia, Nauru, New Zealand, Niue, Papua New Guinea, Philippines, Samoa, Singapore, Solomon Islands, South Korea, Tokelau, Tonga, Tuvalu, Vanuatu and Vietnam.

e Estimate.

Table 4 Hunger, Malnutrition and Poverty

	Undernourished population: Number of undernourished people (millions) 1990-1992	Proportion of population undernourished (%) 1969-1971	Proportion of population undernourished (%) 1990-1992	Relative inadequacy of food supply % below minimum required 1990-1992	% under-5 (1990-1997) suffering from: Underweight moderate & severe	Underweight severe	Wasting moderate & severe	Stunting moderate & severe	% population with access to safe water 1990-1996 Total	Urban	Rural	Population in Poverty (%): Below national poverty line 1984-1996 National	Urban	Rural	Below international poverty line ($1 a day; 1985 PPP$) 1981-1996
Developing Countries	**841.0**	**35**	**20**	**4.7**	**32.0**	**10.0**	**9.0**	**39.0**	..	..	..	..	..	..	**32.0**
Africa (sub-Saharan)	**215.0**	**38**	**43**	..	**30.0**	**9.0**	**8.0**	**41.0**	**47**	..	..	..	..	..	**39.0**h
Angola	5.1	39	54	19.6	..	..	..	..	32	69	15	..	..	..	..
Benin	1.0	36	20	4.3	29.2	7.4	14.3	25.0	70	82	63	33.0	..	..	..
Botswana	0.4	34	29	7.3	15.0x	..	..	44.0x	70	100	53	..	..	..	34.7
Burkina Faso	3.8	66	41	12.4	32.7	9.3	13.2	33.3	78	..	..	..	..	..	..
Burundi	2.9	42	50	17.6	37.5	10.0	5.7	47.4	58	97	55	36.2	..	..	..
Cameroon	5.1	29	43	13.3	15.1	3.8	2.9	26.0	41	71	24	40.0	44.4	32.4	..
Cape Verde	..	..	..	..	18.8	..	3.3	25.8	52	75	34	44.0	..	..	..
Central African Republic	1.9	28	62	25.5	23.2	6.0	6.4	28.4	38	59	23	..	..	..	..
Chad	3.5	40	61	25.0	31.0	..	..	..	24	48	17	..	..	..	..
Comoros	..	..	..	..	25.8	7.9	8.3	33.8	48	..	..	..	..	..	..
Congo (Brazzaville)	0.8	42	34	9.2	23.9	4.7	5.5	27.5	60	94	8	..	..	..	..
Côte d'Ivoire	2.7	24	22	5.0	23.8	6.3	8.3	24.4	82	97	73	..	..	..	17.7
Djibouti	..	..	..	..	22.9	8.8	10.7	22.2	24	27	14	..	..	..	..
Equatorial Guinea	..	..	..	..	..	..	..	..	..	10	48	..	..	..	..
Eritrea	..	..	..	..	41.0	..	10.0	66.0	..	..	7	..	..	..	..
Ethiopia	31.2	59	65	28.0	47.7	16.0	8.0	64.2	27	90	20	..	..	..	33.8
Gabon	0.3	39	24	5.7	..	..	..	..	67	80	30	..	..	..	..
Gambia	0.3	36	29	7.5	..	..	..	..	61	87	86	64.0	..	..	..
Ghana	6.2	34	40	12.0	27.3	7.9	11.3	25.9	56	76	46	31.4	26.7	34.3	..
Guinea	1.5	35	25	5.8	26.0	9.0	12.0	32.0	49	78	51	..	..	..	26.3
Guinea-Bissau	..	..	..	..	23.0x	..	..	..	27	18	47	48.8	24.1	60.9	87.0
Kenya	11.3	33	46	15.1	22.5	5.6	7.8	33.6	49	74	43	42.0	29.3	46.4	50.2
Lesotho	0.6	49	35	10.0	21.4	2x	15.8	32.9	57	90	40	49.2	27.8	53.9	50.4
Liberia	1.6	34	59	23.0	..	..	..	..	46	79	13	..	..	..	..
Madagascar	3.8	20	31	8.0	34.1	9.9	7.4	49.8	32	55	10	59.0	..	..	72.3
Malawi	4.8	26	49	16.4	29.9	8.7	7.0	48.3	54	91	41	..	..	..	..
Mali	3.3	45	34	9.5	40.0	16.5	23.3	30.1	44	42	25	..	..	..	..
Mauritania	0.4	52	20	4.4	23.0	9.2	7.2	44.0	41	49	86	57.0	..	..	31.4
Mauritius	0.2	31	18	4.0	14.9	2.0	13.7	9.7	99	95	100	10.6	..	..	..
Mozambique	9.6	55	66	29.2	27.0	11.0	8.0	55.0	28	44	17	..	..	..	..
Namibia	0.5	36	35	9.6	26.2	5.8	8.6	28.5	57	97	37	..	..	..	..
Niger	2.9	48	37	10.4	42.6	15.0	15.0	39.5	57	58	54	..	..	..	61.5
Nigeria	42.9	26	38	11.1	35.3	11.8	8.9	42.7	43	69	11	34.1	30.4	36.4	28.9
Rwanda	3.4	35	47	14.5	29.4	6.0	3.8	48.7	..	..	79	51.2	..	..	45.7
Senegal	2.3	24	30	7.9	22.2	5.6	8.4	24.7	52	85	28	..	..	..	54.0
Sierra Leone	2.4	34	55	19.9	28.7	..	8.5	34.7	34	58	21	75.0	..	..	..
Somalia	6.4	59	72	35.1	..	..	..	..	31	..	28	..	..	..	..
South Africa	..	..	..	..	9.2	1.4	2.5	22.8	99	99	53	..	..	..	23.7
Sudan	9.7	36	37	10.9	33.9	11.0	13.1	34.3	60	84	41	..	..	..	..
Swaziland	0.1	26	13	2.5	9.7	..	0.9	30.3	60	80	42	..	..	..	..
Tanzania	10.3	60	38	11.1	28.9	7.2	6.0	43.2	49	65	45	51.1	..	..	16.4
Togo	1.1	30	30	7.8	24.5	5.9	5.3	29.2	67	64	54	32.3	..	..	..
Uganda	5.8	29	32	8.5	25.5	6.7	5.3	38.3	38	60	35	55.0	..	..	50.0
Zaire (Congo-Kinshasa)	14.9	36	39	11.2	34.4	10.2	9.6	45.2	42	89	26	..	..	..	..
Zambia	3.6	34	43	13.3	25.2	5.7	5.1	39.8	47	76	43	86.0	..	..	84.6
Zimbabwe	4.2	35	41	12.4	15.5	3.0	5.5	21.4	74	99	65	25.5	..	..	41.0
South Asia	**267.9**e	**33**f	**23**e	..	**52.0**	**20.0**	**16.0**	**53.0**	**63**	**84**	**80**	..	..	..	**43.0**
Afghanistan	12.9	37	73	34.2	..	..	..	..	10	38	17	..	..	..	..
Bangladesh	39.4	23	34	8.8	68.3	24.9	16.7	64.2	83	47	85	47.5	46.7	47.6	29.0
Bhutan	..	..	..	..	37.9	..	4.1	56.1	21	54	26	..	..	..	..
India	184.5	36	21	4.9	53.4	20.6	17.5	52.0	63	87	85	..	..	..	52.5
Maldives	..	..	..	..	39.0	8.3	16.0	30.1	69	57	85	..	..	..	..
Nepal	5.9	45	29	7.3	46.9	16.1	11.2	48.4	48	64	49	42.0	23.0	44.0	53.1
Pakistan	20.5	24	17	3.5	38.2	12.8	9.0	50.0	60	85	47	34.0	28.0	36.9	11.6
Sri Lanka	4.6	21	26	6.4	37.7	7.0	15.5	23.8	57	87	49	22.4	18.3	24.4	4.0
East Asia and the Pacific	**269.0**	**41**	**16**	..	**23.0**	**4.0**	**5.0**	**34.0**	**49**	..	..	..	..	..	**26.0**
Brunei	..	..	..	..	..	..	..	..	..	100	90	..	..	..	..
Burma (Myanmar)	5.2	34	12	2.3	42.9	15.8	8.0	45.0	39	38	36	..	..	..	..
Cambodia	2.5	13	29	7.1	40.0	7.0	8.0	38.0	13	20	12	..	..	..	..
China	188.9	45	16	3.5	17.4	2.9	3.4	31.4	67	97	56	8.6	0.4	11.5	29.4

Table 4, continued: **Hunger, Malnutrition and Poverty**

	Undernourished population			Relative inadequacy of food supply	% under-5 (1990-1997) suffering from:				% population with access to safe water			Population in Poverty (%)			
	Number of undernourished people (millions)	Proportion of population undernourished (%)			Underweight		Wasting	Stunting	1990-1996			Below national poverty line 1984-1996			Below international poverty line ($1 a day; 1985 PPP$)
	1990-1992	1969-1971	1990-1992	% below minimum required 1990-1992	moderate & severe	severe	moderate & severe	moderate & severe	Total	Urban	Rural	National	Urban	Rural	1981-1996
Fiji	..	..	..	..	7.9	0.8	8.2	2.7	77	..	..	..	..	..	..
Hong Kong[a]	0.3	13	5	0.8	0.3	..	2.0	3.0	100	100	96	..	..	..	..
Indonesia	22.1	34	12	2.2	39.9	7.5	..	..	63	86	56	15.1	16.8	14.3	14.5
Korea, N.	2.0	20	9	1.6	..	..	..	..	100	100	100	..	..	..	..
Korea, S.	0.3	2	1	0.1	..	..	..	..	93	100	76	..	..	..	..
Laos	1.1	29	24	5.6	40.0	11.7	10.5	47.3	41	34	36	46.1	24.0	53.0	..
Malaysia	1.3	14	7	1.1	20.1	0.6	..	..	90	100	80	15.5	..	..	5.6
Mongolia	0.7	23	32	8.4	12.3	2.4	1.7	26.4	80	100	58	36.3	38.5	33.1	..
Papua New Guinea	0.4	27	10	1.9	29.9	6.4	5.5	43.2	31	97	18	..	..	..	..
Philippines	13.1	54	21	4.5	29.6	5.0	7.5	32.7	86	92	80	54.0	39.0	71.0	27.5
Singapore	..	..	..	..	..	..	..	..	100x	100x	..	..	..	..	..
Solomon Islands	..	..	..	..	21.3	3.6	6.6	27.3	..	80	62	..	..	..	..
Thailand	14.4	28	26	6.5	25.3	4.0	5.3	21.5	81	89	72	13.1	10.2	15.5	0.1
Vietnam	17.2	24	25	6.0	44.9	11.0	11.6	46.9	38	100	66	50.9	25.9	57.2	..
Latin America and the Caribbean	**64.0**	**19**	**15**	..	**11.0**	**2.0**	**3.0**	**20.0**	**80**	**89**	**57**	..	..	..	**24.0**
Argentina	2.9	4	9	1.6	1.9	0.0	1.1	4.7	64	73	17	25.5	..	..	..
Belize	..	..	..	..	6.2	1.3	..	..	82	95	53	35.0	..	..	..
Bolivia	2.9	43	40	11.9	14.9	3.4	4.2	26.8	60	82	21	..	..	..	7.1
Brazil	9.7	14	6	1.1	5.7	0.6	2.3	10.5	92	99	68	17.4	13.1	32.6	28.7
Chile	2.9	17	22	5.1	0.9	..	0.3	2.4	96	100	31	..	..	..	15.0
Colombia	5.9	38	18	3.9	8.4	0.9	1.4	15.0	96	90	90	18.8	9.9	31.2	7.4
Costa Rica	0.4	25	12	2.2	2.2	0.2	2.0	8.0	96	100	92	11.0	..	..	18.9
Cuba	1.0	15	9	1.7	1.5	0.1	0.4	3.1	94	100	91	..	..	..	..
Dominican Republic	2.4	44	32	8.6	10.3	1.7	1.4	16.5	79	75	40	20.6	..	..	19.9
Ecuador	2.0	32	19	4.1	16.5	0.0x	1.7	34.0	70	79	45	35.0	25.0	47.0	30.4
El Salvador	1.0	50	19	4.1	11.2	1.2	1.3	23.1	62	95	16	48.3	43.1	55.7	..
Guatemala	2.4	35	26	6.3	26.6	5.9	3.3	49.7	64	84	51	58.0	..	..	53.3
Guyana	0.2	22	24	5.6	18.3	2.2	..	..	83	100	75	43.0	..	..	..
Haiti	4.6	56	69	32.4	27.5	8.1	7.8	31.9	28	55	34	65.0	..	..	..
Honduras	1.1	27	21	4.6	18.3	3.2	2.0	39.6	70	90	54	50.0	56.0	46.0	46.5
Jamaica	0.6	21	23	5.6	10.2	2.7	3.5	9.6	70	92	48	34.2	..	..	4.7
Mexico	7.2	15	8	1.4	14.2	2.9	6.0	22.8	87	90	66	10.1	..	..	14.9
Nicaragua	1.0	22	25	5.9	11.9	1.0	1.9	23.7	57	74	30	50.3	31.9	76.1	43.8
Panama	0.5	12	19	4.1	7.0	1.0	1.0	9.0	82	..	..	..	..	..	25.6
Paraguay	0.6	12	15	2.9	3.7	0.5	0.3	13.9	42	70	10	21.8	19.7	28.5	..
Peru	10.7	20	49	15.9	10.7	1.7	1.7	31.8	60	76	24	54.0	50.3	68.0	49.4
Suriname	0.1	31	21	4.9	..	..	..	..	72	78	54	..	..	..	..
Trinidad and Tobago	0.1	15	11	2.1	6.5	0.4	3.8	4.8	82	83	80	21.0	..	..	..
Uruguay	0.3	3	8	1.5	4.4	0.7	1.4	9.5	83	93	5x	..	..	..	..
Venezuela	4.0	25	20	4.6	4.5	0.7	2.9	13.2	88	68	67	31.3	..	..	11.8
Middle East & North Africa	**24.1**e	**27**g	**8**e	..	**16.0**	**4.0**	**7.0**	**24.0**	**85**	**98**	**70**	..	..	..	**4.0**h
Algeria	2.4	52	9	1.6	12.8	3.4	8.9	18.3	78	91	64	..	..	..	1.6
Bahrain	..	..	..	..	7.2	0.8	5.5	9.9	100	100	100	..	..	..	..
Cyprus	..	..	..	..	..	..	..	..	100	100	99	..	..	..	..
Egypt	3.2	24	6	0.9	12.4	2.6	4.6	29.8	84	95	74	..	..	..	7.6
Iran	4.2	32	7	1.2	15.7	..	6.6	18.9	89	100	75	..	..	..	..
Iraq	4.0	21	21	4.8	11.9	2.3	3.4	21.8	45	100	85	..	..	..	..
Jordan	0.1	11	3	0.5	6.4	0.8	3.1	15.8	89	98	94	15.0	..	..	2.5
Kuwait	0.3	7	16	4.1	6.4	..	2.6	12.2	..	..	..	..	..	..	..
Lebanon	0.1	27	5	0.8	3.0	..	2.9	12.2	94	96	88	..	..	..	..
Libya	0.2	20	3	0.5	4.7	..	2.8	15.1	97	97	97	..	..	..	..
Morocco	2.6	23	10	1.8	9.5	2.0	2.2	24.2	59	100	18	13.1	7.6	18.0	1.1
Oman	..	..	..	..	14.1	0.9	9.1	15.7	56	98	56	..	..	..	..
Qatar	..	..	..	..	5.5	..	1.5	8.1	100	100	100	..	..	..	..
Saudi Arabia	1.9	51	12	2.4	..	..	..	..	93	98	54	..	..	..	..
Syria	0.4	20	3	0.4	12.1	3.0	8.1	26.6	87	95	77	..	..	..	..
Tunisia	0.2	23	3	0.4	9.0	2x	3.9	22.5	86	100	67	14.1	..	..	3.9
Turkey	1.8	9	3	0.5	10.3	3.4	3.0	21.0	92	100	85	..	..	..	..
United Arab Emirates	0.1	5	4	0.6	..	..	..	..	98	98	98	..	..	..	..
West Bank and Gaza[a]	..	..	..	..	..	..	..	..	..	..	..	..	..	..	..
Yemen	3.0	51	24	5.6	30.0	4.3	12.7	44.1	52	88	17	19.1	18.6	19.2	..
Countries in Transition[b]	..	..	..	..	..	..	..	..	..	..	..	..	..	..	..
Albania	..	..	..	..	..	..	..	..	..	..	..	19.6	..	..	..
Armenia	..	..	..	..	..	..	..	..	..	..	..	..	..	..	..

Table 4, continued: **Hunger, Malnutrition and Poverty**

	Undernourished population			**Relative inadequacy of food supply**	**% under-5 (1990-1997) suffering from:**				**% population with access to safe water**			**Population in Poverty (%)**			
	Number of undernourished people (millions)	Proportion of population undernourished (%)		% below minimum required	**Underweight**		**Wasting**	**Stunting**	1990-1996			Below national poverty line 1984-1996			Below international poverty line ($1 a day; 1985 PPP$)
	1990-1992	1969-1971	1990-1992	1990-1992	moderate & severe	severe	moderate & severe	moderate & severe	Total	Urban	Rural	National	Urban	Rural	1981-1996
Azerbaijan	..	..	..	..	10.1	2.3	2.9	22.2	..	..	..	..	..	..	..
Belarus	..	..	..	..	..	..	..	..	..	..	..	37.0	..	..	23.0d
Bosnia and Herzegovina	..	..	..	..	..	..	..	..	..	..	..	..	..	..	..
Bulgaria	..	..	..	..	..	..	..	..	..	..	..	..	..	..	2.6
Croatia	..	..	..	..	..	..	..	..	96	98	74	..	..	..	..
Czech Republic	..	..	..	..	1.0	0.0	2.1	1.9	..	..	..	..	..	..	3.1
Estonia	..	..	..	..	..	..	..	..	..	..	..	8.9	6.8	14.7	6.0
Georgia	..	..	..	..	..	..	..	..	..	..	..	30.0	..	..	..
Hungary	..	..	..	..	2.2	0.2	1.6	2.9	..	..	..	25.3	..	..	0.7
Kazakhstan	..	..	..	..	8.3	1.5	3.3	15.8	..	..	..	..	..	..	50.0d
Kyrgyzstan	..	..	..	..	..	..	7.0	..	75	84	..	45.4	32.0	52.2	18.9
Latvia	..	..	..	..	..	..	..	..	..	..	..	..	..	..	23.0d
Lithuania	..	..	..	..	..	..	..	..	..	..	..	..	..	..	2.1
Macedonia	..	..	..	..	..	..	..	..	..	..	..	..	24.0	28.0	..
Moldova	..	..	..	..	..	..	..	..	55	98	18	..	..	..	6.8
Poland	..	..	..	..	..	..	..	..	..	..	..	23.8	..	..	6.8
Romania	..	..	..	..	5.7	0.6	2.5	7.8	..	..	..	21.5	15.6	28.0	17.7
Russia	..	..	..	..	3.0	0.5	3.9	12.7	..	..	..	30.9	..	..	1.1
Slovakia	..	..	..	..	..	..	..	..	..	..	..	..	..	..	12.8
Slovenia	..	..	..	..	..	..	..	..	..	..	..	..	..	..	1.0d
Tajikistan	..	..	..	..	..	..	..	30.0	..	82	49	..	..	..	..
Turkmenistan	..	..	..	..	..	..	..	..	85	..	..	..	..	..	4.9
Ukraine	..	..	..	..	..	..	..	..	97	..	..	31.7	..	..	41.0d
Uzbekistan	..	..	..	..	..	..	..	..	62	82	49	..	..	..	29.0d
Yugoslavia	..	..	..	..	..	..	..	..	..	..	..	..	..	..	..
Industrial Countries	**..**	**..**	**..**	**..**	**..**	**..**	**..**	**..**	**..**	**..**	**..**	**..**	**..**	**..**	**..**
Australia	..	..	..	..	..	..	..	..	95	..	..	..	..	..	8.0c
Austria	..	..	..	..	..	..	..	..	..	..	..	..	..	..	..
Belgium	..	..	..	..	..	..	..	..	..	..	..	..	..	..	12.0c
Canada	..	..	..	..	..	..	..	..	100	..	..	..	..	..	6.0c
Denmark	..	..	..	..	..	..	..	..	100	..	100	..	..	..	8.0c
Finland	..	..	..	..	..	..	..	..	100	100	100	..	..	..	4.0c
France	..	..	..	..	..	..	..	..	100	100	100	..	..	..	12.0c
Germany	..	..	..	..	..	..	..	..	..	..	..	..	..	..	12.0c
Greece	..	..	..	..	..	..	..	..	..	..	..	..	..	..	..
Ireland	..	..	..	..	..	..	..	..	..	..	..	..	..	..	37.0c
Israel	..	..	..	..	..	..	..	..	99	..	..	..	..	..	..
Italy	..	..	..	..	..	..	..	..	..	..	..	..	..	..	2.0c
Japan	..	..	..	..	..	..	..	..	97	100	85	..	..	..	5.0c
Luxembourg	..	..	..	..	..	..	..	..	..	..	..	..	..	..	4.0c
Netherlands	..	..	..	..	..	..	..	..	100	100	100	..	..	..	14.0c
New Zealand	..	..	..	..	..	..	..	..	97	100	82	..	..	..	..
Norway	..	..	..	..	..	..	..	..	100	..	..	..	..	..	3.0c
Portugal	..	..	..	..	..	..	..	..	..	..	..	..	..	..	..
Spain	..	..	..	..	..	..	..	..	99	..	..	..	..	..	21.0c
Sweden	..	..	..	..	..	..	..	..	..	..	..	..	..	..	5.0c
Switzerland	..	..	..	..	..	..	..	..	100	100	..	..	..	..	..
United Kingdom	..	..	..	..	..	..	..	..	100	100	100	..	..	..	13.0c
United States	..	..	..	..	..	..	..	..	90	..	..	..	..	..	14.0c
World	**..**	**..**	**..**	**..**	**28.7**	**9.0**	**8.5**	**35.3**	**76**	**..**	**..**	**..**	**..**	**..**	**..**

.. Data not available.
a Territory.
b Central and Eastern European countries and the newly independent states of the former Soviet Union.
c Poverty line is $14.40 (1985 PPP$) per person per day.
d Poverty line is $4.00 (1990 PPP$) per person per day.
e Bread for the World Institute estimate.
f Afghanistan not included.
g Afghanistan included.
h Djibouti, Somalia and Sudan are included in Middle East and North Africa.
The number '0' (zero) means zero or less than half the unit of measure.
x Indicates data that refer to years or periods other than those specified in the column heading, differ from the standard definition or refer to only part of a country.

Table 5 **Economic and Development Indicators**

	GNP per capita: US$ 1995	GNP per capita: Purchasing Power Parity (PPP$) 1995	GNP per capita: GNP per capita real growth rate (%) 1970-1995	Human Development Index (HDI) rank[c] 1997	Distribution of income or consumption by quintiles[k] 1978-1995: Lowest 20%	Second quintile	Third quintile	Fourth quintile	Highest 20%	Ratio of highest 20% to lowest 20%[*]	Central government expenditure (% of GDP) 1995	Education & health[*] (% of central government expenditure) 1992-1995	Military expenditure (% of combined education and health expenditure) 1990-1991	Per capita energy consumption (kg. of oil equivalent) 1994	Annual deforestation (% of total forest) 1990-1995
Developing Countries	..	..	..	..	..	..	..	..	..	..	..	..	**63**	..	..
Africa (sub-Saharan)	..	..	..	**8**	**5.2**	..	..	..	**52.4**	**10.08**	..	..	..	**237**	**0.7**e
Angola	410	1,310	..	157	..	..	..	..	..	..	..	..	208	89	1.0
Benin	370	1,760	0.1	146	..	..	..	..	..	..	..	..	..	20	1.2
Botswana	3,020	5,580	7.3	97	..	..	..	..	..	..	46.2x	25.2	22	387	0.5
Burkina Faso	230	780	1.5	172	..	..	..	..	..	..	..	24.2	30	16	0.7
Burundi	160	630	0.6	169	..	..	..	..	..	..	..	..	42	23	0.4
Cameroon	650	2,110	1.5	133	..	..	..	..	..	..	15.9x	22.8	48	103	0.6
Cape Verde	960	1,870	5.7x	123	..	..	..	..	..	..	..	..	..	..	-24.0
Central African Republic	340	1,070	-1.6	151	..	..	..	..	..	..	..	..	33	29	0.4
Chad	180	700	-0.1	164	..	..	..	..	..	..	..	..	74	16	0.8
Comoros	470	1,320	-0.6x	140	..	..	..	..	..	..	..	..	..	..	5.6
Congo (Brazzaville)	680	2,050	1.7	130	..	..	..	..	..	..	..	..	37	331	0.2
Côte d'Ivoire	660	1,580	-1.9	145	6.8	11.2	15.8	22.2	44.1	6.49	..	..	14	103	0.6
Djibouti	i	..	..	162	..	..	..	..	..	..	..	..	..	..	0.0
Equatorial Guinea	380	..	..	135	..	..	..	..	..	..	..	..	..	..	0.5
Eritrea	f	..	..	168	..	..	..	..	..	..	..	..	..	..	0.0
Ethiopia	100	450	..	170	..	..	..	..	..	..	27.4x	13.8	190	22	0.5
Gabon	3,490	..	-2.8	120	..	..	..	..	..	..	..	..	51	652	0.5
Gambia	320	930	0.2x	165	..	..	..	..	..	..	20.4x	19.2	11	56	0.9
Ghana	390	1,990	-1.2	132	7.9	12.0	16.1	21.8	42.2	5.34	20.6x	29.0	12	93	1.3
Guinea	550	..	..	167	3.0	8.3	14.6	23.9	50.2	16.73	..	..	37	65	1.1
Guinea-Bissau	250	790	0.1	163	2.1	6.5	12.0	20.6	58.9	28.05	..	..	..	37	0.4
Kenya	280	1,380	1.0	134	3.4	6.7	10.7	17.0	62.1	18.26	27.5x	24.3	24	110	0.3
Lesotho	770	1,780	2.3	137	2.8	6.5	11.2	19.4	60.1	21.46	47.3x	33.4	48	..	0.0
Liberia	f	..	-3.0x	..	..	..	..	..	..	..	..	..	..	..	0.6
Madagascar	230	640	-2.4	152	5.8	9.9	14.0	20.3	50.0	8.62	17.2	23.7	37	36	0.8
Malawi	170	750	-0.2	161	..	..	..	..	..	..	..	..	24	39	1.6
Mali	250	550	0.2	171	..	..	..	..	..	..	..	..	53	22	1.0
Mauritania	460	1,540	-0.7	150	3.6	10.6	16.2	23.0	46.5	12.92	..	..	40	103	0.0
Mauritius	3,380	13,210	0.5x	61	..	..	..	..	..	..	23.3	25.8	4	387	0.0
Mozambique	80	810	-0.2x	166	..	..	..	..	..	..	..	..	121	40	0.7
Namibia	2,000	4,150	..	118	..	..	..	..	..	..	40.7x	..	23	..	0.3
Niger	220	750	-2.6x	173	7.5	11.8	15.5	21.1	44.1	5.88	..	..	11	37	0.0
Nigeria	260	1,220	-0.9	141	4.0	8.9	14.4	23.4	49.3	12.33	..	..	33	162	0.9
Rwanda	180	540	-0.2	174	9.7	13.2	16.5	21.6	39.1	4.03	24.2x	..	25	34	0.2
Senegal	600	1,780	-0.6x	160	3.5	7.0	11.6	19.3	58.6	16.74	..	..	33	97	0.7
Sierra Leone	180	580	-1.1	175	..	..	..	..	..	..	20.2x	22.9	23	77	3.0
Somalia	f	..	-0.3x	..	..	..	..	..	..	..	..	..	..	..	0.2
South Africa	3,160	5,030	-0.6x	90	3.3	5.8	9.8	17.7	63.3	19.18	33.3x	..	41	2,146	0.2
Sudan	f	..	-0.7x	158	..	..	..	..	..	..	..	..	44	66	0.8
Swaziland	1,170	2,880	1.2	114	..	..	..	..	..	..	..	..	11	..	0.0
Tanzania	120	640	..	149	6.9	10.9	15.3	21.5	45.4	6.58	..	..	77	34	1.0
Togo	310	1,130	-1.1	147	..	..	..	..	..	..	..	..	39	46	1.4
Uganda	240	1,470	..	159	6.8	10.3	14.4	20.4	48.1	7.07	..	..	18	23	0.9
Zaire (Congo-Kinshasa)	120	490	-4.0x	142	..	..	..	..	..	..	..	1.3	71	45	0.7
Zambia	400	930	-2.6	143	3.9	8.0	13.8	23.8	50.4	12.92	16.8	29.2	63	149	0.8
Zimbabwe	540	2,030	-0.3	129	4.0	6.3	10.0	17.4	62.3	15.58	..	..	66	438	0.6
South Asia	..	..	..	**7**	**8.8**	..	..	..	**39.9**	**4.53**	..	**4.5**	**61**	**222**	**0.3**e
Afghanistan	f	..	..	..	..	..	..	..	..	..	..	..	..	..	6.8
Bangladesh	240	1,380	1.5	144	9.4	13.5	17.2	22.0	37.9	4.03	..	..	41	64	0.8
Bhutan	420	1,260	5.5x	155	..	..	..	..	..	..	..	18.5	..	..	0.3
India	340	1,400	2.4	138	8.5	12.1	15.8	21.1	42.6	5.01	16.1	3.7	65	248	0.0
Maldives	990	3,080	..	111	..	..	..	..	..	..	..	..	..	..	..
Nepal	200	1,170	1.3	154	7.6	11.5	15.1	21.0	44.8	5.89	17.5	15.5	35	28	1.1
Pakistan	460	2,230	2.9	139	8.4	12.9	16.9	22.2	39.7	4.73	23.2	..	125	254	2.9
Sri Lanka	700	3,250	3.2	91	8.9	13.1	16.9	21.7	39.3	4.42	28.3	17.0	107	97	1.1
East Asia and the Pacific	..	..	..	..	**6.9**	..	..	..	**44.3**	**6.42**	..	..	..	**593**	**0.5**e
Brunei	h	..	..	38	..	..	..	..	..	..	..	..	125	..	0.6
Burma (Myanmar)	f	..	1.2x	131	..	..	..	..	..	..	11.0x	20.0	222	49	1.4
Cambodia	270	..	..	153	..	..	..	..	..	..	..	..	..	52	1.6
China	620	2,920	6.9	108	5.5	9.8	14.9	22.3	47.5	8.64	9.4x	3.3	114	664	0.1
Fiji	2,440	5,780	0.9	46	..	..	..	..	..	..	27.5	27.8	37	..	0.4

Table 5, continued: **Economic and Development Indicators**

	GNP per capita: US$ 1995	GNP per capita: Purchasing Power Parity (PPP$) 1995	GNP per capita: GNP per capita real growth rate (%) 1970-1995	Human Development Index (HDI) rank[c] 1997	Distribution of income or consumption by quintiles[k] 1978-1995: Lowest 20%	Second quintile	Third quintile	Fourth quintile	Highest 20%	Ratio of highest 20% to lowest 20%[e]	Central government expenditure (% of GDP) 1995	Education & health[a] (% of central government expenditure) 1992-1995	Military expenditure (% of combined education and health expenditure) 1990-1991	Per capita energy consumption (kg. of oil equivalent) 1994	Annual deforestation (% of total forest) 1990-1995
Hong Kong[a]	22,990	22,950j	5.7	22	5.4	10.8	15.2	21.6	47.0	8.70	..	..	10	2,185	..
Indonesia	980	3,800	4.7	99	8.7	12.3	16.3	22.1	40.7	4.68	16.3x	12.7	49	366	1.0
Korea, N.	i	..	..	75	..	..	..	..	..	..	..	..	..	1,129	0.0
Korea, S.	9,700	11,450	10.0	32	..	..	..	..	..	..	17.7	20.9	60	2,982	0.2
Laos	350	..	..	136	9.6	12.9	16.3	21.0	40.2	4.19	..	..	..	38	1.2
Malaysia	3,890	9,020	4.0	60	4.6	8.3	13.0	20.4	53.7	11.67	23.0	27.4	38	1,699	2.4
Mongolia	310	1,950	..	101	..	..	..	..	..	..	23.6	10.4	..	1,058	0.0
Papua New Guinea	1,160	2,420	0.2	128	..	..	..	..	..	..	29.4x	26.5	41	236	0.4
Philippines	1,050	2,850	0.6	98	6.5	10.1	14.4	21.2	47.8	7.35	18.4x	18.9	41	316	3.5
Singapore	26,730	22,770	5.7	26	5.1	9.9	14.6	21.4	48.9	9.59	17.7x	30.8	129	8,103	0.0
Solomon Islands	910	2,190	2.8x	122	..	..	..	..	..	..	..	..	..	..	0.2
Thailand	2,740	7,540	5.2	59	5.6	8.7	13.0	20.0	52.7	9.41	15.8	29.2	71	769	2.6
Vietnam	240	..	..	121	7.8	11.4	15.4	21.4	44.0	5.64	..	..	..	101	1.4
Latin America & the Caribbean	**..**	**..**	**..**	**2**	**4.5**	**..**	**..**	**..**	**52.9**	**11.76**	**..**	**..**	**29**	**960**	**0.6**e
Argentina	8,030	8,310	-0.4	36	..	..	..	..	..	..	..	12.2	51	1,504	0.3
Belize	2,630	5,400	3.0	63	..	..	..	..	..	..	31.1	32.3	..	..	0.3
Bolivia	800	2,540	-0.7	113	5.6	9.7	14.5	22.0	48.2	8.61	23.1	25.6	57	373	1.2
Brazil	3,640	5,400	..	68	2.1	4.9	8.9	16.8	67.5	32.14	37.4x	8.8	23	718	0.5
Chile	4,160	9,520	1.8	30	3.5	6.6	10.9	18.1	61.0	17.43	19.2	26.1	68	1,012	0.4
Colombia	1,910	6,130	1.9	51	3.6	7.6	12.6	20.4	55.8	15.50	14.5x	24.4	57	622	0.5
Costa Rica	2,610	5,850	0.7	33	4.0	9.1	14.3	21.9	50.7	12.68	28.4	43.4	5	558	3.0
Cuba	i	..	..	86	..	..	..	..	..	..	..	..	125	923	1.2
Dominican Republic	1,460	3,870	1.4	87	4.2	7.9	12.5	19.7	55.7	13.26	17.1x	20.9	22	337	1.6
Ecuador	1,390	4,220	1.5	72	5.4	8.9	13.2	19.9	52.6	9.74	15.7x	29.6	26	565	1.6
El Salvador	1,610	2,610	-1.0	112	..	..	..	..	..	..	14.5x	21.5	66	370	3.3
Guatemala	1,340	3,340	-0.3	117	2.1	5.8	10.5	18.6	63.0	30.00	8.9x	29.6	31	210	2.0
Guyana	590	2,420	-2.6	104	..	..	..	..	..	..	..	..	21	..	0.0
Haiti	250	910.00	-1.3	156	..	..	..	..	..	..	..	..	30	29	3.4
Honduras	600	1,900	0.2	116	3.8	7.4	12.0	19.4	57.4	15.11	..	..	92	204	2.3
Jamaica	1,510	3,540	-0.8	83	5.8	10.2	14.9	21.6	47.5	8.19	..	..	8	1,083	7.2
Mexico	3,320	6,400	0.9	50	4.1	7.8	12.5	20.2	55.3	13.49	16.8x	15.8	5	1,561	0.9
Nicaragua	380.0	2,000	-5.3	127	4.2	8.0	12.6	20.0	55.2	13.14	32.8	28.9	97	300	2.5
Panama	2,750	5,980	0.7	45	2.0	6.3	11.6	20.3	59.8	29.90	28.2x	40.2	34	618	2.1
Paraguay	1,690	3,650	2.1	94	..	..	..	..	..	..	13.0x	29.4	42	299	2.6
Peru	2,310	3,770	-1.1	89	4.9	9.2	14.1	21.4	50.4	10.29	19.0	..	39	367	0.3
Suriname	880	2,250	4.3	66	..	..	..	..	..	..	..	..	27	..	0.1
Trinidad and Tobago	3,770	8,610	-0.1	40	..	..	..	..	..	..	..	..	9	5,436	1.5
Uruguay	5,170	6,630	0.2	37	..	..	..	..	..	..	31.2	12.3	38	622	0.0
Venezuela	3,020	7,900	-1.1	47	3.6	7.1	11.7	19.3	58.4	16.22	18.8x	..	33	2,186	1.1
Middle East & North Africa	**..**	**..**	**..**	**..**	**6.9**	**..**	**..**	**..**	**45.4**	**6.58**	**..**	**..**	**..**	**1,220**	**0.4**e
Algeria	1,600	5,300	0.6	82	6.9	11.0	15.1	20.9	46.1	6.68	..	..	11	906	1.2
Bahrain	7,840	13,400	-2.2x	43	..	..	..	..	..	..	..	20.6	41	..	0.0
Cyprus	h	..	5.5	24	..	..	..	..	..	..	..	17.2	17	..	0.0
Egypt	790	3,820	3.7	109	8.7	12.5	16.3	21.4	41.1	4.72	42.8x	14.7	52	600	0.0
Iran	i	..	-2.4	70	..	..	..	..	..	..	25.2x	24.8	38	1,505	1.7
Iraq	i	..	..	126	..	..	..	..	..	..	..	..	271	1,213	0.0
Jordan	1,510	4,060	..	84	5.9	9.8	13.9	20.3	50.1	8.49	30.7x	23.4	138	1,067	2.5
Kuwait	17,390	23,790	-3.5	53	..	..	..	..	..	..	51.4	16.6	88	8,622	0.0
Lebanon	2,660	..	..	65	..	..	..	..	..	..	35.1x	..	..	964	7.8
Libya	h	..	-4.8x	64	..	..	..	..	..	..	..	..	71	2,499	0.0
Morocco	1,110	3,340	1.8	119	6.6	10.5	15.0	21.7	46.3	7.02	..	20.9	72	327	0.3
Oman	4,820	8,140	3.3	88	..	..	..	..	..	..	42.3	18.9	293	2,392	0.0
Qatar	11,600	17,690	-5.9	55	..	..	..	..	..	..	..	..	192	..	0.0
Saudi Arabia	7,040	..	-2.9x	73	..	..	..	..	..	..	..	..	151	4,566	0.8
Syria	1,120	5,320	1.4	78	..	..	..	..	..	..	26.6x	12.1	373	997	2.2
Tunisia	1,820	5,000	2.3	81	5.9	10.4	15.3	22.1	46.3	7.85	..	24.1	31	595	0.5
Turkey	2,780	5,580	1.7	74	..	..	..	..	..	..	22.8	16.6	87	957	0.0
United Arab Emirates	17,400	16,470	-4.0x	44	..	..	..	..	..	..	11.8x	24.4	44	10,531	0.0
West Bank and Gaza[a]	i	..	..	..	..	..	..	..	..	..	..	..	..	..	..
Yemen	260	..	..	148	..	..	..	..	..	..	38.4x	25.4	197	206	0.0
Countries in Transition[b]	**..**	**..**	**..**	**..**	**8.8**	**..**	**..**	**..**	**37.8**	**4.30**	**..**	**..**	**..**	**2,647**	**-0.1**e
Albania	670	..	..	102	..	..	..	..	..	..	34.1	..	51	341	0.0
Armenia	730d	2,260d	-0.3	103	..	..	..	..	..	..	..	..	..	384	-2.7
Azerbaijan	480d	1,460d	..	106	..	..	..	..	..	..	..	..	..	2,182	0.0
Belarus	2,070d	4,220d	..	62	11.1	15.3	18.5	22.2	32.9	2.96	..	20.1	..	2,392	-1.0

Table 5, continued: **Economic and Development Indicators**

	GNP per capita US$ 1995	Purchasing **Power Parity (PPP$) 1995**	GNP per capita real growth rate (%) 1970-1995	**Human Development Index (HDI)** rank[c] 1997	**Distribution of income or consumption** by quintiles[k] 1978-1995 Lowest 20%	Second quintile	Third quintile	Fourth quintile	Highest 20%	Ratio of highest 20% to lowest 20%[e]	**Central government expenditure** (% of GDP) 1995	**Education & health**[e] (% of central government expenditure) 1992-1995	**Military expenditure** (% of combined education and health expenditure) 1990-1991	**Per capita energy consumption** (kg. of oil equivalent) 1994	**Annual deforestation** (% of total forest) 1990-1995
Bosnia and Herzegovina	f	..	..	..	..	..	..	..	..	..	..	..	..	348	0.0
Bulgaria	1,330	4,480	0.2x	69	8.3	13.0	17.0	22.3	39.3	4.73	43.1	6.1	29	2,438	0.0
Croatia	3,250	..	..	77	..	..	..	..	..	..	46.5	20.6	..	1,395	0.0
Czech Republic	3,870	9,770	..	39	10.5	13.9	16.9	21.3	37.4	3.56	42.0	27.9	17	3,868	0.0
Estonia	2,860d	4,220d	-1.8x	71	6.6	10.7	15.1	21.4	46.3	7.02	31.9x	25.7	..	3,709	-1.0
Georgia	440d	1,470d	-1.9x	105	..	..	..	..	..	..	..	..	..	614	0.0
Hungary	4,120	6,410	1.1x	48	9.5	14.0	17.6	22.3	36.6	3.85	..	11.2	18	2,383	-0.5
Kazakhstan	1,330d	3,010d	..	93	7.5	12.3	16.9	22.9	40.4	5.39	..	..	..	3,371	-1.9
Kyrgyzstan	700d	1,800d	..	107	..	..	..	..	..	..	..	..	..	616	0.0
Latvia	2,270d	3,370d	0.1x	92	9.6	13.6	17.5	22.6	36.7	3.82	30.3	20.6	..	1,569	-0.9
Lithuania	1,900d	4,120d	..	76	8.1	12.3	16.2	21.3	42.1	5.20	27.4	11.7	..	2,030	-0.6
Macedonia	860	..	..	80	..	..	..	..	..	..	..	..	..	1,279	0.0
Moldova	920d	..	..	110	6.9	11.9	16.7	23.1	41.5	6.01	..	..	..	1,095	0.0
Poland	2,790	5,400	1.2x	58	9.3	13.8	17.7	22.6	36.6	3.94	43.4	..	30	2,401	-0.1
Romania	1,480	4,360	0.0x	79	9.2	14.4	18.4	23.2	34.8	3.78	31.9x	17.8	25	1,733	0.0
Russia	2,240d	4,480d	1.3x	67	3.7	8.5	13.5	20.4	53.8	14.54	22.2	4.6	132	4,014	..
Slovakia	2,950	3,610	..	42	11.9	15.8	18.8	22.2	31.4	2.64	..	..	..	3,243	-0.1
Slovenia	8,200	..	..	35	9.5	13.5	17.1	21.9	37.9	3.99	..	..	..	2,612	0.0
Tajikistan	340d	920d	..	115	..	..	..	..	..	..	..	..	..	616	0.0
Turkmenistan	920d	..	..	85	6.7	11.4	16.3	22.8	42.8	6.39	..	..	..	2,361	0.0
Ukraine	1,630d	2,400d	..	95	9.5	14.1	18.1	22.9	35.4	3.73	..	..	..	3,180	-0.1
Uzbekistan	970d	2,370d	..	100	..	..	..	..	..	..	..	..	..	1,869	-2.7
Yugoslavia	i	..	..	..	..	..	..	..	..	..	..	..	..	1,110	0.0
Industrial Countries	..	..	..	..	..	..	..	..	..	..	..	..	..	..	**-0.2**e
Australia[l]	18,720	18,940	1.4	14	4.4	11.1	17.5	24.8	42.2	9.59	27.6	20.7	24	5,341	0.0
Austria	26,890	21,250	2.2	12	..	..	..	..	..	..	40.5x	22.7	9	3,301	0.0
Belgium[l]	24,710	21,660	1.9	13	7.9	13.7	18.6	23.8	36.0	4.56	50.4x	..	20	5,120	0.0
Canada[l]	19,380	21,130	1.7	1	5.7	11.8	17.7	24.6	40.2	7.05	..	8.6	15	7,854	-0.1
Denmark[l]	29,890	21,230	1.7	18	5.4	12.0	18.4	25.6	38.6	7.15	43.5	11.7	18	3,977	0.0
Finland[l]	20,580	17,760	1.9	8	6.3	12.1	18.4	25.5	37.6	5.97	43.8x	22.5	15	5,997	0.1
France[l]	24,990	21,030	1.8	2	5.6	11.8	17.2	23.5	41.9	7.48	46.4	22.5	29	4,042	-1.1
Germany[l]	27,510	20,070	..	19	7.0	11.8	17.1	23.9	40.3	5.76	33.8	17.6	29	4,128	0.0
Greece	8,210	11,710	1.5	20	..	..	..	..	..	..	43.1x	15.9	71	2,260	-2.3
Ireland	14,710	15,680	2.6	17	..	..	..	..	..	..	42.6x	26.8	12	3,137	-2.7
Israel[l]	15,920	16,490	2.0	23	6.0	12.1	17.8	24.5	39.6	6.60	44.8	19.3	106	2,717	0.0
Italy[l]	19,020	19,870	2.4	21	6.8	12.0	16.7	23.5	41.0	6.03	49.9x	..	21	2,707	-0.1
Japan[l]	39,640	22,110	3.2	7	8.7	13.2	17.5	23.1	37.5	4.31	23.8	7.6	12	3,856	0.1
Luxembourg	41,210	37,930	3.0	27	..	..	..	..	..	..	..	11.5	10	..	0.0
Netherlands[l]	24,000	19,950	1.5	6	8.2	13.1	18.1	23.7	36.9	4.50	50.8	24.4	22	4,580	0.0
New Zealand[l]	14,340	16,360	0.8	9	5.1	10.8	16.2	23.2	44.7	8.76	36.1	30.8	16	4,245	-0.6
Norway[l]	31,250	21,940	2.9	3	6.2	12.8	18.9	25.3	36.7	5.92	41.1x	19.9	22	5,318	-0.3
Portugal	9,740	12,670	2.5	31	..	..	..	..	..	..	42.5x	..	32	1,827	-0.9
Spain[l]	13,580	14,520	2.0	11	8.3	13.7	18.1	23.4	36.6	4.41	39.4x	10.6	18	2,458	0.0
Sweden[l]	23,750	18,540	1.1	10	8.0	13.2	17.4	24.5	36.9	4.61	45.0	5.2	16	5,723	0.0
Switzerland[l]	40,630	25,860	1.1	16	5.2	11.7	16.4	22.1	44.6	8.58	27.1x	..	14	3,629	0.0
United Kingdom[l]	18,700	19,260	1.8	15	4.6	10.0	16.8	24.3	44.3	9.63	41.8	17.3	40	3,772	-0.5
United States[l]	26,980	26,980	1.7	4	4.7	11.0	17.4	25.0	41.9	8.91	22.9	19.9	46	7,819	-0.3
World[n]	..	..	..	..	**4.6**	**6.0**	**7.0**	**20.5**	**61.9**	**13.54**	..	..	**38**	**1,433**	**0.3**e

.. Data not available.
a Territory.
b Central and Eastern European countries and the newly independent states of the former Soviet Union.
c Regional ranking compares developing region: 1 highest, 8 lowest.
d Preliminary.
e Bread for the World Institute estimate.
f Estimated to be low-income ($765 or less).
g Estimated to be upper middle income ($3,036 to $9,385).
h Estimated to be high income ($9,386 or more).
i Estimated to be lower middle income ($766 to $3,035).
j GDP data.
k Distribution of income or consumption on per capita basis, except as noted "l".
l Based on distribution of income among households.
m Positive data indicate loss of forest; negative data indicate gain in forest.
n Distribution of income represented by percentage of GDP (1990) held by each quintile, estimated by Dr. Robert Summers, University of Pennsylvania (personal communication).
The number '0' (zero) means zero or less than half the unit of measure.
x Data refer to a period other than specified in the column heading.

Table 6 **Economic Globalization**

	Trade: Exports of goods and services (% of GDP) 1970	Trade: Exports of goods and services (% of GDP) 1995	Trade: Manufactured exports (% of merchandise exports) 1993	Trade: Food trade[c]: Food exports (% of merchandise exports) 1995	Trade: Food trade[c]: Food imports (% of merchandise imports) 1995	Trade: Food trade[c]: Food imports (% of total consumption) 1995	Trade: Imports of goods and services[c,e] (% of consumption) 1995	Investment 1995: Gross domestic investment (GDI) (% of GDP)	Investment 1995: International capital flows: Net capital flows[d,e] (% of GDI)	Investment 1995: International capital flows: Aid (% of GDI)	Investment 1995: International capital flows: Net private capital flows[e,f] (% of GDI)	Investment 1995: International capital flows: Foreign direct investment net inflows (% of GDI)	Investment 1995: International capital flows: Foreign direct investment net inflows (% of GDP)	Debt: Total external debt (US$ billions) 1995	Debt: Debt service (% of exports of goods and services) 1993-1995	Workers' remittances, receipts (US$ millions) 1995
Developing Countries	..	..	..	**5.7**	**6.5**	..	..	..	..	..	..	..	..	**2,065.7**	**17**	..
Africa (sub-Saharan)	**20.5**	**28.4**	..	**11.5**	**14.1**	..	..	**19.4**	..	..	..	..	..	**226.5**	**15**	..
Angola	..	73.9	..	..	18.3	14.7	102.2	27.3	92.8	41.3	51.5	39.4	10.7	11.5	9	..
Benin	22.1	..	..	9.0	23.2	..	..	..	..	..	..	..	..	1.6	7	88.00
Botswana	22.7	49.4	..	3.8	12.3	6.8	66.7	24.8	14.5	8.6	5.9	6.5	1.6	0.7	4	..
Burkina Faso	6.2	..	..	26.4	14.0	..	..	..	..	..	..	..	0.0	1.3	12	80.00
Burundi	10.7	12.4	..	..	18.0	3.8	28.5	11.0	162.8	161.8	0.9	1.7	0.2	1.2	35	0.00
Cameroon	26.2	25.9	..	15.6	13.5	2.3	24.9	14.5	42.8	38.6	4.3	8.9	1.3	9.4	18	38.70
Cape Verde	..	..	..	0.7	18.1	..	..	..	..	..	..	..	..	0.2	4	95.88
Central African Republic	28.0	18.5	..	0.6	16.3	2.9	29.2	15.1	96.3	..	1.8	..	0.3	0.9	8	..
Chad	23.1	..	..	18.0	7.1	..	..	..	..	..	..	..	0.6	0.9	8	..
Comoros	..	19.3	..	58.5	44.5	11.3	41.1	17.1	115.0	109.8	5.1	5.1	0.9	0.2	3	9.00
Congo (Brazzaville)	34.7	61.8	..	0.8	18.9	5.3	85.6	27.1	13.0	21.3	-8.3	0.2	0.0	6.0	26	..
Côte d'Ivoire	35.8	41.4	..	41.8	13.5	4.9	43.2	13.2	93.0	90.3	2.7	1.4	0.2	19.0	31	0.00
Djibouti	..	41.7	..	26.3	22.2	11.7	56.0	12.0	180.7	173.9	6.7	6.7	0.8	0.3	4	1.02
Equatorial Guinea	35.7	..	..	4.4	10.5	..	..	..	..	..	..	..	0.6	0.3	2	..
Eritrea	..	29.6	..	6.2	14.7	..	..	20.5	..	..	..	..	..	..	..	..
Ethiopia	..	14.7	..	6.8	25.6	4.7	26.9	17.2	91.7	98.3	-4.6	0.8	0.1	5.2	13	311.50
Gabon	49.7	61.1	..	0.1	11.6	4.3	75.8	26.3	1.5	11.6	-10.1	-4.1	-1.1	4.5	11	..
Gambia	33.1	53.4	..	51.5	41.7	..	..	..	..	..	..	..	2.6	0.4	13	..
Ghana	21.3	25.0	..	26.1	12.0	3.6	37.3	18.6	99.5	54.8	44.7	19.6	3.6	5.9	25	13.62
Guinea	..	21.0	..	2.7	23.1	5.3	28.1	14.8	75.8	72.2	3.7	6.4	0.9	3.2	17	0.50
Guinea-Bissau	4.0	13.0	..	65.0	41.8	10.3	32.9	16.4	284.5	282.1	2.4	2.4	0.4	0.9	22	..
Kenya	29.8	32.6	..	13.6	9.6	3.7	44.7	19.2	38.0	40.4	-2.4	1.8	0.4	7.4	28	0.00
Lesotho	10.8	20.8	..	2.9	14.7	10.4	107.5	87.3	16.3	12.7	3.6	2.6	2.2	0.7	6	..
Liberia	58.8	..	..	0.5	25.0	..	..	..	..	..	..	..	..	2.1	3	..
Madagascar	19.2	23.3	..	26.7	13.8	2.4	32.3	10.8	88.4	80.9	1.2	2.7	0.3	4.3	11	8.95
Malawi	24.2	28.8	..	14.3	20.2	6.8	41.3	14.7	192.5	198.8	-6.3	0.5	0.1	2.1	22	..
Mali	13.2	22.3	..	23.4	15.0	3.7	42.4	26.0	86.5	86.4	0.2	158.2	0.0	3.1	15	106.22
Mauritania	40.8	50.4	..	8.1	49.2	12.7	60.5	14.5	145.3	143.4	1.9	1.9	0.3	2.5	25	8.04
Mauritius	43.2	58.4	..	26.2	12.5	8.0	79.1	25.4	32.9	2.3	30.6	1.5	0.4	1.8	8	..
Mozambique	..	..	..	28.2	26.6	..	..	..	..	..	..	..	2.5	5.8	34	0.00
Namibia	..	..	..	13.6	7.1	..	..	..	..	..	..	..	1.5	..	..	8.82
Niger	10.8	..	..	13.5	18.8	..	..	..	..	..	..	..	0.1	1.6	25	..
Nigeria	8.4	..	..	1.7	9.0	2.3	17.6	..	8.9	3.1	6.1	9.7	2.4	35.0	14	657.00
Rwanda	13.6	6.1	..	0.6	35.7	7.0	24.4	13.1	412.7	412.0	0.7	0.7	0.1	1.0	9	..
Senegal	27.4	31.6	..	17.7	30.0	9.2	41.2	15.6	83.9	87.1	-3.2	0.1	0.0	3.8	14	81.32
Sierra Leone	30.1	12.7	..	2.9	87.5	14.6	25.1	5.7	375.2	435.7	-60.5	2.1	0.1	1.2	62	..
Somalia	11.5	..	..	49.9	35.0	..	..	..	..	..	..	..	..	2.7	1	..
South Africa	22.0	22.1	28.1	5.6	5.1	1.2	27.0	18.3	..	1.5	..	0.0	0.0	..	..	0.00
Sudan	16.5	..	..	48.4	20.1	..	..	..	..	..	..	..	..	17.6	5	..
Swaziland	66.6	83.2	..	32.2	7.8	8.1	100.3	17.1	61.2	..	31.5	..	5.4	0.3	2	0.00
Tanzania	..	29.8	..	13.9	10.3	4.1	63.4	31.0	90.6	76.6	12.3	13.1	4.2	7.3	22	0.00h
Togo	49.6	30.8	..	6.0	15.7	3.9	39.2	13.6	109.8	..	0.0	..	..	1.5	10	12.00
Uganda	22.2	12.0	..	9.5	5.7	1.1	22.6	16.4	98.8	86.8	12.0	13.1	2.1	3.6	43	0.00
Zaire (Congo-Kinshasa)	15.5	..	..	1.5	61.5	..	..	..	..	..	..	..	..	13.1	1	..
Zambia	53.6	31.5	..	2.2	5.5	1.3	41.3	11.7	431.1	424.9	6.3	13.8	1.6	6.9	89	..
Zimbabwe	..	..	..	13.8	3.8	..	..	..	..	..	..	..	0.6	4.9	27	..
South Asia	**5.4**	**13.9**	..	**8.0**	**8.6**	..	..	**23.2**	..	..	..	..	..	**156.8**	**25**	..
Afghanistan	9.8	..	..	30.6	31.7	..	..	..	..	..	..	..	..	..	..	..
Bangladesh	8.3	14.2	..	0.3	15.5	3.4	24.5	16.6	26.4	26.2	0.2	0.0	0.0	16.4	14	1,198.00
Bhutan	..	..	..	9.7	13.3	..	..	..	..	..	..	..	0.0	0.1	8	..
India	3.7	12.2	..	8.9	4.7	0.6	19.1	24.5	6.7	2.2	4.5	1.6	0.4	93.8	27	6,000.00
Maldives	..	..	..	..	16.5	..	..	..	..	..	..	..	3.3	0.2	6	..
Nepal	4.9	24.3	..	14.1	7.5	2.6	40.4	23.5	43.1	41.6	-0.2	0.8	0.2	2.4	8	101.39
Pakistan	7.8	16.4	84.6	9.9	16.7	3.3	23.0	18.7	19.8	6.9	12.7	3.5	0.7	30.2	29	1,866.00
Sri Lanka	25.5	35.9	..	3.4	10.4	5.0	54.6	25.1	21.2	16.9	4.3	1.9	0.5	8.2	8	772.36
East Asia & the Pacific	**5.7**	**29.5**	..	..	..	..	..	**39.0**	..	..	..	..	..	**404.5**	**13**	..
Brunei	..	..	..	0.3	8.1	..	..	..	..	..	..	..	..	..	..	..
Burma (Myanmar)	5.2	..	..	42.5	23.7	..	..	..	..	..	..	..	..	5.8	14	..
Cambodia	5.8	..	..	0.6	13.9	..	..	..	..	..	..	..	5.4	2.0	3	10.00
China	2.7	21.0	80.6	3.7	4.7	2.8	33.5	40.5	16.9	1.2	15.7	12.7	5.1	118.1	10	350.00

Table 6, continued: **Economic Globalization**

	Trade: Exports of goods and services (% of GDP) 1970	Trade: Exports of goods and services (% of GDP) 1995	Trade: Manufactured exports (% of merchandise exports) 1993	Trade: Food trade[a]: Food exports (% of merchandise exports) 1995	Trade: Food trade[a]: Food imports (% of merchandise imports) 1995	Trade: Food trade[a]: Food imports (% of total consumption) 1995	Trade: Imports of goods and services[c,e] (% of consumption) 1995	Investment 1995: Gross domestic investment (GDI) (% of GDP)	Investment 1995: International capital flows: Net capital flows[d,e] (% of (GDI)	Investment 1995: International capital flows: Aid (% of GDI)	Investment 1995: International capital flows: Net private capital flows[e,f] (% of GDI)	Investment 1995: International capital flows: Foreign direct investment net inflows (% of GDI)	Investment 1995: International capital flows: Foreign direct investment net inflows (% of GDP)	Debt: Total external debt (US$ billions) 1995	Debt: Debt service (% of exports of goods and services) 1993-1995	Workers' remittances, receipts (US$ millions) 1995
Fiji	48.4	51.2	..	43.6	12.6	6.0	60.1	13.5	32.2	15.5	16.7	24.0	3.2	0.3	7	0.00
Hong Kong[a]	94.6	147.1	93.5	1.4	3.1	6.3	221.7	34.9	..	0.0	..	..	..	..	..	..
Indonesia	13.0	25.5	53.1	5.0	8.1	2.6	42.8	37.8	17.4	1.9	15.6	5.8	2.2	107.8	32	629.00
Korea, N.	..	..	..	2.5	20.1	..	..	..	..	..	..	..	..	..	..	..
Korea, S.	13.9	33.2	93.1	0.8	3.7	1.7	53.5	37.1	..	0.0	..	..	..	..	..	618.00
Laos	..	..	..	12.0	5.0	..	..	..	..	..	..	..	5.0	2.2	..	..
Malaysia	42.0	95.5	..	8.1	3.6	5.3	157.5	40.6	34.8	0.3	34.4	16.8	6.8	34.4	9	..
Mongolia	..	..	..	3.2	14.5	..	..	..	..	..	..	..	1.2	0.5	8	..
Papua New Guinea	18.5	60.5	..	7.7	15.6	6.7	74.6	24.1	80.3	31.4	48.9	38.3	9.2	2.4	27	0.00
Philippines	21.6	36.3	41.6	9.1	6.3	2.8	51.6	22.5	32.9	5.3	27.6	8.9	2.0	39.4	20	432.00
Singapore	102.1	..	78.5	1.7	2.8	8.2	..	33.2	..	0.1	..	..	..	..	..	..
Solomon Islands	..	..	..	18.3	11.6	..	..	..	..	..	..	..	4.8	0.2	4	..
Thailand	15.0	41.5	71.1	9.6	1.5	1.0	75.9	43.1	13.9	1.2	12.7	2.9	1.2	56.8	12	0.00
Vietnam	..	35.9	..	14.2	5.3	2.3	55.8	27.1	41.9	..	27.0	..	6.9	26.5	9	..
Latin America and the Caribbean	**12.2**	**16.7**	**..**	**14.8**	**8.6**	**..**	**..**	**19.5**	**..**	**..**	**..**	**..**	**..**	**636.6**	**26**	**..**
Argentina	5.6	8.5	31.9	37.5	3.9	0.3	10.4	18.3	14.4	..	14.0	..	0.5	89.7	34	0.00
Belize	..	..	20.6	66.9	13.9	..	..	..	..	..	..	..	3.6	0.3	9	13.90
Bolivia	24.7	..	18.7	14.7	10.7	..	..	..	..	..	..	..	2.4	5.3	31	1.00
Brazil	7.0	7.0	58.9	15.1	8.6	0.9	9.9	21.9	12.9	0.2	12.7	3.2	0.7	159.1	31	2,891.00
Chile	14.6	29.3	16.5	10.9	4.9	1.6	38.7	27.4	23.8	1.0	23.0	10.4	2.5	25.6	23	..
Colombia	14.0	15.4	39.8	8.6	7.2	1.6	23.3	20.0	26.1	1.5	24.5	16.4	3.3	20.8	28	172.20
Costa Rica	28.2	40.9	..	42.9	8.2	3.7	55.1	24.8	17.9	0.2	16.8	3.8	4.3	3.8	16	0.00
Cuba	..	..	..	46.5	20.3	..	..	..	..	..	..	..	..	..	..	..
Dominican Republic	17.2	25.9	..	34.6	13.7	4.1	35.1	19.7	16.2	5.6	10.6	12.2	2.4	4.3	13	400.00
Ecuador	14.0	28.8	7.3	23.1	6.2	1.8	33.7	18.7	23.8	7.0	16.7	14.0	2.6	14.0	24	0.00
El Salvador	24.8	21.0	..	11.3	9.8	3.2	36.5	19.4	16.9	16.5	0.4	2.1	0.4	2.6	12	1,060.82
Guatemala	18.6	..	..	34.2	9.6	..	..	..	..	..	..	..	0.5	3.3	12	357.50
Guyana	56.5	73.0	..	40.2	9.0	..	..	..	..	..	..	..	0.5	2.1	17	..
Haiti	13.8	..	..	5.7	46.9	..	..	..	..	..	..	..	0.1	0.8	8	..
Honduras	27.9	35.5	..	17.4	10.5	4.9	51.8	22.9	52.8	45.6	7.2	5.6	1.3	4.6	30	120.00
Jamaica	33.2	68.9	..	14.6	7.6	5.4	84.7	17.4	38.5	14.1	24.4	21.8	3.8	4.3	19	443.20
Mexico	6.4	25.5	74.6	8.2	8.7	2.0	27.3	15.3	35.2	1.0	34.2	18.2	2.8	165.7	56	3,672.00
Nicaragua	26.5	..	..	25.3	16.5	..	..	..	..	..	..	..	3.7	9.3	36	75.00
Panama	..	38.6	16.4	46.2	8.5	3.7	51.5	23.5	15.9	2.9	13.1	12.6	3.0	7.2	4	19.00
Paraguay	14.9	..	16.7	43.1	6.3	..	..	..	..	..	..	..	2.6	2.3	8	..
Peru	17.9	11.9	17.0	3.2	12.0	1.8	20.2	16.8	41.1	4.4	36.6	19.6	3.3	30.8	30	334.00
Suriname	60.3	..	..	11.2	17.0	..	..	..	..	..	..	..	4.5	..	..	..
Trinidad and Tobago	42.8	39.5	34.3	4.9	13.8	5.9	38.3	14.2	39.2	3.4	35.8	39.5	5.6	2.6	24	30.40
Uruguay	14.4	19.1	42.3	38.8	7.3	1.3	23.0	14.1	11.8	..	8.6	..	0.7	5.3	19	0.00
Venezuela	20.9	26.7	13.5	1.5	10.1	2.1	27.8	15.9	7.5	0.4	7.1	7.6	1.2	35.8	21	..
Middle East and North Africa	**..**	**..**	**..**	**..**	**..**	**..**	**..**	**..**	**..**	**..**	**..**	**..**	**..**	**216.0**	**15**	**..**
Algeria	22.0	26.7	..	0.9	26.5	9.4	42.0	32.0	3.3	2.3	1.0	0.0	0.0	32.6	51	350.00
Bahrain	..	..	..	0.3	7.6	..	..	..	..	..	..	..	-0.5	..	..	0.00
Cyprus	..	..	57.7	17.2	7.4	..	..	..	..	..	..	..	..	..	..	88.41
Egypt	14.2	21.3	32.9	9.3	23.8	6.3	34.3	16.9	28.6	24.9	3.7	7.5	1.3	34.1	14	5,059.72
Iran	..	20.6	..	4.8	24.2	..	..	29.3	..	..	..	..	..	21.9	20	..
Iraq	..	..	..	1.6	38.3	..	..	..	..	..	..	..	..	..	..	..
Jordan	..	..	..	9.5	18.5	..	..	..	..	..	..	..	..	7.9	14	1,244.00
Kuwait	59.8	54.7	..	0.2	13.2	4.7	59.8	12.3	..	0.2	..	..	..	..	..	0.00
Lebanon	..	..	..	12.1	11.6	..	..	..	..	..	..	..	0.3	3.0	12	350.00
Libya	61.0	..	..	0.2	18.1	..	..	..	..	..	..	..	..	..	..	..
Morocco	17.6	27.3	56.8	14.0	15.5	4.7	40.3	21.0	15.7	7.3	8.4	4.3	0.9	22.1	34	1,904.40
Oman	73.7	..	67.8	2.0	13.2	..	..	..	..	..	..	..	1.2	3.1	9	39.01
Qatar	..	..	..	0.5	9.0	..	..	..	..	..	..	..	..	..	..	..
Saudi Arabia	66.3	..	..	0.7	11.3	..	..	..	..	..	..	..	-1.5	..	..	0.00
Syria	17.5	..	..	14.1	14.9	..	..	..	..	..	..	..	0.4	21.3	6	400.00
Tunisia	22.0	44.8	75.1	7.2	10.3	5.7	60.9	24.0	19.0	1.6	17.4	6.1	1.5	9.9	19	679.88
Turkey	4.2	20.3	71.8	16.3	5.7	1.5	31.3	24.9	5.6	0.7	4.9	2.2	0.5	73.6	29	3,327.00
United Arab Emirates	..	..	..	1.3	7.0	..	..	..	..	..	..	..	..	..	..	..
West Bank and Gaza[a]	..	..	..	..	..	..	..	..	..	..	..	..	..	..	..	..
Yemen	..	..	..	2.9	55.3	..	..	..	..	..	..	..	0.0	6.2	4	1,080.00
Countries in Transition[b]	**..**	**..**	**..**	**..**	**..**	**..**	**..**	**..**	**..**	**..**	**..**	**..**	**..**	**425.3**	**14**	**..**

Table 6, continued: **Economic Globalization**

	Trade							Investment 1995						Debt		Workers' remittances, receipts (US$ millions) 1995
	Exports of goods and services (% of GDP)		Manufactured exports (% of merchandise exports) 1993	Food trade[c]			Imports of goods and services[c,e] (% of consumption) 1995	Gross domestic investment (GDI) (% of GDP)	International capital flows					Total external debt (US$ billions) 1995	Debt service (% of exports of goods and services) 1993-1995	
	1970	1995		Food exports (% of merchandise exports) 1995	Food imports (% of merchandise imports) 1995	Food imports (% of total consumption) 1995			Net capital flows[d,e] (% of (GDI)	Aid (% of GDI)	Net private capital flows[e,f] (% of GDI)	Foreign direct investment net inflows (% of GDI)	Foreign direct investment net inflows (% of GDP)			
Albania	..	13.8	..	2.1	23.4	6.1	35.4	16.5	68.8	49.5	19.4	19.4	3.2	0.7	1	384.60
Armenia	..	23.7	..	0.4	20.7	3.8	47.8	8.8	87.9	114.2	3.2	4.3	0.4	0.4	2	12.35
Azerbaijan	..	27.0	..	4.8	40.6	8.1	40.7	15.9	38.7	18.7	20.0	19.9	3.2	0.3	..	..
Belarus	..	42.7	..	4.4	7.2	2.1	59.6	25.2	6.3	4.2	2.0	0.4	0.1	1.6	3	..
Bosnia and Herzegovina	..	..	..	..	..	..	..	..	..	..	..	..	..	..	..	..
Bulgaria	..	49.1	..	10.0	6.1	3.4	60.0	20.9	23.2	4.2	18.9	5.2	1.1	10.9	13	..
Croatia	..	40.3	71.1	7.2	9.1	3.8	53.6	14.0	..	..	13.6	3.2	0.4	3.7	6	..
Czech Republic	..	51.6	..	5.2	5.1	3.0	70.4	24.7	51.9	1.3	50.6	23.2	5.7	16.6	10	0.00
Estonia	..	75.5	..	8.7	9.2	0.5	102.9	26.9	1.6	4.9	1.3	17.9	5.0	0.3	1	0.02
Georgia	..	16.8	..	7.5	68.7	9.5	26.9	3.5	251.9	251.9	0.0	0.0	0.0	1.2	..	..
Hungary	30.1	34.9	68.0	18.5	3.1	1.4	46.8	22.8	76.1	-2.5	78.7	44.0	10.3	31.2	42	6.27
Kazakhstan	..	34.5	..	10.0	7.0	1.5	46.0	22.0	11.8	1.6	10.6	8.1	1.3	3.7	2	..
Kyrgyzstan	..	26.3	..	3.8	29.7	5.5	35.6	15.7	62.1	59.5	3.1	3.2	0.5	0.6	..	..
Latvia	..	42.7	..	5.4	6.5	2.5	56.8	20.8	24.0	4.7	19.0	14.3	3.0	0.5	1	..
Lithuania	..	57.8	..	15.2	5.0	2.5	72.5	19.2	27.1	11.4	14.2	4.8	1.0	0.8	2	1.10
Macedonia	..	37.3	..	12.6	16.7	13.2	50.7	15.4	..	..	0.0	0.0	0.0	1.2	5	..
Moldova	..	35.2	..	41.6	5.0	1.2	42.3	6.7	60.0	26.5	33.5	27.1	1.8	0.7	4	..
Poland	..	27.9	..	8.6	5.4	1.6	32.3	17.0	44.1	17.6	25.3	17.0	3.1	42.3	12	46.00
Romania	..	27.6	75.8	5.9	6.1	2.1	40.7	25.7	10.4	2.9	7.5	4.6	1.2	6.7	8	4.00
Russia	..	22.3	..	0.8	19.7	3.6	29.2	25.0	3.1	1.8	1.3	2.3	0.6	120.5	5	..
Slovakia	..	62.9	..	4.8	5.1	3.6	87.5	28.3	15.1	1.9	13.2	3.7	1.1	5.8	9	0.00
Slovenia	..	55.7	85.4	2.8	5.9	3.8	72.3	22.5	..	..	20.1	4.2	0.9	3.5	6	54.20
Tajikistan	..	114.3	..	2.8	21.5	10.5	138.7	17.4	22.9	18.6	4.3	4.3	0.8	0.7	..	..
Turkmenistan	..	..	..	0.6	24.6	..	..	..	..	..	..	..	0.0	0.4	..	..
Ukraine	..	..	..	13.5	5.5	..	..	..	..	..	..	..	0.3	8.4	3	..
Uzbekistan	..	..	..	4.6	17.6	..	..	..	..	..	..	..	0.5	1.6	3	..
Yugoslavia	..	..	..	5.1	4.7	..	..	..	..	..	..	..	..	13.8	..	..
Industrial Countries	..	..	..	..	..	..	..	..	..	..	..	..	..	..	..	..
Australia	14.5	19.8	..	16.5	2.8	0.6	26.1	22.7	..	..	..	..	..	..	..	..
Austria	31.1	38.1	88.9	3.0	4.5	1.7	52.5	26.6	..	..	..	..	..	..	..	297.57
Belgium	51.9	74.4	..	8.9g	8.2g	6.4	89.9	17.9	..	..	..	..	..	..	..	..
Canada	22.7	36.9	62.0	5.3	3.9	1.4	43.9	18.9	..	..	..	..	..	..	..	..
Denmark	27.9	34.9	..	15.8	5.2	1.7	37.2	15.5	..	..	..	..	..	..	..	..
Finland	25.7	38.0	82.6	1.8	3.8	1.2	39.7	16.4	..	..	..	..	..	..	..	..
France	15.8	22.9	77.5	9.6	6.8	1.6	25.6	17.7	..	..	..	..	..	..	..	1,781.84
Germany	..	23.5	86.4	3.3	6.6	1.6	28.8	21.5	..	..	..	..	..	..	..	..
Greece	10.0	22.4	45.7	20.7	12.0	3.5	36.7	18.7	..	..	..	6.2	1.2	..	..	2,982.00
Ireland	35.5	75.5	68.1	16.7	5.9	4.2	83.8	12.8	..	..	..	..	..	..	..	..
Israel	25.0	29.4	90.6	4.4	4.6	1.6	45.8	23.5	..	1.6	..	..	..	..	..	0.00
Italy	16.4	26.4	88.2	4.6	7.4	1.8	29.5	18.5	..	..	..	..	..	..	..	345.57
Japan	10.8	9.5	95.8	0.2	8.1	0.8	11.4	29.0	..	..	..	..	..	..	..	..
Luxembourg	87.7	96.3	..	..	..	..	..	..	..	..	..	..	..	..	..	..
Netherlands	43.5	53.0	59.2	11.9	8.3	5.5	64.9	22.0	..	..	..	..	..	..	..	..
New Zealand	22.6	31.6	26.0	33.3	4.9	1.6	40.3	24.0	..	..	..	..	..	..	..	274.94
Norway	38.2	38.3	30.9	0.6	3.8	..	..	23.0	..	..	..	..	..	..	..	..
Portugal	21.5	28.3	76.9	2.9	8.2	..	..	28.0	..	..	..	..	..	..	..	3,791.02
Spain	13.2	23.7	76.7	11.7	7.9	2.0	29.9	21.5	..	..	..	..	..	..	..	2,588.46
Sweden	23.8	40.6	84.7	1.4	3.8	1.3	44.7	14.4	..	..	..	..	..	..	..	121.83
Switzerland	32.8	35.7	93.3	2.0	4.0	1.5	43.8	23.4	..	..	..	..	..	..	..	160.68
United Kingdom	23.1	28.0	80.4	3.5	6.1	..	..	16.0	..	..	..	..	..	..	..	..
United States	5.8	11.3	77.7	7.2	2.5	..	..	..	..	..	..	..	..	..	..	..
World	**14.1**	**22.5**	..	**5.8**	**6.0**	..	..	**22.7**	..	..	..	..	..	..	..	..

.. Data not available.

a Territory.

b Central and Eastern European countries and the newly independent states of the former Soviet Union.

c Consumption is the sum of private (market value of all goods and services, including durable products, such as cars, washing machines and home computers) and general government consumption (current expenditures to purchase goods and services and capital expenditures on national defense and security).

d Net capital flows include net private capital flows (private debt and nondebt flows) and aid (official development assistance and official aid – including emergency aid).

e Bread for the World Institute estimate.

f Net private capital flows consist of private debt flows (commercial bank lending, bonds and other private credits) and nondebt private flows (foreign direct investment and portfolio equity investment).

g Luxembourg included.

h Data cover mainland Tanzania only.

The number '0' (zero) means zero or less than half the unit of measure.

Table 7 U.S. National Hunger and Poverty Trends

	1970	1980	1982	1984	1985	1986	1987	1988	1989	1990	1991	1992	1993	1994	1995	1996
Total population (millions)	**205.1**	**227.8**	**232.5**	**237.0**	**239.3**	**241.6**	**243.9**	**246.3**	**248.3**	**249.4**	**252.1**	**255.0**	**257.8**	**260.4**	**262.9**	**265.3**
Northeastern region population	..	..	..	..	..	..	..	..	..	50.9	51.0	51.1	51.3	51.4	51.5	51.6
Midwestern region population	..	..	..	..	..	..	..	..	..	59.8	60.2	60.6	61.0	61.3	61.7	62.1
Southern region population	..	..	..	..	..	..	..	..	..	85.7	86.9	88.2	89.5	90.7	92.0	93.1
Western region population	..	..	..	..	..	..	..	..	..	53.0	54.1	55.1	56.0	56.8	57.7	58.5
Total food insecure population (millions)	..	..	..	..	**20.0**	..	..	..	..	..	**30.0**	..	..	..	..	..
Children under 12 hungry (millions)	..	..	..	..	..	..	..	..	..	..	5.5	..	..	..	4.0	..
Children under 12 at risk of hunger (millions)	..	..	..	..	..	..	..	..	..	..	6.0	..	..	..	9.6	..
Percent of federal budget spent on food assistance[a]	**0.5**	**2.4**	**2.1**	**2.1**	**2.0**	**1.9**	**1.9**	**1.9**	**1.9**	**1.9**	**2.0**	**2.3**	**2.5**	**2.47**	**2.48**	**2.43**
Total infant mortality rate (per 1,000 live births)	**20.0**	**12.6**	**11.5**	**10.8**	**10.6**	**10.4**	**10.1**	**10.0**	**9.7**	**9.1**	**8.9**	**8.5**	**8.4**	**8.0**	**7.6**	..
White infant mortality rate	17.8	11.0	10.1	9.4	9.3	8.9	8.6	8.5	8.5	7.7	7.3	6.9	6.8	6.6	6.3	..
African American infant mortality rate	32.6	21.4	19.6	18.4	18.2	18.0	17.9	17.6	17.6	17.0	17.6	16.8	16.5	15.8	15.1	..
Hispanic infant mortality rate	..	..	..	..	..	..	7.9	8.1	8.5	7.8	7.5	6.8	..	..	..	..
Total poverty rate (%)	**12.6**	**13.0**	**15.0**	**14.4**	**14.0**	**13.6**	**13.4**	**13.1**	**12.8**	**13.5**	**14.2**	**14.8**	**15.1**	**14.5**	**13.8**	..
Northeastern region poverty rate	..	..	..	..	..	..	..	..	10.2	10.2	11.3	12.6	13.3	12.9	12.5	
Midwestern region poverty rate	..	..	..	..	..	..	..	..	12.0	11.9	12.8	13.3	13.4	13.0	11.0	
Southern region poverty rate	..	..	..	..	..	..	..	..	15.6	15.9	16.2	17.1	17.1	16.1	15.7	
Western region poverty rate	..	..	..	..	..	..	..	..	12.8	11.6	12.4	14.8	15.6	15.3	14.9	
White poverty rate	9.9	10.2	12.0	11.5	11.4	11.0	10.4	10.1	10.0	10.7	11.3	11.9	12.2	11.7	11.2	..
African American poverty rate	33.5	32.5	35.6	33.8	31.1	31.1	32.6	31.6	30.7	31.9	32.7	33.4	33.1	30.6	29.3	..
Hispanic poverty rate	..	25.7	29.9	28.4	29.0	27.3	28.1	26.8	26.2	28.1	28.7	29.6	30.6	30.7	30.3	..
Elderly poverty rate	24.6	15.7	14.6	12.4	12.6	12.4	12.5	12.0	11.4	12.2	12.4	12.9	12.2	11.7	10.5	..
Female-headed households poverty rate	38.1	36.7	40.6	38.4	37.6	38.3	38.3	37.2	32.2	33.4	39.7	39.0	38.7	34.6	32.4	..
Total child poverty rate (%)	**15.1**	**18.3**	**21.9**	**21.5**	**20.7**	**20.5**	**20.5**	**19.7**	**19.6**	**20.6**	**21.1**	**22.3**	**22.7**	**21.8**	**20.8**	..
White child poverty rate	..	13.9	17.0	16.7	16.2	16.1	15.4	14.6	14.8	15.9	16.1	17.4	17.8	16.9	16.2	..
African American child poverty rate	..	42.3	47.6	46.6	43.6	43.1	45.6	44.2	43.7	44.8	45.6	46.6	46.1	43.8	41.9	..
Hispanic child poverty rate	..	33.2	39.5	39.2	40.3	37.7	39.6	37.9	36.2	38.4	39.8	40.0	40.9	41.5	40.0	..
Unemployment rate (%)	**4.9**	**7.1**	**9.7**	**7.5**	**7.2**	**7.0**	**6.2**	**5.5**	**5.3**	**5.6**	**6.8**	**7.5**	**6.9**	**6.1**	**5.6**	**5.4**
White unemployment rate	4.5	6.3	8.6	6.5	6.2	6.0	5.3	4.7	4.5	4.8	6.1	6.6	6.1	5.3	4.9	4.7
African American unemployment rate	..	14.3	18.9	15.9	15.1	14.5	13.0	11.7	11.4	11.4	12.5	14.2	13.0	11.5	10.4	10.5
Hispanic unemployment rate	..	10.1	13.8	10.7	10.5	10.6	8.8	8.2	8.0	8.2	10.0	11.6	10.8	9.9	9.3	8.9
Household income distribution (per quintile in %)																
All races																
Lowest 20 percent	4.1	4.2	4.0	4.0	3.9	3.8	3.8	3.8	3.8	3.9	3.8	3.8	3.6	3.6	3.7	..
Second quintile	10.8	10.2	10.0	9.9	9.8	9.7	9.6	9.6	9.5	9.6	9.6	9.4	9.0	8.9	9.1	..
Third quintile	17.4	16.8	16.5	16.3	16.2	16.2	16.1	16.0	15.8	15.9	15.9	15.8	15.1	15.0	15.2	..
Fourth quintile	24.5	24.8	24.5	24.6	24.4	24.3	24.3	24.3	24.0	24.0	24.2	24.2	23.5	23.4	23.3	..
Highest 20 percent	43.3	44.1	45.0	45.2	45.6	46.1	46.2	46.3	46.8	46.6	46.5	46.9	48.9	49.1	48.7	..
Ratio of highest 20 percent to lowest 20 percent[e]	10.6	10.5	11.3	11.3	11.7	12.1	12.2	12.2	12.3	11.9	12.2	12.3	13.6	13.6	13.2	..
White																
Lowest 20 percent	4.2	4.4	4.2	4.3	4.1	4.1	4.1	4.1	4.1	4.2	4.1	4.1	3.9	3.8	4.0	..
Second quintile	11.1	10.5	10.3	10.2	10.1	10.0	10.0	10.0	9.8	10.0	9.9	9.7	9.3	9.2	9.3	..
Third quintile	17.5	17.0	16.6	16.5	16.4	16.3	16.3	16.2	16.0	16.0	16.0	15.9	15.3	15.1	15.3	..
Fourth quintile	24.3	24.6	24.4	24.4	24.3	24.2	24.2	24.1	23.8	23.9	24.1	24.1	23.3	23.2	23.3	..
Highest 20 percent	42.9	43.5	44.4	44.6	45.1	45.4	45.5	45.6	46.3	46.0	45.8	46.2	48.2	48.6	48.1	..
Ratio of highest 20 percent to lowest 20 percent[e]	10.2	9.9	10.6	10.4	11.0	11.1	11.1	11.1	11.3	11.0	11.2	11.3	12.4	12.8	12.0	..
African American																
Lowest 20 percent	3.7	3.7	3.6	3.6	3.5	3.1	3.3	3.3	3.2	3.1	3.1	3.1	3.0	3.0	3.2	..
Second quintile	9.3	8.7	8.6	8.4	8.3	8.0	7.9	7.7	8.0	7.9	7.8	7.8	7.7	7.9	8.2	..
Third quintile	16.3	15.3	15.3	15.0	15.2	14.9	14.8	14.6	15.0	15.0	15.0	14.7	14.3	14.3	14.8	..
Fourth quintile	25.2	25.2	25.3	24.7	25.0	25.0	24.4	24.7	24.9	25.1	25.2	24.8	23.7	24.3	24.2	..
Highest 20 percent	45.5	47.1	47.1	48.4	48.0	49.0	49.7	49.7	48.9	49.0	48.9	49.7	51.3	50.5	49.6	..
Ratio of highest 20 percent to lowest 20 percent[e]	12.3	12.7	13.1	13.4	13.7	15.8	15.1	15.1	15.3	15.8	15.8	16.0	17.1	16.8	15.5	..
Hispanic origin																
Lowest 20 percent	..	4.3	4.2	3.9	4.1	3.9	3.7	3.7	3.8	4.0	4.0	4.0	3.9	3.7	3.8	..
Second quintile	..	10.1	9.6	9.5	9.4	9.5	9.1	9.3	9.5	9.5	9.4	9.4	9.1	8.7	8.9	..
Third quintile	..	16.4	16.1	16.2	16.1	15.8	15.5	15.6	15.7	15.9	15.8	15.7	15.1	14.8	14.8	..
Fourth quintile	..	24.8	24.6	24.9	24.8	24.8	24.1	24.2	24.4	24.3	24.3	24.1	23.1	23.3	23.3	..
Highest 20 percent	..	44.5	45.5	45.5	45.6	46.1	47.6	47.2	46.6	46.3	46.5	46.9	48.7	49.6	49.3	..
Ratio of highest 20 percent to lowest 20 percent[e]	..	10.3	10.8	11.7	11.1	11.8	12.9	12.8	12.3	11.6	11.6	11.7	12.5	13.4	13.0	..

.. Data not available.

a Data refer to fiscal year.

e Bread for the World Institute estimate.

Table 8 United States – State Hunger and Poverty Statistics

	Total Population (millions) July 1996	% children under 12 hungry 1993	% children under 12 hungry or at risk 1991	% children under 12 hungry or at risk 1993	Infant mortality rate per 1,000 live births 1995 Total	Infant mortality rate 1995 White	Infant mortality rate 1995 African American	% population in poverty 1995	Unemployment rate (%) (seasonally adjusted)[a] May 1997
Alabama	4.27	8.6	35.0	29.5	9.8	7.1	15.2	20.1	4.6
Alaska	0.61	5.5	17.7	20.3	7.7	6.1	..	7.1	6.9
Arizona	4.43	9.0	25.8	30.4	7.5	7.2	17.0	16.1	4.7
Arkansas	2.51	10.0	38.5	36.1	8.8	7.2	14.3	14.9	4.6
California	31.88	11.8	27.8	37.1	6.3	5.8	14.4	16.7	6.3
Colorado	3.82	6.0	21.0	21.0	6.5	6.0	16.8	8.8	3.5
Connecticut	3.27	6.1	16.2	19.4	7.2	6.5	12.6	9.7	5.2
Delaware	0.72	5.9	21.8	21.8	7.5	6.0	13.1	10.3	4.1
District of Columbia	0.54	11.3	33.7	40.0	16.2	..	19.6	22.2	6.8
Florida	14.40	11.8	27.5	39.5	7.5	6.0	13.0	16.2	4.9
Georgia	7.35	7.3	27.1	24.5	9.4	6.5	15.1	12.1	4.5
Hawaii	1.18	5.4	23.7	19.1	5.8	..	..	10.3	5.9
Idaho	1.19	8.2	34.4	30.6	6.1	5.8	..	14.5	4.9
Illinois	11.85	7.9	28.0	26.3	9.4	7.2	18.7	12.4	4.4
Indiana	5.84	7.2	25.3	28.1	8.4	7.3	17.5	9.6	3.2
Iowa	2.85	6.4	31.7	23.2	8.2	7.8	21.2	12.2	3.0
Kansas	2.57	8.1	22.8	29.1	7.0	6.2	17.6	10.8	4.0
Kentucky	3.88	9.2	29.8	33.7	7.6	7.4	10.7	14.7	5.1
Louisiana	4.35	12.1	32.1	39.1	9.8	6.2	15.3	19.7	6.3
Maine	1.24	9.9	24.3	35.0	6.5	6.3	..	11.2	4.8
Maryland	5.07	5.9	16.4	19.9	8.9	6.0	15.3	10.1	4.7
Massachusetts	6.09	6.5	19.3	22.5	5.2	4.7	9.0	11.0	4.2
Michigan	9.59	8.4	27.6	29.9	8.3	6.2	17.3	12.2	4.0
Minnesota	4.66	6.7	21.2	24.4	6.7	6.0	17.6	9.2	3.3
Mississippi	2.72	10.3	38.7	37.3	10.5	7.0	14.7	23.5	4.9
Missouri	5.36	9.2	26.9	32.4	7.4	6.4	13.8	9.4	4.0
Montana	0.88	7.9	31.5	30.3	7.0	7.0	..	15.3	4.9
Nebraska	1.65	6.9	28.6	24.8	7.4	7.3	..	9.6	2.3
Nevada	1.60	6.7	27.9	22.9	5.7	5.5	..	11.1	4.4
New Hampshire	1.16	6.3	12.6	22.8	5.5	5.5	..	5.3	2.8
New Jersey	7.99	7.1	20.3	22.7	6.6	5.3	13.3	7.8	5.3
New Mexico	1.71	8.7	36.1	31.4	6.2	6.1	..	25.3	6.3
New York	18.18	9.5	29.7	30.7	7.7	6.2	13.9	16.5	6.3
North Carolina	7.32	8.3	26.3	29.5	9.2	6.7	15.9	12.6	3.5
North Dakota	0.64	5.3	27.9	21.2	7.2	6.7	..	12.0	3.2
Ohio	11.17	7.1	24.3	26.5	8.7	7.3	17.5	11.5	4.5
Oklahoma	3.30	10.6	28.7	38.7	8.3	8.0	15.1	17.1	3.5
Oregon	3.20	6.9	24.1	25.2	6.1	5.9	..	11.2	5.0
Pennsylvania	12.06	7.6	25.6	28.1	7.8	6.2	17.6	12.2	5.2
Rhode Island	0.99	6.9	25.6	25.8	7.2	7.0	..	10.6	5.7
South Carolina	3.70	10.0	31.3	35.8	9.6	6.7	14.6	19.9	4.8
South Dakota	0.73	8.0	28.6	29.9	9.5	7.9	..	14.5	2.6
Tennessee	5.32	10.6	30.7	36.8	9.3	6.8	17.9	15.5	4.9
Texas	19.13	10.1	28.6	30.6	6.5	5.9	11.7	17.4	5.4
Utah	2.00	7.0	25.5	24.7	5.4	5.3	..	8.4	3.0
Vermont	0.59	5.2	20.5	21.9	6.0	6.2	..	10.3	3.8
Virginia	6.68	5.8	20.5	20.7	7.8	5.7	15.3	10.2	4.3
Washington	5.53	7.4	22.7	27.5	5.9	5.6	16.2	12.5	4.9
West Virginia	1.83	10.2	38.6	37.3	7.9	7.6	..	16.7	6.0
Wisconsin	5.16	7.8	24.7	28.6	7.3	6.3	18.6	8.5	3.4
Wyoming	0.48	8.9	22.6	28.9	7.7	6.8	..	12.2	4.8
United States	**265.28**	**8.9**	**26.8**	**29.0**	**7.6**	**6.3**	**15.1**	**13.8**	**4.8**

.. Data not available.

a Preliminary.

Sources for Tables

TABLE 1: Global Hunger – Life and Death Indicators

Total population, projected population, projected population growth rate, projected total fertility rate, urban population, life expectancy: United Nations Fund for Population Activities, *The State of World Population 1997* (New York: UNFPA, 1997).

Population below age 15: Statistics Division and Population Division of the United Nations Secretariat, "Indicators on Youth and Elderly Populations," posted at http://www.un.org/Depts/unsd/social/youth.htm.

Infant mortality, low birthweight, percent immunized, under-5 mortality, maternal mortality: U.N. Children's Fund (UNICEF), *The State of the World's Children 1997* (New York: Oxford University Press, 1997 – "*SWC*").

Refugees: U.S. Committee for Refugees, *World Refugee Survey 1997* (Washington: Immigration and Refugee Services of America, 1997).

TABLE 2: Food, Nutrition and Education

Per capita dietary energy supply, annual growth rate: Food and Agriculture Organization of the United Nations (FAO), *The Sixth World Food Survey* (Rome: FAO, 1996).

Daily per capita calorie supply as percent of requirements, food expenditures as percent of household consumption: *SWC, 1996.*

Food production per capita: FAO, FAOSTAT TS software, 1996.

Iodine Deficiency: World Health Organization, "Global Prevalence of Iodine Deficiency Disorders," *Micronutrient Deficiency Information System Working Paper* Number 1 (Geneva: WHO, 1993).

Adult literacy rate, combined primary, secondary and tertiary educational enrollment ratio: U.N. Development Programme, *Human Development Report 1997* (New York: Oxford University Press, 1997 – "*HDR*").

Gross primary enrollment: The World Bank, *1997 World Development Indicators* [CD-ROM] (Washington: The World Bank, 1997 – "*WDI*").

TABLE 3: Regional Prevalence of Anemia

C. Abouzahr, E. Ahman and K. Bailey, "Malnutrition and the Burden of Disease: the Global Epidemiology of Protein-energy Malnutrition, Anaemias and Vitamin Deficiencies," in *The Global Burden of Disease and Injury Series*, vol. 8 (WHO/World Bank Global Burden of Disease Publication, 1997).

TABLE 4: Hunger, Malnutrition and Poverty

Undernourished population: FAO, *Mapping Undernutrition – An Ongoing Process* (Rome: FAO, 1996).

Relative inadequacy of food supply: FAO, *The Sixth World Food Survey.*

Underweight, wasting, stunting: WHO Global Database on Child Growth and Malnutrition, 1997; *SWC.*

Access to safe water: *WDI*; *SWC.*

Population in poverty: *WDI*; *HDR.*

TABLE 5: Economic and Development Indicators

GNP per capita, distribution of income or consumption, government expenditure as percent of GDP, per capita energy consumption: *WDI.*

HDI rank, education and health as percent of government expenditure, military expenditure as percent of combined education and health expenditure: *HDR.*

Annual deforestation: FAO, *State of the World's Forests 1997* (Rome: FAO, 1997).

TABLE 6: Economic Globalization

Exports as percent of GDP, manufactured exports as percent of merchandise exports, imports as percent of consumption, investment, workers' remittances: *WDI.*

Food as percent of total merchandise exports, imports: FAO data posted at http://www.fao.org.

Food imports as percent of consumption: FAO data posted at http://www.fao.org; *WDI.*

Debt: The World Bank, *Global Development Finance 1997, Volume 1* (Washington: The World Bank, 1997).

TABLE 7: U.S. National Hunger and Poverty Trends

Total population, poverty data, household income distribution: U.S. Bureau of the Census.

Total food insecure population: Center on Hunger, Poverty and Nutrition Policy, Tufts University.

Children under 12 hungry, at risk of hunger: Food Research and Action Center (FRAC).

Percent of federal budget spent on food assistance: Congressional Budget Office.

Infant mortality: National Center for Health Statistics, *Monthly Vital Statistics Report* 45:11, Supplement 2 (June 12, 1997).

Unemployment: U.S. Bureau of Labor Statistics.

TABLE 8: United States – State Hunger and Poverty Statistics

Population, population in poverty: U.S. Bureau of the Census.

Unemployment: U.S. Bureau of Labor Statistics.

Infant mortality: National Center for Health Statistics, *Monthly Vital Statistics Report* 45:11, Supplement 2 (June 12, 1997).

Children under 12 hungry, at risk of hunger: FRAC.

Abbreviations

CAS – Country Assistance Strategy
CERES – Coalition for Environmentally Responsible Economies
CGIAR – Consultative Group on International Agricultural Research
CSO – Civil Society Organization
DES – Dietary Energy Supply
EU – European Union
FAO – Food and Agriculture Organization of the United Nations
FDI – Foreign Direct Investment
FRAC – Food Research and Action Center
GATT – General Agreement on Tariffs and Trade
GDI – Gross Domestic Investment
GDP – Gross Domestic Product
GNP – Gross National Product
GSP – Generalized System of Preferences
HDI – Human Development Index
HIPC – Highly Indebted Poor Country
IBRD – International Bank for Reconstruction and Development
ICCR – Interfaith Center on Corporate Responsibility
IDA – International Development Association
IFAD – International Fund for Agricultural Development
IFAP – International Federation of Agricultural Producers
IFI – International Financial Institution
IFPRI – International Food Policy Research Institute
ILEP – International Program for the Elimination of Child Labor
ILO – International Labor Organization
IMF – International Monetary Fund
IMR – Infant Mortality Rate
IUF – International Union of Food, Agricultural, Hotel, Restaurant, Catering, Tobacco and Allied Workers' Associations
LIFDC – Low-Income Food Deficit Country
LIS – Luxembourg Income Study
MAI – Multilateral Agreement on Investing
MDB – Multilateral Development Bank
MFN – Most Favored Nation
NAFTA – North American Free Trade Agreement
NGO – Nongovernmental Organization
NIC – Newly Industrializing Country
NIS – Newly Independent States of the former Soviet Union
OECD – Organization for Economic Cooperation and Development
PPP – Purchasing Power Parity
PVO – Private Voluntary Organization
SAP – Structural Adjustment Program
SEWA – Self-Employed Women's Association
TNC – Transnational Corporation
U.K. – United Kingdom
U.N. – United Nations
U.S. – United States
UNCTAD – U.N. Conference on Trade and Development
UNDP – U.N. Development Programme
UNFPA – U.N. Fund for Population Activities
UNHCR – U.N. High Commissioner for Refugees
UNICEF – U.N. Children's Fund
USAID – U.S. Agency for International Development
USDA – U.S. Department of Agriculture
WHO – World Health Organization
WIC – Special Supplemental Nutrition Program for Women, Infants and Children

Glossary

Absolute poverty – The income level below which a minimally nutritionally adequate diet plus essential non-food requirements are not affordable.

Anemia – A condition in which the hemoglobin concentration (the number of red blood cells) is lower than normal due to disease or as a result of a deficiency of one or more essential nutrients such as iron.

Bilateral aid – Financial or material assistance provided to an individual developing country by a single donor country (as distinguished from multilateral aid).

Biodiversity – Diversity of animal and plant species within an environment.

Civil society organizations (CSOs) – Voluntary popular organizations and associations through which individuals work together to pursue interests, values and ideas for their perceptions of the common good.

Collective agriculture – Agriculture on a farm or group of farms managed and worked by laborers under state supervision.

Combined gross enrollment ratio – A comparison of the enrollment of all schools and colleges with the population of the relevant age groups.

Comparative advantage – A doctrine of classical economics in which a nation or business specializes in producing those goods it can produce more efficiently, while importing or exchanging for goods which can be more efficiently produced elsewhere, benefiting both trading partners.

Competitiveness – In an economic sense, the ability of a firm or economy to act independently to secure business by offering favorable terms.

Daily calorie requirement – The average number of calories needed to sustain normal levels of activity and health, taking into account age, sex, body weight and climate; on average, about 2,350 calories per person per day.

Debt service – The sum of repayments of principal and payments of interest on debt.

Deforestation – Clearing of forest lands for human use, including all forms of agriculture, settlements, other infrastructure and mining.

Developing countries – Countries in which most people have a low economic standard of living. Also known as the "Third World," the "South" and the "less-developed countries."

Dietary energy supply (DES) – The total daily food supply, expressed in calories, available within a country for human consumption.

Economic globalization – The integration of world markets for goods, services and finance.

Exchange rate – The official international value of a country's currency, usually expressed in U.S. dollars.

Export credits – Industrial-country government loans at favorable interest rates aimed at promoting exports to developing countries.

Export zones – Specialized areas in which export-oriented businesses receive tax, tariff and other concessions from the host government.

Fair trade organizations – Organizations that provide market outlets for small-scale, low-income producers. "Fairly traded" products support living wages and safe working conditions for workers in developing countries.

Fertility rate – The average number of children borne by women during their lifetimes; used as a measure of long-term population changes.

Food security – Assured access for every person, primarily by production or purchase, to enough nutritious food to sustain an active and healthy life with dignity. Includes food availability, food access and appropriate food utilization.

Food self-reliance – A strategy whereby countries boost yields, employing sustainable and efficient farming practices, and diversify their agricultural production, some for export and some for domestic consumption.

Food self-sufficiency – A strategy whereby countries, communities or regions rely exclusively on their own food production.

Food sovereignty – The right of each nation to maintain and develop its own capacity to produce its basic foods, respecting cultural and productive diversity.

Foreign direct investment (FDI) – Investment from abroad in ownership and control of productive activities, as opposed to more passive stock and bond investment.

Free markets – Markets where competition is not restricted by government policies, private monopolies or private price-fixing agreements.

Genetic erosion – Loss of diversity among plant varieties.

Germ plasm – The hereditary material of plant or animal species.

"Green box" policies – Under the Uruguay Round agreement (see below), government agricultural policies that support farming with only minimal effects on trade.

Green revolution – A term used to describe technological changes in agricultural production methods since World War II. The technologies include improved, high-yielding plant varieties, often combined with irrigation, chemical fertilizers and pesticides.

Gross domestic investment (GDI) – Total investment in new facilities or productive capacity, usually expressed as a proportion of gross domestic product.

Gross domestic product (GDP) – The value of all goods and services produced within a nation during a specified period, usually a year.

Gross national product (GNP) – The value of all goods and services produced by a country's citizens, wherever they are located.

Group of 8 – The wealthiest industrial countries: Canada, France, Germany, Italy, Japan, Russia, United Kingdom and United States (formerly the Group of 7, excluding Russia).

Human Development Index (HDI) – As used by the United Nations Development Programme, a measure of well-being based on economic growth, educational attainment and health.

Human rights – The basic rights and freedoms due all human beings, including the right to food and other basic necessities, the right to life and liberty, freedom of thought and expression, and equality before the law.

Hunger – A condition in which people do not get enough food to provide the nutrients (carbohydrate, fat, protein, vitamins, minerals and water) for fully productive, active and healthy lives.

Import quota – A limit on the quantity of a product that can be imported during a particular period.

Industrial countries – Countries in which most people have a high economic standard of living (though there are often significant poverty populations). Also called the "developed countries" or the "North."

Infant mortality rate (IMR) – The annual number of deaths of infants under one year of age per 1,000 live births.

Informal sector – Economic activities beyond the effective reach of taxing or regulatory authorities, also known as *"underground," "hidden," "gray"* or *"shadow"* market activities.

Infrastructure – The basic facilities, services and installations needed for the functioning of a community or society such as transportation, communications, financial, educational and health care systems.

Intellectual property rights – Guarantees to individuals, businesses or organizations of exclusive rights to the intangible creations, such as an invention, an industrial process or an artistic work – patents, copyrights, trademarks and legally protected trade secrets.

International financial institutions (IFIs) – Intergovernmental agencies, including the International Monetary Fund and the World Bank, which make loans to governments.

International Monetary Fund (IMF) – An international organization that makes loans to countries that have short-term foreign exchange and monetary problems. These loans are conditioned upon the willingness of the borrowing country to adopt IMF-approved economic policies.

Labor market flexibility – As used in current economic parlance, policies intended to weaken guarantees of job security and wage rates, in order to make an economy competitive internationally.

Least developed countries – According to the United Nations, low-income countries that are suffering from long-term handicaps to economic growth, in particular low levels of human resource development and/or severe structural weaknesses.

Liberalization – Permitting greater play of market forces, including fiscal balance, removal of trade barriers, and elimination of controls on interest and exchange rates.

Livelihood security – The ability of a household to meet *all* its basic needs – for food, shelter, water, sanitation, health care and education.

Low birth-weight infants – Babies born weighing 2,500 grams (five pounds, eight ounces) or less who are especially vulnerable to illness and death during the first months of life.

Macroeconomic policies – Policies related to general levels of production and income, and the relationship among economic sectors. "Microeconomics" deals with individual units of activity, such as a firm, household or prices for a specific product.

Malnutrition – A condition resulting from inadequate consumption (undernutrition) or excessive consumption of a nutrient; can impair physical and mental health, and can contribute to or result from infectious diseases.

Maquiladoras – Foreign-owned assembly plants in tax-favored Mexican export zones.

Market economy – An economy in which prices for goods and services are set primarily by private markets rather than by government planning or regulation.

Marshall Plan, The – A coordinated effort by the United States and many nations of Europe to foster European economic recovery after World War II; also known as the European Recovery Program.

Mega-cities – Cities with more than 10 million people in their metropolitan area.

Microcredit – Small, short-term loans to low-income people, too poor to borrow from commercial banks, to help them start their own businesses, generate income and raise their standard of living.

Microenterprises – Very small economic ventures owned and managed by one entrepreneur and employing fewer than five people.

Micronutrients – Vitamins, major minerals and trace elements needed for a healthy, balanced diet. Micronutrient deficiencies are also called "hidden hunger." "Macronutrients" are protein, carbohydrates and fat.

Multilateral aid – Financial or material assistance channeled to developing countries via international organizations such as the World Bank, the European Union or U.N. agencies (as distinguished from bilateral aid).

Newly Industrializing Countries (NICs) – Developing countries with high levels of per capita income, that have experienced rapid growth and industrialization, primarily for export. These countries are mainly located in East and Southeast Asia and are sometimes called *"tigers"* or *"dragons."*

Non-tariff barriers – Rules and regulations a country establishes to make it difficult for foreign goods or services to compete with domestic products.

Participation – People's involvement in making decisions that affect their lives.

Portfolio investment – Investment in stocks and bonds as opposed to direct ownership of, and management control over, productive facilities.

Poverty line – An official measure of poverty defined by national governments. In the United States, it is calculated as three times the cost of the U.S. Department of Agriculture's "Thrifty Food Plan," which provides a less-than-adequate diet.

Prevailing wage – The usual compensation for a particular type of work in a given area.

Private investment – Commitment of funds by private individuals or corporations.

Privatization – The transfer of ownership of companies and delivery of services from government to private agencies.

Protectionism – Trade policy that protects domestic producers by impeding or limiting, as through tariffs or quotas, the importation of foreign goods and services.

Public investment – Investment of funds by governments and inter-governmental organizations.

Purchasing Power Parity (PPP) – An estimate of the amount of money required to purchase comparable goods in different countries, usually expressed in U.S. dollars.

Responsible trade – As used in this report, trade policies that seek the efficiencies possible through freer trade, complemented by measures to promote broad-based economic growth and more secure livelihoods for all.

Slash and burn agriculture – A system of shifting cultivation in which trees and wild vegetation are cleared or burned before planting crops.

Social safety nets – Government and private charitable programs to meet the needs of low-income, disabled and other vulnerable people.

Structural adjustment program (SAP) – Economic policy changes, often negotiated as a condition for loans, intended to stimulate economic growth. These generally involve reducing the role of government in the economy and increasing exports.

Stunting – Failure to grow to normal height caused by chronic undernutrition during the formative years of childhood.

Subsistence farming – Agriculture which produces exclusively to feed the farming household.

Sustainability – Society's ability to shape its economic and social systems so as to maintain both natural resources and human life.

Sustainable development – The reduction of hunger and poverty in environmentally sound ways. It includes: meeting basic human needs, expanding economic opportunities, protecting and enhancing the environment, and promoting pluralism and democratic participation.

Sweatshop – A shop or factory in which employees work long hours at low wages under poor conditions.

Tariff – A tax imposed on imported items, usually to raise their prices relative to domestic goods.

Transition economies – Former communist states in Eastern Europe and Central Asia.

Transnational corporation (TNC) – A firm that engages in international commerce and investment through affiliates and subsidiaries located outside its home country.

Underemployment – The situation of not being fully employed year round. Underemployed people include unemployed, discouraged (those who have stopped looking for work) and involuntary part-time workers.

Under-5 mortality rate – The annual number of deaths of children under five years of age per 1,000 live births; a high rate correlates closely with hunger and malnutrition.

Undernutrition – Inadequate consumption of nutrients, often adversely affecting children's physical and mental development, undermining their future as productive and creative members of their communities.

Underweight – A condition in which a person is seriously below normal weight for her or his age.

Uruguay Round – The eighth round of global trade negotiations under the informal General Agreement on Tariffs and Trade to reduce tariffs and non-tariff barriers, launched in that South American country in 1986. The resulting agreement, approved in 1994, establishes the World Trade Organization, calls for significant cuts in industrial tariffs, sets down new rules for trade in services and agriculture, and adds protections for intellectual property.

Vulnerability to hunger – A condition of individuals, households, communities or nations who have enough to eat most of the time, but whose poverty makes them especially susceptible to hunger due to changes in the economy, climate, political conditions or personal circumstances.

Wasting – A condition in which a person is seriously below the normal weight for her or his height due to acute undernutrition or a medical condition.

World Bank – An intergovernmental agency that makes long-term loans to the governments of developing nations.

World Trade Organization (WTO) – An international organization established to enforce the Uruguay Round global trade agreement.

Notes

Introduction

1. David Korten, "Corporate Control or Democratic Development?," *Why*, Spring 1997, 37.
2. "61 Ways of Looking at Poverty," *Choices*, October 1996, 9.
3. Daniel Finn, *Just Trading: On the Ethics and Economics of International Trade* (Nashville: Abingdon Press, 1996), 258. While Finn describes Christian beliefs, most religions would, to some extent, affirm these core values.
4. Arthur Simon, *Bread for the World* (New York: Paulist Press, 1975), 205-206.
5. Adapted from William Schweiker, "Against the Skeptics: On Getting Real About Morality," *Criterion*, Winter 1997, 22-31. See also William Schweiker, *Responsibility and Christian Ethics* (Cambridge: Cambridge University Press, 1996).
6. "61 Ways, ...", 7.
7. Vine Deloria, Jr., *God is Red* (Cutchogue, NY: Buccaneer Books, 1973).

Chapter 1

1. United Nations Conference on Trade and Development, *World Investment Report 1996* (New York and Geneva: UNCTAD, 1996).
2. Fred Barbash, "Former Empire Yields 'Cheap Labor,'" *Washington Post*, December 30, 1996.
3. Keith B. Richburg, "Tide of Foreign Capital Helps Lift World Poor," *Washington Post*, December 29, 1996.
4. The World Bank, *World Development Indicators 1997* (Washington: The World Bank, 1997), 295.
5. This section is based primarily on Food and Agriculture Organization of the United Nations, *The Sixth World Food Survey* (Rome: FAO, 1996), and additional data posted at <www.fao.org>. The *Survey* is the most comprehensive study of hunger in developing countries currently available. However, according to Dr. Lisa C. Smith, a Science, Engineering and Diplomacy Fellow of the American Association for the Advancement of Science, the *Survey*'s measure of chronic undernutrition is biased toward national food availability and does not adequately account for the problem of poor access to food (the most widespread cause of food insecurity), as intended.
6. <www.worldbank.org>.
7. Henry Sender, "Sprinting to the Forefront," *Far Eastern Economic Review*, August 1, 1996, 50-51; Sandra Sugawara, "As China's Auto Market Accelerates, GM Jumps On," *Washington Post*, January 2, 1997.
8. Michael Richardson, "Poverty Marches to Forefront in Thailand," *International Herald Tribune*, March 21, 1997.
9. United Nations Commission for Social Development, *1997 Report on the World Social Situation*, E/CN.5/1997/8 (Part II) (New York: United Nations, 1997), 19.
10. According to the International Food Policy Research Institute's initiative, *A 2020 Vision for Food, Agriculture and the Environment*; see IFPRI, *Feeding the World, Preventing Poverty and Protecting the Earth: A 2020 Vision* (Washington: IFPRI, 1996).
11. *World Development Indicators 1997*; Dr. Flavio Luiz Schieck Valente, General Coordinator, Association for Projects Against Hunger, Brasilia, personal communication, April 7, 1997.
12. Luther Tweeten *et al.*, *Food Security Discussion Paper*, prepared for the U.S. Agency for International Development, n.d.
13. Sarah Anderson and John Cavanagh, *Top 200: The Rise of Global Corporate Power* (Washington: Institute for Policy Studies, 1996).
14. ACTIONAID, *Hunger and the Global Agenda: Who Wins?...Who Loses?...Who Cares?* (London: ACTIONAID, 1996).
15. U.N. Commission for Social Development, Part II; Anderson and Cavanagh.
16. Jean Drèze and Amartya Sen, *Hunger and Public Action* (Oxford: Clarendon Press, 1989); FAO, "Mapping Undernutrition," November 1996; United Nations Development Programme, *Human Development Report 1996* (New York: Oxford University Press, 1996).
17. FAO, *FAO: What It Is, What It Does*, posted at <www.fao.org>.
18. Lee Swenson, President, U.S. National Farmers Union, presentation to U.S. nongovernmental organizations attending the World Food Summit, November 1996.
19. Information provided by Lutheran World Relief.
20. Marilee Karl, *Partners for Food Security* (Rome: FAO, 1996).
21. U.N. Commission for Social Development, Part II.
22. Karl.
23. Jessica T. Mathews, "Power Shift," *Foreign Affairs* 76:1 (January/February 1997): 56.
24. Karl; Via Campesina statement to NGO Forum on Food Security, 1996.
25. *Why*, Spring 1995; Renato S. Maluf, Francisco Menezes and Flavio L. Valente, *Contribution to the Food Security Theme in Brazil* (Brasilia: Agora, REDCAPA and RIAD, 1995).
26. Drèze and Sen.
27. Morris David Morris, "The Changing Condition of the World's Poor, 1960-1990: Some Development Policy Implications," Unpublished Paper, September 14, 1996, provided by the author.
28. Drèze and Sen; Amartya Sen, *Public Action to Remedy Hunger: Fourth Annual Arturo Tanco Memorial Lecture* (New York: The Hunger Project, 1990); Commision on Social Development, Part II.

Chapter 2

1. Francis Fukuyama, *The End of History and the Last Man* (New York: Free Press, 1992).
2. William Greider, *One World, Ready or Not: The Manic Logic of Global Capitalism* (New York: Simon and Schuster, 1997).
3. This section and the next two are based on Isabelle Grunberg, "Employment, Governments and the Global Economy," in Marc J. Cohen, ed., *What Governments Can Do: Hunger 1997* (Silver Spring, MD: Bread for the World Institute, 1996), 54-68.
4. Paul Hirst and Gahame Thompson, *Globalization in Question* (London: Blackwell, 1996); Charles P. Kindleberger, *The World in Depression, 1929-1939* (Berkeley: University of California Press, 1986).
5. United Nations Development Programme, *Human Development Report 1996* (New York: Oxford University Press, 1996), 20.
6. *Ibid.*, 2.
7. See Izumi Ohno, "Beyond the `East Asian Miracle': An Asian View," *UNDP/Office of Development Studies Discussion Paper* No. 5 (January 1996).
8. "Mexican Church Leaders Speak Out Against the 'God of Profit,' " *Financial Times*, April 8, 1996; Manuel Agosin and Ricardo Ffrench-Davis: "Managing Capital Inflows in Latin America," *UNDP/ODS Discussion Paper* No. 8 (January 1996).
9. United Nations, *World Economic and Social Survey 1995 – Current Trends and Policies in the World Economy* (New York: U.N. Department of Economic and Social Information and Policy Analysis, 1995), 2, 35.
10. Richard B. Freeman, *When Earnings Diverge: Causes, Consequences and Cures for the New Inequality in the United States* (Washington: National Policy Association, 1997).
11. International Labor Organization, *World Employment 1995, An ILO Report* (Geneva: ILO, 1995), 65-66.
12. " 'Feel Bad' Factor Grips the Western World," *Financial Times*, June 11, 1996.
13. "An Unhealthy Workweek," *Financial Times*, December 27, 1995.
14. Daniel P. McMurrer, Isabel V. Sawhill and Robert I. Lerman, "Welfare Reform and Opportunity in the Low-Wage Labor Market," *Opportunity in America*, July 1997.
15. Rebecca M. Blank, "The Misdiagnosis of Eurosclerosis," *The American Prospect*, January/February 1997, 84.
16. Dani Roderick, *Has Globalization Gone Too Far?* (Washington: Institute for International Economics, 1997); Neal R. Peirce, "Does the Nation-State Have a Future?," *International Herald Tribune*, April 4, 1997.
17. Peter L. Berger, *The Sacred Canopy* (Garden City, New York: Doubleday, 1967), 138, 147.

Chapter 3

1. Martin Ravallion and Shaohua Chen, "What Can New Survey Data Tell Us About Recent Changes in Distribution and Poverty?" *World Bank Economic Review*, May 1997.
2. Michael T. Rock, " 'Twenty-five Years of Economic Development' Revisited," *World Development* 21:11 (1993): 1787-1801; G. Fields, "Growth and Income Distribution," in G. Psacharopoulos, ed., *Essays on Poverty, Equity and Growth* (New York: Pergamon Press, 1991); The World Bank, *World Development Report 1990: Poverty* (New York: Oxford University Press, 1990), 3.
3. Nancy Birdsall, Thomas C. Pinckney and Richard H. Sabot, "Why Low Inequality Spurs Growth: Savings and Investment by the Poor," *Inter-American Development Bank Working Paper Series* No. 327 (1996); Rock; Fields; *World Development Report 1990*.
4. The World Bank classifies countries in four groups according to per capita gross national product. In 1995, the groups were: low-income, $765 or less; lower middle-income, $766-$3,035; upper middle-income $3,036-9,385; and high-income, $9,386 or more. See The World Bank, *World Development Report 1997: The State in a Changing World* (New York: Oxford University Press, 1997), 265.
5. International Labor Organization, *Child Labour: Targeting the Intolerable*, (Geneva: ILO, 1996), 7.
6. ILO, "ILO and Industry Form Child Labor Pact," *ILO Focus*, Winter/Spring 1997.
7. Richard B. Freeman, *When Earnings Diverge: Causes, Consequences and Cures for the New Inequality in the U.S.* (Washington: National Policy Association, 1997); Peter Gottschalk and Timothy M. Smeeding, "Cross-National Comparisons of Levels and Trends in Inequality," *Luxembourg Income Study Working Paper* No. 126 (July 1995), 19-20.
8. U.N. Centre for Human Settlements (Habitat), *An Urbanizing World: Global Report on Human Settlements, 1996* (Oxford: Oxford University Press, 1996).
9. Marc J. Cohen, ed., *Hunger 1993: Uprooted People* (Washington: Bread for the World Institute, 1992) and *Countries in Crisis: Hunger 1996* (Silver Spring, MD: BFW Institute, 1995).
10. P. Stalker, *The Work of Strangers: A Survey of International Labour Migration*, (Geneva: ILO, 1994).
11. The World Bank, *1997 World Development Indicators* (Washington: International Bank for Reconstruction and Development, 1997), Table 4.21, 210-212.
12. Bob Benenson, "Provisions: GATT Implementing Bill," *Congressional Quarterly*, November 26, 1994, 3410-3416.
13. Renato Ruggiero, "The State of World Trade, Trade Policy and the WTO," summary of special report to the Singapore WTO Ministerial Meeting, 9 December 1996 (Geneva: World Trade Organization, 1997), 4-10; Christophe Bellmann and Richard Gerster, "Accountability in the World Trade Organization," *Journal of World Trade* 30:6 (December 1996).
14. Ralph Estes, *Tyranny of the Bottom Line: Why Corporations Make Good People Do Bad Things* (San Francisco: Berrett-Koehler, 1995).
15. Benjamin Hollister, Rosalyn Will and Alice Tepper Marlin, *Shopping for a Better World: The Quick and Easy Guide to All Your Socially Responsible Shopping* (San Francisco: Sierra Club Books, 1994); see also Council on Economic Priorities' monthly *Research Report*, or updates on website: http://www.accesspt.com/cep.

Chapter 4

1. GATT 1994 is officially titled: "The Final Act Embodying the Results of the Uruguay Round of Multilateral Trade Negotiations," signed in Marrakesh, 15 April 1994. See *The Results of the Uruguay Round of Multilateral Trade Negotiations: The Legal Texts* (Geneva: World Trade Organization, 1995); a summary can be found on the World Trade Organization's website, <www.wto.org>.
2. Renée Marlin-Bennett, *Food Fights: International Regimes and the Politics of Agricultural Trade Disputes* (New York: Gordon and Breach, 1993), Chapter 4.
3. <www.fao.org>; ACTIONAID, *Hunger and the Global Agenda: Who Wins . . . Who Loses . . . Who Cares?* (London: ACTIONAID, 1996).
4. FAO, "Food Supply Outlook in Africa Improves, But 17 Countries Face Exceptional Food Emergencies," *Global Watch Report*, 1997, <www.fao.org/news/global/GW9710-e.htm>.
5. Summarized at <www.wto.org/wto/ursum_wpf.html#Decision>.
6. These are roughly the same countries as the Food and Agriculture Organization's Low-Income Food Deficit Countries; see Table 1.2, p. 10.
7. Penny Fowler, "The Marrakesh Decision: Honouring the Commitment to Net Food-Importing Developing Countries," *CIIR Briefing* (London: Catholic Institute for International Relations, 1996).
8. Judith Randel and Tony German, eds., *The Reality of Aid 1995* and *1996* (London: EARTHSCAN, 1995, 1996).
9. World Trade Organization, "Singapore Ministerial Declaration," WT/MIN(96)/DEC, adopted on 13 December 1996, <www.wto.org/wto/whats_new/wtodec.htm>.
10. The TRIPS Agreement, formally known as the Agreement on Trade Related Aspects of Intellectual Property Rights, Including Trade in Counterfeit Goods, is summarized at <www.wto.org/wto/ursum_wpf.html#Agreement>. Several other international treaties govern intellectual property.
11. Vandana Shiva, "Caliber of Destruction: Globalization, Food Security and Women's Livelihoods," *No Short-Cut to Food Security Monograph* No. 3 (Manila: Isis International-Manila, 1996); "Dwindling Diversity," *Washington Post*, February 15, 1997; Cary Fowler and Pat Mooney, *Shattering: Food, Politics and the Loss of Genetic Diversity* (Tucson: University of Arizona Press, 1990).
12. Per Pinstrup-Andersen, Mattias Lundberg and James L. Garrett, "Foreign Assistance to Agriculture: A Win-Win Proposition," *Food Policy Report* No. 20 (Washington: International Food Policy Research Institute, 1995).
13. National Center for Food and Agricultural Policy, *Development, Trade Expansion and U.S. Agriculture: Policies for the 21st Century, Report of the Working Group on International Trade and Development*, Robert Paarlberg, Chair, February, 1997, 7.
14. Agnes R. Quisumbing, Lynn R. Brown, Hilary Sims Feldstein, Lawrence Haddad and Christine Peña, "Women: The Key to Food Security," *Food Policy Report* No. 21 (Washington: International Food Policy Research Institute, 1995).

Chapter 5

1. The World Bank, *1997 World Development Indicators* (Washington: The World Bank, 1997), 238; James Michel, *Development Co-operation: Efforts and Policies of the Members of the Development Assistance Committee, 1996 Report* (Paris: Organisation for Economic Co-operation and Development, 1997).
2. Except as noted, this section is based on United Nations Conference on Trade and Development, *World Investment Report 1996* (Geneva: UNCTAD, 1996), *UNCTAD96*; also, *UNCTAD94* and *UNCTAD95*.
3. The World Bank, *Labor and the Growth Crisis in Sub-Saharan Africa* (Washington: The World Bank, 1995).
4. *UNCTAD95*, 57.
5. "Building on Africa's Progress," *IMF Survey*, July 7, 1997, 1.
6. Various organizations and periodicals assist investors in assessing the risks of operations. Standard and Poor's and other agencies rate government and corporate bonds. *The Global Competitiveness Report 1997* (Davos, Switzerland: World Economic Forum, 1997) rates economies based on economic and political criteria. The current report rated Singapore and Hong Kong one and two, respectively, ahead of the United States. The United Kingdom moved up to seventh place, while Indonesia rose from 30th to 15th. China went from 36th to 29th, and Chile moved up to 13th. No African nations were mentioned in the upper levels.
7. *UNCTAD94*.
8. *UNCTAD94;* Sarah Anderson and John Cavanagh, *The Top 200: The Rise of Global Corporate Power* (Washington: Institute for Policy Studies, 1996).
9. *Ibid.*
10. *Ibid.*; William Greider, *One World Ready or Not: The Manic Logic of Global Capitalism* (New York: Simon and Schuster, 1997); John Cavanagh and Robin Broad, "Don't Neglect the Impoverished South," *Foreign Policy* No. 101 (Winter 1995-1996): 18-35; Lance Taylor and Ute Pieper, "Reconciling Economic Reform and Sustainable Human Development: Social Consequences of Neo-liberalism," *United Nations Development Programme Office of Development Studies Discussion Paper* No. 2 (January 1996). More mainstream economists such as Paul Krugman, Lester Thurow and others are also critical of TNCs, but see them as important engines of growth in the world economy, as do most governments.
11. "The Poor Start Businesses and Make Big Changes with Small Loans," *Christian Science Monitor*, March 26, 1997; "Micro-Loans for the Very Poor," editorial, *New York Times*, February 16, 1997; Barbara MkNelly and Christopher Dunford, "Are Credit and Savings Service Effective against Hunger and Malnutrition? A Literature Review and Analysis," *Freedom from Hunger Research Paper* No. 1 (February 1996); Barbara MkNelly, Chatree Watetip, Cheryl A. Lassen and Christopher Dunford, "Preliminary Evidence that Integrated Financial and Educational Services Can be Effective against Hunger and Malnutrition," *Freedom from Hunger Research Paper* No. 2 (April 1996).
12. Statement text provided by Microcredit Summit Secretariat, RESULTS Educational Fund.
13. James Tobin, "A Tax on International Currency Transactions" in U.N. Development Programme, *Human Development Report 1994* (New York: Oxford University Press, 1994), 70.
14. "Corporate Responsibility Challenges 1997," *The Corporate Examiner* 25:7-8 (February 28, 1997).

Chapter 6

1. Harvard University economist, cited in World Bank documents.
2. United Nations Development Programme, *Human Development Report 1996* (New York: Oxford University Press, 1996), 2.
3. The Security Council, which gives veto rights to the United States, United Kingdom, France, China and Russia, is a notable exception.
4. This guarantee, called "paid in" capital, is very modest – often on the order of $50 million per year. "Callable" capital is the amount for which the creditor government would be liable in the event of a default or other emergency.
5. Jean Drèze and Amartya Sen, *Hunger and Public Action* (Oxford: Clarendon Press, 1989).
6. The World Bank, *The Participation Sourcebook* (Washington: The World Bank, 1996), xi.
7. A recent review of 123 projects by the Bank's Environment Department found that only 8 percent of projects with good social analysis were unsatisfactory; 70 percent of those projects rated as unsatisfactory on completion had little or no social analysis.
8. Kunibert Raffer and H.W. Singer, *The Foreign Aid Business* (Cheltenham, UK: Edward Elgar Publishing, 1996).

Chapter 7

1. "61 Ways of Looking at Poverty," *Choices*, October 1996, 7.
2. *Ibid.*, 9-10.
3. According to the International Food Policy Research Institute's initiative, A 2020 Vision for Food, Agriculture and the Environment; see IFPRI, *Feeding the World, Preventing Poverty and Protecting the Earth: A 2020 Vision* (Washington: IFPRI, 1996).
4. Bread for the World, *Tell Congress Hunger Has a Cure: 1997 Offering of Letters Kit* (Silver Spring, MD: BFW, 1997), 4.
5. This section is based on Food and Agriculture Organization of the United Nations, *The Sixth World Food Survey* (Rome: FAO, 1996) and United Nations Commission for Social Development *1997 Report on the World Social Situation*, E/CN.5/1997/8, 2 parts (New York: United Nations, 1997). Regional classifications in this chapter are those of FAO, unless otherwise noted – "industrial countries" are Australia, New Zealand, Japan, Israel, the United States, Canada and Western Europe; "transition economies" are in Central and Eastern Europe and the newly independent states of the former Soviet Union; "Middle East" refers to Asian countries from Afghanistan west and Africa north of the Sahara; "South Asia" includes Bangladesh, India, Nepal, Pakistan and Sri Lanka; other regional classifications are self-explanatory.
6. U.N. Commission for Social Development, Part II, 15, 18; U.N. Department of Public Information, "Poverty and Development: An (Im)balance Sheet," May 1996.
7. U.N. Commission for Social Development, Part II, 15-16; "Children Bear the Brunt of Poverty in Latin America," *World Bank News*, July 18, 1996; FAO data posted at <www.fao.org>.
8. "61 Ways...," 8.
9. Carolyn Campbell, Cornell University Nutrition Professor, personal communication, December 15, 1996.
10. This section is based on U.N. Commission for Social Development; Barbara Boyle Torrey, Timothy M. Smeeding and Debra Bailey, "Rowing Between Scylla and Charybdis: Income Transitions in Central European Households," *Luxembourg Income Study Working Paper* No. 132 (February 1996); Timothy M. Smeeding and Peter Gottschalk, "The International Evidence on Income Distribution in Modern Economies: Where Do We Stand?," *LIS Working Paper* No. 137 (December 1995); Jonathan Bradshaw and Jun-Rong Chen, "Poverty in the UK: A Comparison with Nineteen Other Countries," *LIS Working Paper* No. 147 (October 1996); Peter Gottschalk and Timothy M. Smeeding, "Empirical Evidence on Income Inequality in Industrialized Countries," *LIS Working Paper* No. 154 (February 1997) and data posted at <www.fao.org>. Vietnam and Mongolia are often categorized as "Countries in Transition," but here are considered part of East Asia.
11. Smeeding and Gottschalk, "The International Evidence...," 25; see also Anthony Atkinson, Lee Rainwater and Timothy Smeeding, "Income Distribution in Advanced Economies: Evidence from the Luxembourg Income Survey," *LIS Working Paper* No. 120 (October 1995).
12. Gary Craig and Elizabeth Dowler, "Let Them Eat Cake! Poverty, Hunger and the U.K. State," in Graham Riches, ed., *First World Hunger: Food Security and Welfare Politics* (New York: St. Martin's, 1997), 127.
13. Graham Riches, "Hunger in Canada: Abandoning the Right to Food," Chapter 3 in *First World Hunger*, and *Global Food Security: Canadian Perspectives* (Ottawa: Canadian Hunger Foundation-Partners in Rural Development, 1995).
14. République Française, Comité Interministériel de l'Agriculture et l'Alimentation, *Rapport au Sommet Mondial de l'Alimentation* [Republic of France, Inter-Agency Committee on Agriculture and Food, *Report to the World Food Summit*] (Paris: Ministry of Agriculture, Fisheries and Food, 1996).
15. Data from European Federation of Food Banks and U.N. Commission on Social Development; *Is the European Union Housing Its Poor?* (Brussels: European Federation of National Organizations Working with the Homeless, 1995); Karel Van den Bosch and Ive Marx, "Trends in Financial Poverty in OECD Countries," *LIS Working Paper* No. 148 (December 1996); Isabelle Grunberg, "Rival States, Rival Firms: How Do People Fit In? The Global Unemployment Challenge," *UNDP Office of Development Studies Discussion Paper* No. 4 (January 1996).
16. Tom Buerkle, "Testing the Welfare System: EU Finds Poverty at 17%," *International Herald Tribune*, May 15, 1997.
17. Data on iodine and vitamin A deficiency are reported according to WHO's regional classifications, which differ

significantly from those used elsewhere in this report. "Eastern Mediterranean" includes Middle East, Afghanistan, Pakistan, Djibouti, Somalia and Sudan. "Western Pacific" includes Australia, New Zealand, the Philippines, Cambodia, Japan, Laos, Malaysia, Singapore, Vietnam, China and South Korea, as well as the small Pacific Island countries. "Southeast Asia" includes Mongolia, North Korea, Indonesia and the Indian subcontinent, as well as Thailand and Burma. "Africa" includes North Africa.

18. World Health Organization data.
19. Terry Peel, *America's Partnership with UNICEF* (New York: U.N. Children's Fund, 1997), 40.
20. United Nations Children's Fund, *The State of the World's Children 1996* (New York: Oxford University Press, 1996), 55.
21. FAO Global Information and Early Warning System on Food and Agriculture, *Foodcrops and Shortages* No. 2 (March/April 1997); U.N. Department of Humanitarian Affairs, <www.reliefweb.int>.

Chapter 8

1. United Nations Development Programme, *Human Development Report 1997* (New York: Oxford University Press, 1997), 93.
2. Council on Economic Priorities, *Shopping for a Better World: The Quick and Easy Guide to All Your Socially Responsible Shopping* (San Francisco: Sierra Club Books, 1994), xiii, 1.
3. Daniel Finn, *Just Trading: On the Ethics and Economics of International Trade* (Nashville: Abingdon Press, 1996).
4. *Ibid.*

Sponsors

Bread for the World Institute seeks to inform, educate, nurture and motivate concerned citizens for action on policies that affect hungry people. Based on policy analysis and consultation with poor people, it develops educational resources and activities, including this annual report on the state of world hunger, an anti-hunger leadership development program and a project that empowers civil society organizations in developing countries as they interface with the World Bank. Contributions to the Institute are tax deductible. It works closely with Bread for the World, a Christian citizens' movement of 44,000 members who advocate specific policy changes to help overcome hunger in the United States and overseas.

1100 Wayne Avenue, Suite 1000
Silver Spring, MD 20910
Phone: (301) 608-2400
Fax: (301) 608-2401
E-mail: bread@bread.org

Brot für die Welt is an association of German Protestant churches that seeks to overcome poverty and hunger in developing countries, as an expression of their Christian faith and convictions, by funding programs of relief and development. Founded in 1959, Brot has funded more than 18,000 programs in over 100 nations in Africa, Latin America and Asia. The emphasis of the programs that Brot funds has shifted from relief to development and empowerment. Brot's programs of education in Germany are intended to lead to changes – in understanding and lifestyle at the personal level, and to policy changes at the national, European Community and international levels.

Stafflenbergstrasse 76, Postfach 10 11 42
D-70010 Stuttgart, Germany
Phone: 01-49-711-2159-0
Fax: 01-49-711-2159-110
E-mail: bfdwinformation@brot-fuer-die-welt.org

Christian Children's Fund, founded in Richmond, VA, in 1938, is one of the world's oldest and most respected nonprofit child sponsorship charities. Christian Children's Fund is dedicated to providing long-term sustainable development assistance to approximately 2.5 million needy children and their families in more than 30 countries around the world, including the United States. Services are provided without regard to religion, gender or race. Christian Children's Fund is America's fourth largest relief and development organization.

2821 Emerywood Parkway, P.O. Box 26484
Richmond, VA 23261-6484
Phone: (804) 756-2700
Fax: (804) 756-2718

Congregation of the Sisters of Charity of the Incarnate Word, Houston, Texas. In the early 1860s in Texas, threatening epidemics such as yellow fever, as well as the continuing horror of war, brought suffering and death throughout the state. Bishop Claude Dubuis was determined to find Sisters who would minister to the sick and dying as well as to children left orphaned by epidemics and war. In 1866, three Sisters from the Monastery of the Incarnate Word and Blessed Sacrament in Lyons, France, responding to the call, came to Galveston, Texas, and founded the Congregation of the Sisters of Charity of the Incarnate Word. Since then, the Sisters of Charity have expanded their ministries of prayer, healing and education to California, Utah, Louisiana, Oklahoma, Central America, Ireland and Africa. Sisters of Charity are committed to upholding the dignity of persons and to promoting justice and equality.

P.O. Box 230969
6510 Lawndale
Houston, TX 77223-0969
Phone: (713) 928-6053
Fax: (713) 928-8148

Covenant World Relief is the relief and development arm of The Evangelical Covenant Church. Dr. Timothy C. Ek is vice president of the Covenant and director of Covenant World Relief. The Evangelical Covenant Church has its national headquarters in Chicago, IL. The Covenant's historic commitment to being actively involved in Christ's mission to respond to the spiritual and physical needs of others was the basis for the formation of Covenant World Relief.

5101 North Francisco Avenue
Chicago, IL 60625-3699
Phone: (773) 784-3000
Fax: (773) 784-4366
E-mail: 102167.1330@compuserve.com

The **Evangelical Lutheran Church in America World Hunger Program** is a 24-year-old ministry that confronts hunger and poverty through emergency relief, long-term development, education, advocacy and stewardship of financial resources. Seventy-two percent of the program works internationally and 28 percent within the United States. Lutheran World Relief (New York City) and Lutheran World Federation (Geneva, Switzerland) are key partners in international relief and development. Twelve percent is used for domestic relief and development, 10 percent for education and advocacy work in the United States and 6 percent for fundraising and administration.

8765 West Higgins Road
Chicago, IL 60631-4190
Phone: (800) 638-3522, ext. 2709
Fax: (773) 380-2707
E-mail: jhalvors@elca.org

LCMS World Relief (The Lutheran Church – Missouri Synod) provides relief and development funding for domestic and international projects. Based under the Synod's Department of Human Care Ministries, LCMS World Relief provides domestic grants for Lutheran congregations and social ministry organizations as well as other groups with Lutheran involvement which are engaged in ministries of human care. Domestic support is also provided to Lutheran Disaster Response and Lutheran Immigration and Refugee Service. International relief and development assistance is channeled through the Synod's mission stations and partner churches as well as Lutheran World Relief.

1333 So. Kirkwood Road
St. Louis, MO 63122-7295
Phone: (800) 248-1930, ext. 1392
Fax: (314) 965-0541
E-mail: ic_schroepj@lcms.org

Lutheran World Relief (LWR) acts on behalf of U.S. Lutherans in response to natural disasters, humanitarian crises and chronic poverty in some 50 countries of Asia, Africa, Latin America and the Middle East. In partnership with local organizations, LWR supports over 150 community projects to improve food production, health care, environment and employment, with special emphasis on training and gender. LWR monitors legislation on foreign aid and development, and advocates for public policies which address the root causes of hunger and poverty. LWR values the God-given gifts that each person can bring to the task of promoting peace, justice and human dignity. LWR began its work in 1945.

Lutheran World Relief
390 Park Avenue South
New York, NY 10016
Phone: (212) 532-6350
Resources: (800) LWR-LWR2
Fax: (212) 213-6081
E-mail: lwr@lwr.org

LWR/CWS Office on Development Policy
110 Maryland Avenue, N.E.
Building Mailbox #45
Washington, DC 20002-5694
Phone: (202) 543-6336
Fax: (202) 546-6232
E-mail: csw/lwr@igc.apc.org

For 28 years, the **Presbyterian Hunger Program** has provided a channel for congregations to respond to hunger in the United States and around the world. With a commitment to the ecumenical sharing of human and financial resources, the program provides support for programs of direct food relief, sustainable development and public policy advocacy. A network of 100 Hunger Action Enablers leads the Presbyterian Church (USA) in the study of hunger issues, engagement with communities of need, advocacy for just public policies, and the movement toward simpler corporate and personal lifestyles.

100 Witherspoon Street
Louisville, KY 40202-1396
Phone: (502) 569-5832
Fax: (502) 569-7609

The **RLDS World Hunger Committee** is the official committee responsible for engaging the membership of the Reorganized Church of Jesus Christ of Latter Day Saints (RLDS) in a corporate response to world hunger. Since 1979, the World Hunger Committee, appointedby the First Presidency, has considered grant proposals submitted by such organizations as Outreach

International, World Accord and Oxfam America, among many others. Advocacy, education and direct relief are the committee's main areas of interest. The largest portion of World Hunger funds is used for relief in disaster aid and self-help programs in developing countries. Congregations in the U.S. have also received World Hunger grants to help establish soup kitchens, food pantries and food banks.

P.O. Box 1059
Independence, MO 64051-0559
Phone: (816) 833-1000
Fax: (816) 521-3097
E-mail: ritasmck@rlds.org

Share Our Strength (SOS) is the nation's leading anti-hunger organization that mobilizes industries and individuals to contribute their talents to fight hunger. By supporting food assistance, treating malnutrition and other consequences of hunger, and promoting economic independence among people in need, Share Our Strength meets immediate demands for food while investing in long-term solutions to hunger and poverty. Since its founding in 1984, Share Our Strength has distributed more than $30 million in grants to over 800 anti-hunger organizations in the United States, Canada and around the world. Operation Frontline, a direct service program in more than 10 cities across the United States, trains volunteer culinary professionals to teach cooking, nutrition and food budgeting skills to people at risk of hunger and malnutrition. SOS's fundraising efforts include: Taste of the Nation, an annual series of food and wine tastings held in April in more than 100 cities throughout the United States and Canada; Writers Harvest: The National Reading, an annual event in which hundreds of authors read from their work to support anti-hunger efforts; Dine Across America, an in-restaurant national dining promotion to raise funds for anti-hunger efforts; and Publishing Ventures, which includes original works donated by authors, artists and chefs.

1511 K Street, N.W., Suite 940
Washington, DC 20005
Phone: (202) 393-2925
Fax: (202) 347-5868

Shield-Ayres Foundation

The **United Methodist Committee on Relief (UMCOR)** was formed in 1940 in response to the suffering of people during World War II. It was a "voice of conscience" expressing the concern of the church for the disrupted and devastated lives churned out by the war. UMCOR has expanded its ministry into more than 70 countries to minister with compassion to "persons in need, through programs and services which provide immediate relief and long-term attention to the root causes of their need." Focusing on refugee, hunger and disaster ministries, the work of UMCOR, a program department of the General Board of Global Ministries of the United Methodist Church, is carried out through direct services and a worldwide network of national and international church agencies that cooperate in the task of alleviating human suffering.

475 Riverside Drive, Room 330
New York, NY 10115
Phone: (212) 870-3816
Hotline: (800) 841-1235
Fax: (212) 870-3624
E-mail: wendyw@gbgm-umc.org

The **United Nations Development Programme** (UNDP) is the United Nations' largest provider of technical cooperation grants and the main coordinator of U.N. development assistance. It works with governments, U.N. agencies, organizations of civil society and individuals in 175 countries and territories to build national capacities for sustainable human development. Activities focus on poverty eradication, creation of jobs and sustainable livelihoods, advancement of women, protection and regeneration of the environment and good governance. UNDP's central resources, totaling about $1 billion (U.S.) a year, are derived from the voluntary contributions of governments. UNDP also administers several special purpose funds (U.N. Capital Development Fund, U.N. Development Fund for Women, U.N. Volunteers) and, with the World Bank and the U.N. Environment Programme, the $2 billion Global EnvironmentFacility.

1 United Nations Plaza
New York, NY 10017
Phone: (212) 906-5000
Fax: (212) 906-5001
E-mail: HQ@undp.org
Web site: www.undp.org

Cosponsors

The **Academy for Educational Development** (AED), founded in 1961, is an independent, nonprofit service organization committed to addressing human development needs in the United States and throughout the world. Under contracts and grants, the Academy operates programs in collaboration with policy leaders; nongovernmental and community-based organizations; governmental agencies; international multilateral and bilateral funders; and schools, colleges and universities. In partnership with its clients, the Academy seeks to meet today's social, economic and environmental challenges through education and human resource development; to apply state-of-the-art education, training, research, technology, management, behavioral analysis and social marketing techniques to solve problems; and to improve knowledge and skills throughout the world as the most effective means for stimulating growth, reducing poverty, and promoting democratic and humanitarian ideals. AED is registered with the U.S. Agency for International Development as a private voluntary organization. The Academy is exempt from federal income taxes under Section 501(c)(3) of the Internal Revenue Code. Contributions to the Academy are tax deductible.

1875 Connecticut Avenue, N.W.
Washington, DC 20009-1202
Phone: (202) 884-8000
Fax: (202) 884-8400
E-mail: admindc@aed.org

The **Adventist Development and Relief Agency International** (ADRA) is an international non-governmental organization which operates in more than 140 countries worldwide. ADRA's purpose is to develop human capacity, increase self-reliance, and empower communities to meet crisis or chronic distress. The agency has operated since 1956 (founded as the Seventh-day Adventist Welfare Service, SAWS, by its parent organization the Seventh-day Adventist Church) and has been recognized internationally for its expertise in implementing humanitarian development and relief initiatives. ADRA's major sectors of involvement include primary health care and child survival, food security, economic development, basic education and emergency preparedness and response. ADRA emphasizes sustainable, community based programs which involve active local participation in planning and implementation, as well as monitoring and evaluation. The agency is dedicated to working in partnership with people in need throughout the world, and fostering self-reliance among vulnerable groups, without regard to ethnicity or religious affiliation. ADRA is organized as a network of semi-autonomous country level and regional offices.

12501 Old Columbia Pike
Silver Spring, MD 20904
Phone: (301) 680-6380
Fax: (301) 680-6370

Baptist World Aid (BWAid) is a division of the Baptist World Alliance, a fellowship of almost 200 Baptist unions and conventions around the world, comprising a membership of over 40 million baptized believers. This represents a community of over 80 million Baptists ministering in more than 200 countries. For over 75 years Baptists have been working in partnership to entrust, empower and enable the indigenous Baptist leadership to carry out programs of emergency relief, sustainable development and fellowship assistance.

6733 Curran Street
McLean, VA 22101-6005
Phone: (703) 790-8980
Fax: (703) 893-5160
E-mail: bwaid@baptistnet.org

Call to Action is a Catholic organization of over 18,000 lay people, religious, priests and bishops working together to foster peace, justice and love in our world, our church and ourselves in the spirit of the Second Vatican Council and the U.S. Catholic Bishops' Call to Action (1976). Programs include publications each month (*CTA News*, *ChurchWatch* and *Spirituality/Justice Reprint*); annual We Are the Church national conference, 40 local chapters, a Church Renewal Directory of 400 national and local faith groups committed to church and societal renewal; the Future of Priestly Ministry Dialogue Project; and a Speakers and Artists Referral Service.

4419 North Kedzie
Chicago, IL 60625
Phone: (773) 604-0400
Fax: (773) 604-4719
E-mail: ctaIL@igc.apc.org
Web site: call-to-action.org

Canadian Foodgrains Bank is a 13 member church-based organization that provides food aid and development assistance to countries in need. It utilizes an extensive network of Canadian grain elevators to collect substantial amounts of donated grain and other agricultural commodities from Canadian farmers. These donations are combined with cash contributions - both matched by cost sharing funds from Canadian International Development Agency (CIDA) - to procure and ship food assistance to food deficit countries and provide related services to its member agencies. In 1996, food was provided to 26 countries, with major assistance going to Ethiopia, the Great Lakes region, Guinea/Liberia/Sierra Leone region, North Korea, Cuba, Afghanistan, Angola and Haiti. Other special projects include monetization, food security reserves and household food security monitoring. Canadian Foodgrains Bank also takes an active interest in food security policy. To support this policy dialogue, a number of discussion papers on a variety of food security issues have been prepared. Staff and member agencies were actively involved in preparations for the 1996 World Food Summit and continue to engage both government and other like-minded organizations in post-Summit actions related to the eradication of world hunger.

Box 747, 400-280 Smith Street
Winnipeg, MB, Canada R3C 2L4
Phone: (204) 944-1993
Fax: (204) 943-2597

CARE is one of the world's largest and most effective private relief and development organizations. Each year, CARE reaches more than 35 million people in over 60 nations in Africa, Asia and Latin America. The organization's work began in 1946, when CARE packages helped Europe recover from World War II. Today, CARE provides famine and disaster victims with emergency assistance, improves health care, helps subsistence farmers and small-business owners produce more goods, addresses population and environmental concerns, and helps to develop economies and societies in a sustainable manner. The scope of CARE's work is broad, but its vision focuses on a single concept – helping people help themselves.

151 Ellis Street
Atlanta, GA 30303
Phone: (404) 681-2552
Fax: (404) 577-5977

Catholic Charities USA is the nation's largest network of independent social service organizations. The 1,400 agencies and institutions work to reduce poverty, support families and empower communities. Catholic Charities organizations provide social services ranging from adoption and counseling to emergency food and housing. Nearly 10.8 million people of all religious, national, racial, social and economic backgrounds received services in 1995. Catholic Charities USA promotes public policies and strategies that address human needs and social injustices. The national office provides advocacy and management support for agencies. The Disaster Response Office organizes the Catholic community's response to U.S. disasters.

1731 King Street, Suite 200
Alexandria, VA 22314
Phone: (703) 549-1390
Fax: (703) 549-1656
E-mail: info@catholiccharitiesusa.org
Web site: www.catholiccharitiesusa.org

Catholic Relief Services-USCC (CRS) is the overseas relief and development agency of the U.S. Catholic community. Founded in 1943, CRS provides almost $200 million in development and relief assistance in 80 nations around the world. Working in partnership with the Catholic Church and other local institutions in each country, CRS works to alleviate poverty, hunger and suffering, and supports peacebuilding and reconciliation initiatives. Assistance is given solely on the basis of need. Even while responding to emergencies, CRS supports over 2,000 development projects designed to build local self-sufficiency. CRS works in conjunction with Caritas Internationalis and CIDSE, worldwide associations of Catholic relief and development agencies. Together, these groups build the capacity of local nonprofit organizations to provide long-term solutions. In the United States, CRS seeks to educate and build awareness on issues of world poverty and hunger and serve as an advocate for public policy changes in the interest of the poor overseas.

209 West Fayette Street
Baltimore, MD 21201-3443
Phone: (410) 625-2220
Fax: (410) 685-1635
E-mail: webmaster@catholicrelief.org
Web site: www.catholicrelief.org

The **Center on Hunger, Poverty and Nutrition Policy** was established at Tufts University in 1990. Its purpose is to advance public policy choices which reduce hunger and poverty, and enhance the development and productive capacities of American families and children. The Center carries out policy research and analyses, and works with government leaders and the media to promote greater understanding of policy alternatives for the nation.

11 Curtis Avenue
Medford, MA 02155
Phone: (617) 627-3956
Fax: (617) 627-3020

The **Christian Reformed World Relief Committee** (CRWRC) is a ministry of the Christian Reformed Church in North America. CRWRC shows God's love to people in need through *development* – working with families and communities in food production, income earning, health education, literacy learning, spiritual and leadership skills – through *relief* – working with disaster survivors by providing food, medicines, crisis counseling, rebuilding and volunteer assistance – and through *education* – working with people to develop and act on their Christian perspective of poverty, hunger and justice. CRWRC works with communities in North America and in over 30 countries worldwide to create permanent, positive change in Christ's name.

CRWRC U.S.
2850 Kalamazoo Avenue, S.E.
Grand Rapids, MI 49560-0600
Phone: (800) 552-7972
Fax: (616) 246-0806
E-mail for U.S. & Canada:
CRWRC@crcna.org

CRWRC CANADA
3475 Mainway
P.O. Box 5070 STN LCD1
Burlington, ON L7R 3Y8
Phone: (800) 730-3490
Fax: (905) 336-8344

Church World Service (CWS) is a global relief, development and refugee-assistance ministry of the 33 Protestant and Orthodox communities that work together through the National Council of Churches. Founded in 1946, CWS works in partnership with local church organizations in more than 70 countries worldwide, supporting sustainable self-help development of people which respects the environment, meets emergency needs, and addresses root causes of poverty and powerlessness. Within the United States, CWS resettles refugees, assists communities in responding to disasters, advocates for justice in U.S. policies which relate to global issues, provides educational resources, and offers opportunities for communities to join a people-to-people network of global and local caring through participation in a CROP WALK.

475 Riverside Drive, Suite 678
New York, NY 10115-0050
Phone: (212) 870-2257 or 2175
Fax: (212) 870-3523
E-mail: rodney@ncccusa.org

EuronAid is a European association of nongovernmental organizations (NGOs) which facilitates dialogue with the Commission of the European Union in the areas of food security and food aid. EuronAid cooperates with the Commission in programming and procuring food aid for the NGOs, then arranges and accounts for delivery to Third World NGOs for distribution. In recent years, triangular operations (purchases within Third World nations) have accounted for half of EuronAid's food aid, which meets mainly development purposes. EuronAid assimilates the experiences of NGOs involved in food aid and employs this knowledge in its dialogue with the Commission and the European Parliament to achieve improved management of food aid. EuronAid was created in 1980 by major European NGOs in cooperation with the Commission of the European Union. The association has at present 29 member agencies and services an additional 60 European and Southern NGOs on a regular basis.

P.O. Box 12
NL-2501 CA Den Haag
The Netherlands
Phone: 31 70 330 57 57
Fax: 31 70 362 17 39
E-mail: euronaid@euronaid.nl

Food for the Hungry International (FHI) is an organization of Christian motivation committed to working with poor people to overcome hunger and poverty through development and, where needed, as appropriate relief. Founded in 1971, FHI is incorporated in Switzerland and works in over 20 countries of Asia, Africa and Latin America. As its name implies, FHI focuses on poverty needs that relate to food and nutrition. Its primary emphasis is on long-term development among the extremely poor, recognizing their dignity, creativity and ability to solve their own problems. The international staff numbers more than 1,200 persons. Autonomous Food for the Hungry partner entities in several different countries such as Food for the Hungry (USA) contribute resources.

7807 East Greenway Road, Suite 3
Scottsdale, AZ 85260
Phone: (602) 951-5090
Fax: (602) 951-9035
E-mail: robins@fh.org

Founded in 1946, **Freedom from Hunger** fights chronic hunger with two of the most powerful and flexible resources ever created: money and information. Operating in rural regions of 10 developing nations, our *Credit with Education* program builds on the success of village banking by integrating basic health, nutrition, family planning and microenterprise management education into group meetings. Results from recent studies show beneficial impacts, not only on income and income-generating activities, but also on the health and nutrition of participants and their children. Freedom from Hunger's goal is to bring *Credit with Education* to 2.2 million women by the year 2005.

1644 DaVinci Court
Davis, CA 95617
Phone: (800) 708-2555
Fax: (916) 758-6241
E-mail: info@freefromhunger.org
Web site: www.freefromhunger.org

The **International Fund for Agricultural Development** (IFAD) is an international financial institution headquartered in Rome, Italy. Established in 1977 as a result of the 1974 World Food Conference, IFAD is a Specialized Agency of the United Nations with an exclusive mandate to provide the rural poor of the developing world with cost-effective ways of overcoming hunger, poverty and malnutrition. IFAD advocates a targeted, community-based approach to reducing rural poverty. The fund's task is to help poor farmers raise their food production and improve their nutrition by designing and financing projects which increase their incomes. Since 1978, IFAD has committed $5.1 billion for 461 projects in 110 developing countries. The governance and funding of the institution are the result of a unique partnership among developed and developing countries. With the recent additions of South Africa and Croatia, IFAD now has 160 Member States.

Via del Serafico, 107
00142 Rome, Italy
Phone: 39 6 54591
Fax: 39 6 5043463
E-mail: ifad@ifad.org

Jesuit International and Refugee Ministries is one of the Secretariats of the U.S. Jesuit Conference. The Office of International and Refugee Ministries serves as the national office of the Jesuit Refugee Service in the USA and of Jesuit Missions, Inc., as well as serving as an assistancy wide international justice and peace office for the 10 U.S. Jesuit provinces.

1616 P Street, N.W., Suite 400
Washington, DC 20036-1405
Phone: (202) 462-0400
Fax: (202) 328-9212
E-mail: usajrs@aol.com

MAZON: A Jewish Response to Hunger has granted more than $12 million since 1986 to nonprofit organizations confronting hunger in the United States and abroad. MAZON (the Hebrew word for "food") awards grants principally to programs working to prevent and alleviate hunger in the United States. Grantees include emergency and direct food assistance programs, food banks, multi-service organizations, anti-hunger advocacy/education and research projects, and international hunger-relief and agricultural development programs in Israel and impoverished countries. Although responsive to organizations serving impoverished Jews, in keeping with the best of Jewish tradition, MAZON responds to all who are in need.

12401 Wilshire Boulevard, Suite 303
Los Angeles, CA 90025-1015
Phone: (310) 442-0020
Fax: (310) 442-0030
E-mail: mazonmail@aol.com

Mennonite Central Committee (MCC), founded in 1920, is an agency of the Mennonite and Brethren in Christ churches in North America, and seeks to demonstrate God's love through committed women and men who work among people suffering from poverty, conflict, oppression and natural disaster. MCC serves as a channel for interchange between churches and community groups where it works around the world and North American churches. MCC strives for peace, justice and dignity of all people by sharing experiences, resources and faith. MCC's priorities include disaster relief and refugee assistance, rural and agricultural development, job creation, Ten Thousand Villages (formerly known as SELFHELP Crafts), health and education.

21 South 12th Street
Akron, PA 17501-0500
Phone: (717) 859-1151
Fax: (717) 859-2171
E-mail: mailbox@mcc.org

The mission of the **National Association of WIC Directors** (NAWD) is to provide leadership to the WIC community to promote quality nutrition services, serve all eligible women, infants and children, and assure sound and responsive management of the Special Supplemental Nutrition Program for Women, Infants and Children (WIC). The purpose of the association is to link state WIC directors, local WIC directors, nutrition services coordinators and others in a national forum to act collectively on behalf of the program to include the following functions: A) To promote the improved health, well-being and nutritional status of women, infants and children; B) To provide a national resource network through which ideas, materials and procedures can be communicated to persons working in the WIC community; C) To promote good management practices and to assist WIC program directors at the state and local levels; D) To act as a resource at the request of governmental bodies and individual legislators regarding issues particular to the health and nutrition of women, infants and children and to assist WIC clients; and E) To do whatever is necessary to promote and sustain the WIC program.

P.O. Box 53355
1627 Connecticut Avenue, N.W., Suite 5
Washington, DC 20009-3405
Phone: (202) 232-5492
Fax: (202) 387-5281
E-mail: nawd@tomco.net

Oxfam America fights global poverty and hunger by working in partnership with grassroots organizations promoting sustainable development in Africa, Asia, the Caribbean and the Americas, including the United States. In order to foster an environment supportive of long-term development, Oxfam America also advocates for policy change and produces educational materials for the U.S. public on poverty and hunger issues. Oxfam America is a member of Oxfam International which comprises 10 autonomous Oxfams around the world.

26 West Street
Boston, MA 02111
Phone: (800) 77-OXFAM
Fax: (617) 728-2594
E-mail: oxfamusa@igc.apc.org
Web site: www.oxfamamerica.org

RESULTS is an international, grassroots citizens' lobby dedicated to creating the political will to end hunger and poverty, and committed to breaking through the idea that "I don't make a difference." RESULTS identifies the most cost-effective programs which positively impact the lives of the poorest of the poor, and advocates for increased funding and replication of those programs. RESULTS volunteer activists work with their local media and their elected officials to ensure that governments support cost-effective programs proven to combat hunger and poverty, at home and abroad.

236 Massachusetts Avenue, N.E., Suite 300
Washington, DC 20002
Phone: (800) 900-LEAD
Fax: (202) 543-7512
E-mail: results@action.org
Web site: www.action.org

Save the Children Federation/U.S. works to make lasting, positive change in the lives of disadvantaged children in the United States and 39 countries around the world. International programs in health, education, economic opportunities and humanitarian response place children at the center of activities and focus on women as key decision makers and participants. Key principles are child centeredness, women focus, participation and empowerment, sustainability, scaling up and maximizing impact. Programs in the United States emphasize youth and community service.

54 Wilton Road
Westport, CT 06880
Phone: (203) 221-4000
Fax: (203) 454-3914

Second Harvest is the largest domestic hunger-relief charity in the United States. Through a nationwide network of nearly 200 food banks, Second Harvest distributes surplus food and grocery products to nearly 50,000 charitable agencies. These food pantries, soup kitchens, homeless shelters and other feeding programs serve nearly 26 million people each year, including 11 million children.

116 South Michigan Avenue, Suite 4
Chicago, IL 60603-6001
Phone: (312) 263-2303
Fax: (312) 263-5626
Web site: www.secondharvest.org

The Trull Foundation has been interested in educational, religious, cultural and social programs since 1948. Current priorities include concern for:

1. The needs of the Palacios, Texas, area where the foundation has its roots;
2. Pre-adolescents, opportunities to direct lives away

from child abuse, neglect and hunger, towards an adolescence of good mental and physical growth;

3. Mexican-Americans in South Texas, to help them "catch up," hurdle a language barrier, a poverty barrier and system which has consistently kept them poor, uneducated and unrepresented; and
4. A concern for those persons and families devastated by the results of substance abuse.

404 Fourth Street
Palacios, TX 77465
Phone: (512) 972-5241
Fax: (512) 972-1109

U.S. Committee for UNICEF works for the survival, protection and development of children worldwide through education, advocacy and fund raising. UNICEF is currently in over 140 countries providing needed assistance in the areas of health, nutrition, safe water and sanitation, girls' and women's issues, education, emergency relief and child protection.

333 East 38th Street, 6th Floor
New York, NY 10016
Phone: (212) 686-5522
Fax: (212) 779-1679
E-mail: information@unicefusa.org
Web site: www.unicefusa.org

United Church Board for World Ministries (UCBWM) is the instrumentality of the United Church of Christ for the planning and conduct of its program of global missions, development and emergency relief. The UCBWM's fundamental mission commitment is to share life in partnership with global church partners and ecumenical bodies. Through service, advocacy and mission program, the UCBWM sends as well as receives persons in mission; is committed to the healing of God's creation; engages in dialogue, witness and common cause with people of other faiths; and seeks a prophetic vision of a just and peaceful world order so that all might have access to wholeness of life.

475 Riverside Drive, Fl. 16
New York, NY 10115
Phone: (212) 870-2637
Fax: (212) 932-1236
E-mail: petrucel@ucc.org

United Church of Christ Hunger Action program coordinates and stimulates all UCC hunger and hunger-related ministries; increases awareness and understanding of world hunger and related issues; and promotes, interprets and administrates the Hunger Action Fund of the United Church of Christ. The Hunger Action Program is celebrating its 23rd anniversary in 1998.

700 Prospect Avenue
Cleveland, OH 44115
Phone: (216) 736-3290
Fax: (216) 736-3293
E-mail: millers@ucc.org